Love as Passion

Love as Passion

The Codification of Intimacy

NIKLAS LUHMANN

Translated by Jeremy Gaines and Doris L. Jones

Harvard University Press
Cambridge, Massachusetts
1986

This translation of *Liebe als Passion: Zur Codierung von Intimität* is published by arrangement with Suhrkamp. (© Suhrkamp Verlag Frankfurt am Main, 1982.)

Library of Congress Cataloging in Publication Data

Luhmann, Niklas.
  Love as passion.

  Translation of: Liebe als Passion.
  Includes index.
  1. Love. 2. Intimacy (Psychology) 3. Interpersonal communication. 4. Semantics. I. Title.
HQ801.L8313   1986   128'.4   86—14929
ISBN 0-674-53923-0

Contents

Preface to the English Edition

In writing this book I had the German reader and thus a specific social and intellectual context in mind. The English translation places the text in a different setting, adding to the difficulties of trying to understand a highly demanding theoretical argument. Despite the fact that in recent years there has been a more ready interchange of ideas internationally, many notions in the book retain a local colouring, last but not least because, whereas readers in Germany keep up with works published in English without difficulty, the same cannot be said to an equal degree for English-speaking readers. Since the publisher has kindly allowed me to preface the English edition, I would like to take this opportunity to explain a number of the underlying assumptions of the book which are not dealt with in sufficient detail there. In particular, it is necessary to distinguish between several different theoretical complexes which all serve to place the present work in the framework of current discussion in the field of the social sciences.

The book can be viewed as a case study that attempts to use theoretical tools to describe, if not actually explain, historical material. General discussions in Germany about the relationship between theory and history have not as yet been particularly fruitful. There are a number of different reasons for this. On the one hand, the wealth of historical facts which historians are able to dig up from their sources never fails to dash all attempts at theoretical treatment, unless one concedes from the outset that any theory has to be selective in approach. Moreover, historians and sociologists customarily have their own different ways of treating empirical data, and thus both professions can justifiably accuse each other of making unwarranted generalizations. Finally, sociological theory – or so it seems to me, at any rate – is nowhere near complex enough, and above all is not elaborated in sufficiently abstract terms as to be able really to tackle the wealth of historical data. The only possible path one can take in order to uncover the details (or, as in the present case, the boring, old-fashioned pedantry of a body of often mediocre literature) leads via the detour of theoretical abstraction.

As far as the history of ideas is concerned, I have allowed myself to be guided by the project outlined by the editors of the dictionary of *Geschichtliche Grundbegriffe: Lexikon zur politisch-sozialen Sprache in Deutschland*,[1] and I have adopted their usage of the term 'semantics'.[2] This project starts from the assumption that the basic semantic terms used to describe either society or time underwent a radical change during the second half of the eighteenth century; even words which remained the same took on new meanings. Historians, however, have not explained the reasons for this transformation, but have merely confirmed that it did indeed occur.

Foucault's 'archaeology' and the concept of discourse it employs are equally unsatisfactory in this respect. Disregarding for the moment the philosophical battle lines Foucault draws up, i.e. his attack on both a linear philosophy of history and the programme of enlightenment centred on reason – a stance he uses to justify his methodology – a sociologist would be likely to go one step further and endeavour to establish what restrictions were imposed by the social structure on possible discourse. Moreover, the concept of power does not provide an adequate explanation for the force exerted by discourse over life, the empirical nature of which is also probably overestimated. It seems to me that historical research needs a stronger theoretical basis with respect both to 'historical semantics' and the 'archaeology of discourse'.

It is most probable that the sociologist would try and draw on the classical writings on the 'sociology of knowledge' when attempting to overcome this weakness. However, on closer examination this too does not provide an adequate theoretical foundation. It seems that, since the 1920s, development has come to a standstill in two areas. First of all, even if we ignore the inherent difficulties involved in any theory of social class, relating facts to social classes allows us to observe at best only partial phenomena. The only way out of this predicament is, or so Karl Mannheim suggested, to resort to generalization. Class is replaced as a concept by all forms of social position, a step which, however, should necessitate a process of respecification, because notions such as 'position' or 'relativity of being' must be regarded as poor substitutes for a theory which has not yet been found.

Secondly, the sociology of knowledge has been stranded in epistemological difficulties that it has not been able to solve by means of the classical theory of cognition. The truth content of its own statements, which are intended to relativize true (or supposedly true) statements, has never been unequivocally established. One might conceive of a sociology of knowledge of the sociology of knowledge – or a sociology of knowledge of the free-floating intellectual; but in the end we would only come up against the paradoxes known to us ever since Antiquity as inherent in a Reason that tries to enlighten itself – a process Foucault has attempted to undermine using the spade of archaeology.

But how are we to extricate ourselves from this embarrassing state of affairs? If none of this works, what can one do 'instead'?

I cannot for many reasons share the faith Jürgen Habermas places in the opportunities afforded by resorting to a paradigm of intersubjective understanding.[3] It is above all difficult to conceive of how a sufficiently complex theory of society resulting from an intersubjective understanding could be generated by the discourses of everyday life. Instead, it would seem to me to make more sense to utilize certain of the theoretical resources that have already been quite extensively elaborated in the course of interdisciplinary research on a cybernetics of self-referential orders, on general systems theory, on autopoiesis and on information and communication.[4]

In the following study of the semantics of love, the epistemological problems which could not be solved using a sociology of knowledge are dealt with in a new way: they are treated as a problem of observing observations, of describing descriptions, of calculating calculations within self-referential systems. Heinz von Foerster has called this 'second order cybernetics'. In this context the term 'epistemological constructivism' is also used, but a discussion of this would take up so much space that I must instead refer the reader to the literature in question.[5] This approach at the same time allows us to establish premises on which a theory of society could be based. It is possible, using this methodology, to treat society as a social system that consists solely of communications and therefore as a system that can only reproduce communications by means of communications. This also includes communications by the society about itself (in particular: theories of society). All other conditions for the evolution of society and its day to day functioning, including life and human consciousness, belong to the *environment* of this system.

In current debates it has been this unusual design for a theory that has met with the greatest resistance, owing no doubt to the continued presence of a tradition of humanism. But from the standpoint of systems theory, 'environment' is by no means an area to be considered of secondary importance; on the contrary, it is the single most important condition for systems formation. In other words, the theoretical approach used here proposes to abandon such guiding principles as humankind, the human species, the norms of rational life style, or the telos of intellectual history or of human life, and replace them by a differentiation between system and environment. And this proposal is motivated by the idea that it is much more fruitful and leads to more theoretical constructs if theory is built on a difference, instead of a global unity. This theory begins, as does George Spencer Brown's logic, by obeying the instruction: 'draw a distinction!'[6]

What this theoretical model does have in common with Foucault's work is a clearly post-humanistic perspective, which would appear to have become unavoidable, now that humanism has exhausted itself in its exaltation of the subject. And like Foucault, I am not interested in finding some nice, helpful theory oriented towards the 'Good', and much less in basking in indignation at the current state of affairs. But, whereas Foucault would speak in terms of the power of discourse over our suffering bodies, systems theory analyses a relationship between system and environment. The latter approach also allows us to demonstrate that we love and suffer according to cultural imperatives. Indeed, systems theory additionally makes it possible to create a complex theoretical apparatus that can describe the non-random character of variations in social relations, if not actually explain the individual characteristics of the latter of these. In other words, one does not have to leave the genesis of the particular discourses and their subsequent disappearance unexplained. The dominant semantics of a given period becomes plausible only by virtue of its compatibility with the social structure – not in the sense of a mere 'reflection', and by no means in the sense of a relationship of the superstructure. Compatibility is the more elaborate concept. It also embraces the problems of evolutionary, transitional states in which the losses in plausibility experienced by the old order that is passing have to be compensated for and new figures of meaning tested for their suitability to the changed conditions.

The present work deals with only a minute facet of this enormous theoretical programme and is informed by two hypotheses:

1 that the transition from traditional societies to modern society can be conceived of as the transition from a primarily stratified form of differentiation of the social system to one which is primarily functional
2 that this transformation occurs primarily by means of the differentiation of various symbolically generalized media of communication.

This change destroyed the traditional order of life, which had been based primarily on stratified family households, religious cosmology and morals, i.e. on multifunctional institutions. These were replaced by a primary orientation towards such systems as the economy, politics, science, intimacy, law, art, etc., which thus all acquired a high degree of systemic autonomy, and yet precisely because of this became all the more interdependent.

This conception can be elaborated by means of both systematic and historical analyses. One could, for example, demonstrate systematically that functional systems are able to combine their autonomy, which is based on specific functions, with having to depend greatly on fulfilling other functions in their environment, and describe the manner in which this occurs. In other words, they operate simultaneously as closed and open systems.[7] Historical research is faced with the problem that all evolutionary theory has to contend with: namely, that this radical transformation is effected in small, barely perceptible steps. The present case study serves to show that, while the stratified order and family systems remained intact, a semantics for love developed to accommodate extra-marital relationships, and was then transferred back into marriage itself, thus providing a basis for the latter's differentiation – libertinage as a case of evolutionary good fortune, if you will.

The distinction between the theory of social systems and the theory of symbolically generalized media of communication, two areas that should belong together, runs counter to the distinction between a systematic and an historical perspective. In this context 'media' is not meant in the sense of mass media, but rather in the sense of the *symbolically generalized media of interchange*, as defined in the theory Parsons developed. However, Parsons considers the emergence of media to be a *consequence* of the functional differentiation of the action system (and this differentiation is in turn already implied in the concept of action). This is why Parsons speaks of 'media of interchange' and explains them in terms of the necessity of reconnecting the two differentiated systems.

I feel unable to adopt this theoretical model, because I doubt whether a complete functional matrix (the four-function paradigm) and thus a complete theory of symbolically generalized media can be deduced from the concept of action.[8] Consequently, I see the question of the connection between systems theory and media theory not as a fixed link, but as one open to change. It is not pre-determined by the conceptual structure of systems theory, but rather remains in essence open to evolution. This makes historico-empirical investigations all the more necessary. I think of symbolic media as codes which offer relatively improbable communicative intentions, nevertheless, some prospect of success; or as codes which exclude fairly effectively the danger of abuse or of illusion or of errors in the use of particular symbols.[9] Media underpin relatively improbable communication. They make trust possible, if not in fact necessary.[10] In this capacity, media codes can be conceived of as catalysts which necessarily bring about a differentiation of complex social systems, once their use has become sufficiently dependable and constant enough to be foreseeable. In this manner, the differentiation of the economy is a consequence of the use of money; the differentiation of politics a consequence of the use of power; the differentiation of science a consequence of the use of truth – and in each case this takes place once a sufficiently effective semantics has become available by means of which one can distinguish between the use of money and the use of power, etc. (which, for example, was not possible on the basis of land ownership alone).

The following study of the evolution of a special semantics for passionate love thus draws on theoretical sources of a highly diverse nature. And, above all, it is not so ambitious as to attempt to prove that things had to happen the way they did for reasons that can be clearly understood in terms of theory. There are other, methodologically less rigorous, less demanding ways of deploying theoretical concepts in order to select and interpret historical data and texts. If the aim is to link a very complex theory – and how today could a theory of society be otherwise – to a wide, hopefully representative collection of historical material, then one cannot at the same time set one's methodological sights too high. This is why the form of an historical case study has been chosen here, which has meant not only taking a narrow cross section of material, and one selected with great theoretical care, but also making only highly selective use of the manifold possibilities afforded by the theoretical apparatus. This procedure does not by any means exclude the possibility of the theorist learning in the course of completing historical studies and adjusting his theory to the findings. Historical research is one of the reasons why a theory must be complex, and the aesthetics of the theory suffers if it is dipped into a bath of historical facts. But if a theory is sufficiently complex, it can also itself recognize which of its assumptions it has to change or differentiate if it is to be able to recast those facts in its own theoretical language.

Niklas Luhmann, Bielefeld, August 1985

Introduction

The following investigations into the 'semantics of love' combine two different theoretical complexes. On the one hand, these studies are to be seen in the context of writings on the sociology of knowledge concerning the transition from traditional to modern forms of society. Other writings on this subject have appeared in a previous publication,[1] and I intend to conduct further research in this area. These investigations rest on the assumption that the social system's transformation from a stratified to a functional mode of differentiation generates profound changes in the conceptual resources that enable a society to ensure the continuity of its reproduction and the adaption of one action to another. In the course of such evolutionary transformations, word forms, set phrases, adages and precepts may very well continue to be handed down over the generations; however, their meaning changes and with it the way in which they pinpoint a specific referent, encapsulate particular experiences and open up new perspectives. A shift occurs in the pivotal point from which complexes of meaning direct actions, so that as long as the conceptual resources are rich enough, they can pave the way for and accompany profound changes in social structures quickly enough for these to seem plausible. Such a shift permits structural transformations to proceed with relative rapidity, indeed often in a revolutionary fashion, without these having to create all the necessary preconditions for change beforehand.

The second framework of this investigation will be provided by a preliminary outline of an overall theory of generalized symbolic media of communication. In other words, love will not be treated here as a feeling (or at least only secondarily so), but rather in terms of its constituting a symbolic code which shows how to communicate effectively in situations where this would otherwise appear improbable. The code thus encourages one to have the appropriate feelings. Without this, La Rochefoucauld believed, most people would never acquire such feelings. Indeed, English-women who try to emulate characters in pre-Victorian novels have to wait for visible signs of nuptial love before allowing themselves to discover consciously what love is. In other words, we are not dealing with a pure invention of sociological theory, but rather with something that has long been the subject of consideration in studies of the semantics of love. A generalized theory can only contribute abstract insights, but these in turn enable comparisons to be made between love and things of a completely different nature, such as power, money and truth; accordingly, additional knowledge is gained and love is thus shown to be not a mere anomaly, but indeed a quite normal improbability.

Increasing the probability of the improbable – such is the formula that links social theory, evolutionary theory, and a theory of the media of communication. Any normalization of more improbable social structure makes greater demands on the media of communication, is reflected in their semantics; evolution is the concept that will be used to explain how this phenomenon comes about.

The historical studies on the semantics of love are embedded in this theoretical framework. Naturally they cannot, strictly speaking, claim to provide a methodological verification of evolutionary theory, but with regard to methodology, however, they do provide two complementary, pragmatic insights. The one shows that only highly abstract sociological theories of a very complex nature can bring historical material to life: access to the concrete is only reached by treading the path of abstraction. Sociology is thus far too little developed in terms of theory and abstraction for fruitful historical research to be fully elaborated. The second insight is that temporal sequences possess a unique evidential quality with respect to complex phenomena – a form of proof, however, which has so far not been adequately clarified in methodological terms.

Parsons occasionally toyed with the idea that a differentiated system is only a system because it has arisen from processes of differentiation. Research into historical semantics reinforces such a view. Apparently, evolution experiments with adaptive capacity.

When viewed synchronically, highly complex matters clearly appear to be intertwined. This interconnectedness can be deemed contingent, but it is then nearly impossible to exclude other combinations as being less valid or less probable. An historical investigation uncovers such affinities more readily, in that it demonstrates how an existing system or a thoroughly formulated, consistently ordered semantics predetermines its own future (even though it in principle must be thought of as undetermined). This is most evident in the history of science: it can hardly be pure chance that scientific discoveries are triggered off which subsequently prove themselves to be true. Truth becomes manifest within the process.

This maxim could perhaps be generalized to serve as a heuristic tool, as is illustrated by the following example from the historical case studies. Sociological theory postulates abstractly that a relation obtains between the differentiation of generalized symbolic media of communication and the regulation of their 'real assets' (Parsons), i.e. their symbiotic mechanisms. This approach can be demonstrated by comparing the connections between truth and perception, love and sexuality, money and elementary needs as well as between power and force. Employing this hypothesis, historical research shows further that the differences between the *amour passion* complex of the French and the Puritans' notion of marriage based on 'companionship' created different preconditions for their respective adaptability, spefically in the following context: only the semantics of *amour passion* was sufficiently complex, as we shall show in detail, to absorb the revaluation of sexuality that occurred in the eighteenth century. Despite having provided a preliminary basis for the integration of love and marriage, and under the same conditions as the French, the English were only able to come up with the Victorian malformation of sexual morality. This historical *sequence* reveals an underlying *factual* connection – particularly in the *diversity* of the reactions it uncovers – to *one and the same problem*. Admittedly (despite what Weber says) this offers only an unsatisfactory methodological explanation.

I shall not go into the circumstances and results of this approach here, because the nature of the connections involved is too complex to be summarized briefly. Their sequential presentation in chapters is thus itself something of a compromise. Since factual complexes, historical changes and regional differences are often interwoven, it was not possible to divide the study in such a manner that each chapter would deal with one specific aspect. The literature I worked with is indicated in the notes. I have drawn in addition on seventeenth- and eighteenth-century novels which were at first closely intertwined with aphoristic and discursive literature, only for this link to slowly dissolve. This created certain difficulties in evaluating the material. Although it has been known since the seventeenth century that novels assume the role of providing instruction and orientation in affairs of the heart, it is difficult to break this insight down into individual theses, concepts, theorems and precepts. All that can be determined is that the behaviour of characters in novels is code-oriented, i.e. they tend to animate the code rather than expand upon it. In the case of important works, such as the *Princesse de Clèves* and the subsequent train of novels on the renunciation of worldly pleasure that followed in its wake, the exceptions to the rule will readily meet the eye. I made a point of looking for second- and third-rate literature, and allowed myself to be guided by a very subjective principle in selecting the quotations, namely, that of stylistic elegance. It may therefore be attributed to a personal love of the material that I could not bring myself to translate quotations from widely spoken European languages.

1

Society and Individual

Personal and Impersonal Relationships

It is most assuredly incorrect to characterize modern society as an impersonal mass society and leave it at that. Such a view arises partly owing to an overly narrow conception of society and partly because of a set of optical illusions. If society is conceived of primarily in terms of economic categories, that is, its economic system, then it necessarily follows that impersonal relationships are the rule, for this is indeed the case within the economic system. But the economy is only one of the various factors determining social life. It is true even for individuals, of course, that only impersonal relationships can be established with most other people. If society is therefore taken to be the sum-total of possible relationships, it will appear, for the most part, to be impersonal. At the same time, however, it is *also* possible for individuals in some cases to intensify personal relationships and to communicate to others much of what they believe to be most intimately theirs and find this affirmed by others. Bearing in mind that everyone can enter into such relationships, and indeed many do, these too must be judged to exist on a massive scale.[1] Moreover, in modern society to avail oneself of this option is typically neither subject to any restrictions nor encumbered by the need to make allowances for other relationships.

We shall accordingly assume in the following that modern society is to be distinguished from older social formations by the fact that it has become more elaborate in two ways: it affords more opportunities both for impersonal and for more intensive personal relationships. This double adaptive capacity can be further expanded because present society is, as a whole, more complex, can more effectively regulate interdependencies between different forms of social relations and is better able to filter out potential disturbances.

It is possible to speak in terms of an enhanced capacity for impersonal relationships, in that one can communicate in numerous areas with no risk of misunderstanding, even if one has no personal knowledge whatsoever of the people with whom one is talking, and can only 'size them up' by means of a few hurriedly noted role characteristics (policeman, salesman, switchboard operator). This is the case, moreover, because every individual action depends on innumerable others, the functions of which are not guaranteed by certain personality characteristics that can be known to the person who has to rely on them. Never before has a society exhibited such improbable, contingent dependencies, which can neither be held to be natural, nor interpreted solely on the basis of one's knowledge of other people.

Equally, an enhanced capacity for personal relationships cannot be seen as a simple extension or increase in the number and diversity of effective acts of communication, for such an extension would soon reach a point where it would overwhelm anyone.

The personal element in social relationships cannot therefore become more extensive, only more intensive. In other words, it is a question of laying the basis for social relations in which more of the individual, unique attributes of each person, or ultimately all their characteristics, become significant. We shall term such relationships *interpersonal interpenetration*. By the same token, one can speak of *intimate relationships*.

This concept describes a process. It is based on the supposition that the sum total of everything which goes to form an individual, his memories and attitudes, can never be accessible to someone else, if for no other reason than that the individual himself has no access to them (as can be seen from Tristram Shandy's attempt to write his own biography). Of course, one can to a 'greater or lesser' degree know something about the other person and heed this. Above all, at the communicative level, there are rules or codes which prescribe that in certain social situations one must be receptive in principle to everything about another person, must refrain from displaying indifference towards what the other finds of great personal relevance and in turn must leave no question unanswered, even if and especially when this centres on matters of a personal nature. While interpersonal interpenetration can be enhanced *continuously* in factual terms – given sufficient room for manoeuvre in society and disregarding possible disturbances – the capacity for such enhancement must be fixed *discontinuously* at the level of communicative regulations.

A type of system is thus created for intimate relationships which ensures that the personal level has to be included in the communication.

Judging from what we know or assume about the social genesis of individuality,[2] the need for personal individuality and the capacity for stylizing oneself and others as unique can presumably not be adequately explained simply in terms of anthropological constants. Rather, such a need and its possible expression and affirmation in communicative relationships correspond to a specific socio-structural framework, especially to the complexity and particular form of differentiation adopted by that social system.[3] We shall not treat the sociogenesis of individuality and its attendant semantics *in extenso*, but shall instead confine ourselves to a subordinate question which is nevertheless important to our considerations: namely, the question of the genesis of a generalized symbolic communicative medium assigned specifically to facilitating, cultivating and promoting the communicative treatment of individuality.

It goes without saying that one must assume that individuality in the sense of a self-propelling, psycho-physical unity, and above all in terms of each person's individual death, is something accepted by all societies.

The Christian credo of the indestructability of the soul and the notion that the salvation of the soul is an individual fate irrespective of stratification, family or even the circumstances surrounding each death, do not essentially add anything to this anthropological fact, nor, for that matter, do the Renaissance view of a pronounced individualism, the individualization of affect-management and natural rationality (e.g. Vives) or the Baroque concept of self-assertive individualism. Such notions serve only to strengthen their social legitimacy in the face of increasing difficulties in anchoring the individual person in the respective social structures. People are still defined according to their social status, i.e. by their positions within a stratified social system. At the same time, however, less claim is made to a specific position within the functional areas of politics, economics, religion and the academic world. This did not, at least not initially, lead to the abandonment of the old concept of the individual, i.e. its definition in terms of indivisibility and separateness, or to its being modified when applied to actual living persons.[4]

The development which leads up to the modern world and which cancelled out the traditional concept of the individual and invested the word with new meaning had a number of different aspects to it. These must be carefully distinguished from one another because they not only refer to substantially different things, but also to some extent conflict with each other. First of all, the transition from stratified to functional differentiation within society leads to greater differentiation of personal and social systems (or, to be exact, of system/environment distinctions within personal or social systems). This is the case because with the adoption of functional differentiation individual persons can no longer be firmly located in one single subsystem of society, but rather must be regarded a priori as socially displaced.[5] As a consequence, not only do individuals now consider themselves unique owing to the supposed greater diversity of individual attributes (which may not at all be true), but also a greater differentiation occurs of system/environment relations, necessary for personal systems to refer to specific systems. Accordingly, if persons now nonetheless share common characteristics, this must be attributed to coincidence (and no longer to a characteristic of the species).

This trend towards differentiation, easily comprehensible from the point of view of systems theory, means that individuals are all the more provoked into interpreting the difference between themselves and the environment (and in the temporal dimension, the history and future of this difference) in terms of their own person, whereby the ego becomes the focal point of all their inner experiences and the environment loses most of its contours. Possessing a name and a place within the social framework in the form of general categories such as age, gender, social status and profession no longer suffices as a means both of knowing that one's organism exists and of self-identification – the basis of one's own life experience and action. Rather, individual persons have to find affirmation at the level of their respective personality *systems*, i.e. in the difference between themselves and their *environment* and in the manner in which they deal with this difference – as opposed to the way others do. At the same time, society and the possible worlds it can constitute become much more complex and impenetrable. The need for a world that is still understandable, intimate and close (which, incidentally, means approximately the same thing as does the ancient Greek 'philos') stems from this, a world which one can, furthermore, learn to make one's own.

An individualization of the person and the need for a close world are not necessarily parallel processes; indeed, they tend to contradict one another, for the close world leaves the individual less room for development than do the impersonal macro-mechanisms fixed in terms of legal or monetary, political or scientific principles. Thus, a concept of increasing personal individualization does not adequately pinpoint the problems which individuals have to overcome in the modern world, for they cannot simply fall back on their autonomy and the resulting adaptability this entails. What is more, the individual person needs the *difference* between a close world and a distant, impersonal one, i.e. the *difference* between only personally valid experiences, assessments and reactions and the anonymous, universally accepted world – in order to be shielded from the immense complexity and contingency of all the things which could be deemed possible.

It is by virtue of this difference that individuals can channel the flow of the information they receive. This is only possible if the manner in which one deals with highly personal inner experiences as well as one's inclinations to act in a particular way receive social affirmation and as long as the forms by which such affirmation can be achieved are approved by society. Individuals must be in a position to receive positive feedback not only on what they themselves are, but also on what they themselves see.

These circumstances must be formulated in such a complex manner if we are to comprehend that all communication in areas that have great personal relevance has to do with this double quality of both being oneself and having a personal view of the world, and that the person who takes part in this process of communication as the alter ego is involved in it himself and for others in precisely this double fashion. Thus, in order for a commonly shared private world to become a differentiated entity, each person must be able to lend his support to the world of the other (although his inner experiences are highly individual), because a special role is accorded to him in it: he appears in the other person's world as the one who is loved. Despite all the possible, and indeed already apparent, discrepancies between excessive individualism and the need for a close world (one need think only of the sentiments of both friendship *and* loneliness in the eighteenth century), a common medium of communication has developed to deal with both types of problems – which employs the semantic fields of friendship and love.

Our investigation is concerned with the differentiation of this medium and with assessing the durability of the semantics it created. The differentiation of such a system first assumes a visible shape in the second half of the seventeenth century. It was aided by the fact that both the unique value of individuality and tasks such as self-control and affect-management assigned to the individual as an individual were already socially recognized. But it could not be presumed that individuals oriented themselves towards the difference of personal and impersonal interaction and therefore the medium sought to establish a highly personal form of communication based on intimacy and trust. The need for a close world that could be projected into the world as a whole was entirely absent for such a time as the form of communication was still based on a stratification. How was it thus nevertheless possible for a special medium of communication for intimacy to develop? And what course did it take? These questions must first be elaborated by means of an overall theory of generalized symbolic media of communication before we proceed to the historical case studies.

2

Love as a Generalized Symbolic Medium of Communication

Generalized symbolic media of communication are primarily semantic devices which enable essentially improbable communications nevertheless to be made successfully.[1] In this context 'successfully' means heightening receptivity to the communication in such a way that it can be attempted, rather than abandoned as hopeless from the outset. This threshold of improbability must be overcome above all as social systems would otherwise not be formed, in that they arise only through the agency of communication. Improbabilities, in other words, amount to thresholds which one is discouraged from crossing, and, with regard to evolution, those at which possible variations will again be eradicated. If the point at which one must tread these thresholds can be deferred, then a social system's capacity for forming subsystems increases. At the same time the number of communicable topics grows, as does both the leeway for potential communication in the system and the external adaptability of the system. This has the cumulative effect of enhancing the probability of evolution.[2]

One can assume of all media of communication that the demands placed on them increase in the course of social evolution. If the social system and its possible environments become more complex, then the selectivity of each definition also increases. Communicating something in particular involves selection from among a number of different possibilities. The motivation to transmit and receive selected choices thereby becomes more improbable, and it thus becomes more difficult to motivate receptivity by means of the form of selection taken. It is, however, the function of media of communication to achieve precisely this. Taken together, the theory of social evolution and the proposition that changing the type of differentiation adopted by society effects a sudden increase in the complexity of the social system lead one to suppose not only that society's communicative processes indeed follow such a course of development, but that they will attempt to find a different, at once both more general and more specialized level combining selection and motivation. Love, for example, is now declared – in contrast to the traditional demand that it function solely as a form of social solidarity – to be both unfathomable and personal: 'Par ce que c'estoit luy; par ce que c'estoit moy', as Montaigne's famous epigram would have it.[3]

There is no reason to suppose that the search for new forms will necessarily be successful or that the enhanced complexity in all functional areas of society can be held in check. One must therefore rely on empirical and historical analyses, on analyses of both the social structures and the history of ideas. Each of these is necessary in order not only to clarify the extent to which society can sustain its own evolution and is able to re-form its communications accordingly, but also to specify the degree to which certain functional areas lag behind, as a result of which corresponding deformations have to be taken into account.

The generalized symbolic media which have to solve such problems of combining selection and motivation employ a semantic matrix intimately connected with reality: truth, love, money, power, etc. These terms *designate* particular properties of sentences, feelings, media of exchange, threats and the like. And the use of the media involves precisely these forms of orientation towards such specific circumstances, whereby the factual circumstances themselves are taken to possess a causality of their own. The communicating parties *mean* this; they have this 'in mind'. But the media of communication themselves *are not to be confused* with the circumstances in question; rather, they are communicative instructions which can be manipulated more or less independently of whether such circumstances indeed exist or not.[4] The functions and effects of the media can thus not be adequately comprehended if studied only at this level of factually localized qualities, feelings and causalities, for they are always already socially mediated: by virtue of the agreement reached on the communicative capacities to be adopted.

Understood in terms of the above, love as a medium is not itself a feeling, but rather a code of communication, according to the rules of which one can express, form and simulate feelings, deny them, impute them to others, and be prepared to face up to all the consequences which enacting such a communication may bring with it. As early as the seventeenth century, people were fully aware of the fact, as we shall show in the coming chapters, that, despite all emphasis on love as passion, they were dealing with a model of behaviour that could be acted out and which one had in full view before embarking on the search for love. In other words, the model provided a point of orientation and a source of knowledge as to the importance of the pursuit before one tried to find a partner, made one notice the absence of a partner and indeed made this absence appear as one's fate.[5] Love thus at first seemed to be like running on the spot[6] and to centre on a generalized search pattern which, while facilitating selection, could obstruct any deep emotional fulfilment. It is the enhancement of the meanings anchored in the code which enables love to be learned, tokens of it to be interpreted and small signs of it to convey deep feelings; and it is the code which allows difference to be experienced and makes unrequited love equally exalting.

The following considerations are grounded in a number of related premises. We assume that the thematic choices and guiding principles informing literary, idealizing and mythicizing portrayals of love are not arbitrary, but rather represent reactions to the respective society and the trends for change within it. These portrayals do not necessarily depict the real factual circumstances of love – even if given in descriptive form – but do indeed solve recognizable problems: by lending an historically transferrable form to functional necessities of the social system. The semantics of love can in each case therefore provide an understanding of the relationship between symbolic media and social structure.

Every generalized symbolic medium is differentiated according to a specific threshold problem. In the case of the medium of love, this problem lies in the fact that communication is highly personalized, which is taken to mean that one endeavours to set oneself off from other individuals. This can be achieved by making oneself the topic of conversation, i.e. by talking about oneself; or, in the case of a factual topic, by making one's grasp of the topic the hub of the conversation. The more individual, idiosyncratic or strange one's own standpoint or view of the world, the more improbable that it will find the consensus of others or meet with their interest. It is not merely a question of the characteristics an individual possesses, or claims to possess; in other words, it is not only the person's beauty or virtue which plays a decisive role in the love literature of the seventeenth and eighteenth centuries. It is possible, after all, for personal characteristics to be accepted, admired or simply tolerated as facts. What cannot be treated in this manner is the *personal individual's relation to the world*, which does not emerge as a topic until the end of the eighteenth century. If this relation to the world is also individualized in the process, then it is no longer possible for one to limit oneself in communication to simply according recognition to some fact – pleasant, useful, barely acceptable or otherwise appraised – present in the other person. If the other person lays claim to possessing a world-constitutive individuality, then one has always already been allocated a place in that world and therefore is *ineluctably* faced with *the alternative of either affirming or rejecting the other's egocentric projection of the world*. This complementary role as the affirmer of a particular world is forced upon one, although at the same time that world projection is supposed to be unique, idiosyncratic and therefore cannot serve as a basis for consensus. This also means that one is expected to adopt an affirmative stance which simultaneously cuts him off from the outside world, i.e. the view cannot be upheld elsewhere. Put under such pressure, any sensible addressee will take flight or at least try to ignore the implied personalized communicative frame of reference and tactfully guide the conversation toward the impersonal level of an 'anonymously' constituted world.

Thus, even if this appears to the lovers to be the case at the outset, love can not centre on 'total communication',[7] on concentrating all possible acts of communication on the partner or the love affair. Not a total, but rather a universal frame of reference is expected of the other partner in the sense of a constant consideration of oneself in all possible situations. In other words, the informative content of all communication is constantly being enriched by the ingredient of 'for you'. Accordingly, it is not the *thematic* level of the communicative process that provides the point from which love can be understood and practised, but rather its *codification*.

A special 'code' for love is created once all information is duplicated in terms of the meaning that it possesses on the one hand in the general, anonymously constituted world and on the other for you, for us, and for our world. This difference is not simply that one piece of information can be treated as being part of only the one or the other world, because, needless to say, each private world projects what it regards as its own 'never-endingness' onto the total horizon of that world which is the same for everyone. Rather, the information has to be duplicated, in order for it to gain validity in and stand the test of each of the two worlds (according to the needs of the given moment). As is often the case with the written word, the code is duplicated for special purposes, which does not throw into question the underlying unity of both variants.

An examination of the location in inner experience and action to which selections are attributed reveals that successful communication becomes increasingly improbable, given conditions in which the person's view of the world is increasingly individualized and yet the world is still held to be anonymously constituted.[8] Individuals cannot conceive of their relation to the world in terms of their own actions (that is, unless they have read Fichte); it is impossible for them to attribute everything they experience as selection to their own actions. Rather, the mass of selections, however idiosyncratically these are related to specific expectations, emphasized or accorded importance compared with differences, are nevertheless registered as selections made by the world itself. Other persons, forced into the role of affirming this world, would then have to act in opposition to it, in that they would have to state why they do not share certain views. The distinction of such attributes is thus structured *asymmetrically* in terms of the problem threshold and the improbability of highly personal communication. The lover, who is expected to affirm idiosyncratic selections, is obliged to *act*, because he is confronted with a choice that has to be made; the beloved, on the other hand, has only *experienced* something and expects him to identify with that experience. The one has to become involved, whereas the other (who is also forever tied to a projected world) only had to make the projection. The flow of information, the transfer of selectivity from the alter (the beloved) to the ego (the lover) thus transfers inner experience onto action. The special (and, if one so wishes, tragic) nature of love lies in this asymmetry, in the necessity of responding to inner experience with action, and to already being bound by binding oneself.[9]

On the other hand, in love relationships, the lover (the ego) can only *adapt his actions* to something because the beloved's inner experience prescribes *reductions*. The theme of 'never-endingness' which is forever cropping up in the semantics of love also means that there are no bounds to one's own actions in the other's inner world; at least not for someone who is included in this world as also being loved. The asymmetry of inner experience and action then entails the *possibility of anticipation*: one can orientate oneself towards the inner experience of the other person, even if he has not actually conveyed that expectation, has not expressed a wish of any kind and not undertaken to attribute anything to himself. This is what is meant when in the semantics of love someone is urged to go beyond the call of galant duty, or when mention is made of an 'unspoken' agreement. It is also what is experienced when lovers have no need to rely on procedures for reaching an agreement in order to act in harmony vis-à-vis third parties.

Thus the medium cannot be adequately characterized simply by asserting that love is aimed at a single person, an 'individual', and embraces the indivisible totality of the beloved. Such a conception is analogous to reifying the other person; calling him a 'subject' merely denies this, but does not actually display a new notion. Only by wedding systems theory and a theory of communication is it possible to advance beyond this stage of research.

What has been labelled 'inner experience' can be unravelled further to reveal two distinct areas, in both of which extreme demands are placed on one's ability to observe and to then act accordingly. We will now refer to the alter as a psychic system. Inner experience consequently means that the system refers to its *environment* in the attribution of particular facts and occurrences. It is extraordinarily difficult for an observer to incorporate the environment of the observing system into the field of observation. This is the case because on the one hand inner experience must be regarded not as a fact but as the selective process of another system relating itself to its own environment (whereby relations cannot be observed, but only conceptualized). On the other hand, the observer forms (at least in the case of love) a part, indeed often an important part, of this environment. In other words, not only does one come up against the limits of one's own system, but right in the middle of the world, so to speak, one suddenly comes across one's own compelling references to oneself.[10]

The second area the analysis reveals is centred on the concept of *information*. Normally, all that can be observed in other systems is inputs and outputs. We can see that the other person is listening to, watching, or reading something and then reacts to it, but this does not mean that we can also grasp the information or information processing involved. Information is the selective treatment of differences, whereby the person experiencing something projects occurrences onto a horizon of other possibilities and sets the limits of his own system by the experience of 'this and not something else' or 'this and not that'. Which and when further alternatives function as the comparative matrix for the others can therefore hardly be assessed from outside the respective systems, and yet information is not observable without taking this selective horizon into account. One would have to participate in the other person's self-referential information processing or at least be able to adequately reconstruct it, in order to be able to 'understand' how input works in him as information and how the person in turn reconnects output (what is said, for example) and information processing.

The communicative medium of love functions to make this seemingly improbable step possible. This is what is called 'understanding' in everyday parlance, and finds expression as the wish to be understood and – in the form of the complaint that one is not sufficiently understood – is pushed beyond the bounds of the technically possible. If someone attempts to thus surpass the observable, then it is understandable why ultimately all objective, generalized indicators of love, such as merit, beauty or virtue, are cast aside in favour of an increasing personalization of the principle which will make the improbable possible. To do so, the medium makes use of each person, in the sense that one has to know him as well as possible in order to be able to register or develop a feel for what it is that works both for him as an environment and in him as a comparative matrix. What must also be considered is that the concept of the subject is desubstantialized in the eighteenth century; for it is indeed a question of thinking of the other person in terms of the relations to the environment operative for him and in terms of his relations to himself, and thus of no longer conceiving of him in terms of personal characteristics, but rather as a set of functions. The basis which one needs for such an understanding can only be gained by addressing the person – rather than the person's nature or morals. If one accepts what has come about by chance and foregoes any external foundation for this calculation or assessment, one may make some progress toward adjusting oneself to what constitutes environment and information, to what is more or less compulsion and freedom for one's beloved, and to the functional horizons that delimit the shape her inner experiences and actions take. But such an understanding love is so strenuous in cognitive terms that it is easier to stick to feelings and put up with the instability involved. However, this escape route, as we will show in some detail, prevents any institutional solution to the relation of love and marriage.

This also clearly shows that love solves its own attendant communicative problems in a completely unique manner. To put it paradoxically, love is able to enhance communication by largely doing without any communication. It makes use primarily of indirect communication, relies on anticipation and on having already understood. And love can thus be damaged by explicit communication, by discreet questions and answers, because such openness would indicate that something had not been understood as a matter of course. In this context, one might mention that the classical code makes use of 'eye language' as well as the idea of lovers talking for hours on end with one another without really having anything to say.[11] In other words, the lover does not need to be tuned in by action, questions or requests on the part of the beloved: the latter's inner experience is supposed to immediately trigger off the lover's actions.

The concept of love would nevertheless not be complete if it were seen merely as a form of reciprocally satisfying action or as the willingness to fulfil wishes. Love initially colours an experience of someone's inner experience and thus transforms the world as the horizon of inner experience and action. Being in love thus means to internalize another person's subjectively systematized view of the world; it thereby lends a special power of conviction to the other person's experience or possible experience in terms of the objects and even occurrences involved. And it is only of secondary importance that love motivates one to act, not for concrete effect, but because such action has, or is assumed to have, a symbolically expressive, love-exhibiting meaning and is judged to complete the uniqueness of the world in which the lover knows himself to be in harmony with the beloved (and with no one else). This is a world of a common taste and a history in common, of common deviations, of topics discussed and occurrences jointly evaluated. One acts thus not owing to some intention to profit from the action in question, but because of the fact that such a projection of the world as an entity completely tailored to the individuality of a person is not just a matter of course. To the extent that love revolves around 'giving', it therefore implies 'enabling the other to give, by virtue of the fact that he is as he is'.

This function is not clearly formulated, but rather symbolized within the semantics of the medium of love. There is nothing which says a lover has to approve of a private world that is not in accordance with public opinion; but love is normally described by symbols which express that this is indeed the case when one loves. The primary symbol governing the thematic structure of the medium of love is initially called 'passion', and passion means that one is subjected to something, something unalterable and for which one cannot be held accountable. Other images, some of which go back a long way, have the same symbolic value – as in the saying that love is a type of disease; that love is madness, *folie à deux*;[12] that love puts one in chains. Other expressions say that love is a mystery, or a miracle, that it defies explanation or requires no justification, etc.[13] All these images point to a deviation from normal social controls, nevertheless tolerated as a sort of disease and honoured by being assigned a special role.[14]

When outlining a generalized symbolic medium of communication, we must also bear in mind that people live together, a physical and organic fact which must be examined more closely. No communicative system can be devised totally disregarding the physical existence of the communicators within it, and the functional specialization of a media-semantics thus requires that this physical, organic relation also be transformed into symbols. We shall term symbols that fulfil this function symbiotic symbols or symbiotic mechanisms – 'mechanisms' in the sense that they can be expected to designate organic processes which can be consummated.[15] Various possibilities come into consideration, but on the whole we need only distinguish between a small number of them in order to differentiate between the communicative media. Perception (including a perception of perceptions), sexuality, the satisfaction of (initially basic) needs as well as physical force are distinct, and all highly graphic, organic processes; they influence one another, can upset or further each other and form, if more than two parties are present, a diffuse basis for communication.[16] If a situation is to be reserved for one, and only one, communicative medium, then potential disturbances have to be eliminated. This is accomplished by concentrating on one and only one symbiotic mechanism. For the power complex, this mechanism would be force, for truth it would be perception based on theoretically relevant data, for money the (increasingly abstracted) need satisfaction and for love, sexuality. Although communication in the respective media sphere is in no way limited by the symbiotic mechanism to which it is allocated, this mechanism is all the more a precondition for differentiation and enhancement. It is thus no coincidence that the most important social communicative media are each based on selective and at the same time highly graphic reference to organic processes and wherever this is not possible, the association of media with functional systems creates problems.[17]

In the case of sexually based intimacy, the relationship of symbiotic base to symbolic generalization takes on particular traits which can be described in greater detail.[18] Initially this basis in sexuality explains why the partners set such great store on 'being together', on immediacy and closeness; and why they prefer to be in places where they can hope to see each other. Furthermore, it is peculiar to sexual relations that they are not realized with outsiders or their approval in mind. Instead they are meaningful in themselves and their further refinement does not require the outside world. Giving and taking, rewarding and holding back, affirmation and correction are all possible, but cannot be easily discerned or attributed to some particular interest or intention, for that matter. An intention to exchange, sanction, teach and learn, as well as elements of these acts, all fulfil their particular function, but can hardly be kept apart from one another, accorded to some individual characteristic or submitted for discussion. They blend together into an amorphous mass. This prevents, other than in extreme cases, an exact evaluation of advantages and disadvantages, the optimization of one's own position, and also prevents the relationship from developing into the asymmetry of a given construct of performance, hierarchy or interests. Thanks to this elusiveness of sexual contact, even relatively unbalanced relationships can still be experienced by both sides as favourable and incomparable. This, in turn, permits a broad range of mental and spiritual interests to be drawn into the relationship without them being traded off against each other.[19] Thus, to a degree otherwise barely attainable, one can assume that one's own inner experience is also that of one's partner. This is ultimately the case because of the reflexivity of reciprocal desire. In physical interplay one discovers that, beyond one's own desire and its fulfilment, one also desires the other's desire and thus learns that the other wishes to be desired. This makes it impossible for 'selflessness' to provide a foundation for one's actions and the form they take; rather the strength of one's own wish becomes the measure of what one is able to give.[20] As a result of all this, sexuality breaks out of the schematism of egoism/ altruism and the hierarchization of human relationships according to sensuality/reason. Last but not least, historical evidence for this is to be found in the fact that these two distinctions, common in traditional European morals and anthropology, are rendered invalid by the differentiation of sexually based intimate relationships within the code of love, as we shall show in detail.

What is more, the non-verbal communication just outlined can also be effected with reference to sexuality and can enrich itself from it. However, it is not as if all 'already understanding each other' can be attributed to it! But the non-linguistic communication in physical contact provides an important non-logical field of interpretation for linguistic messages. It offers access to a structure beneath language and the opportunity to supplement language, i.e. it generates an interpretation of the spoken word which concretizes what opinions and intentions the word manifests. The different forms of communication used by love enable one to express the ineffable; to strengthen or weaken, belittle, retract or thwart what has already been said, iron out misunderstandings and *faux pas* by changing the level of communication; and one can hit upon a rejoinder or even a block at this metalevel below articulated communication.

As is always the case with symbolization, negation is not excluded here, but rather appropriated. Thus, the code of force is based on the exclusion of all physical force – except to enforce justice. And in the semantics of love the exclusion of possible sexual relationships plays a considerable role – taking forms that range from the *amour lointain* of Medieval courtly love via such stages as the lengthy puzzles and games of hide-and-seek of the giant seventeenth-century novels, the moment of pleasure being shifted to the level of the 'not yet' and the preservation of virtue as a tactical means of foisting marriage on someone,[21] to a positive doctrine of sexuality.[22] The latter had gradually been established from the eighteenth century on, but still hinged on feelings, the existence of which was as a whole denied and only desired in secret. The use of negation in the context of the linguistic realization of a medium may appear as 'ambiguity', but as an element of the semantic structure it has a very precise meaning in terms of a differentiation and enhancement of the specific ways of communicating and communicative successes. Inhibiting what is actually possible is a prerequisite for the semantic conditioning that grants access to such a linguistic realization, and the progressive degrees of freedom within the communicative processes are founded on this conditioning.[23]

In addition, before turning to historical analyses, some attention must be paid to *self-referentiality* within a communicative medium. We have to do here with another general requirement of all communicative media. With the differentiation of structure and process, self-referentiality also doubles up, so that we have to distinguish between two levels. At the level of the semantic structure of the medium, self-reference appears as the systematization of themes. Each individual characterization of love must be understood as referring back to all others. As this is true of *every* characterization, and thus holds true for *all the others*, every theme occurs in all the others as *the other of the others*. Via self-referentiality, in other words, codification becomes (at the semantic level) a closed system. It is in this manner that the references of the symbiotic mechanism are incorporated: in love one cannot not think of sensuality, and yet conversely, advances in the direction of sexual relations raise the question of whether true or only pretended love is involved.[24]

Self-referential systematization increases in importance in direct proportion to the improbability of communicative success and the uncertain fate of the social relationship. The more uncertain one is of how the other will adapt to expectations, the more indispensable it becomes to have a system within which one can interpret one's own utterances and the ensuing reactions to them, i.e. where one can read them as indicators of something else, something further, something hoped for. This can be demonstrated most clearly by looking at the seventeenth century. The recognition that a woman was free to enter into a relationship of love led to a systematization of the code of *amour passion*. To put it in theoretical terms, a *double contingency is differentiated* in a particular area of interest, resulting in a *self-referential systematization* of a special code for love. The *uncertainty* which arises from this double contingency can then become *thematized* within this code, for example as the alternatives of either true or false love. Uncertainty then becomes the basis for the validity and use of the semantics in question, which, in turn gives it some sort of tolerable form.

Once a special semantics has become sufficiently differentiated, the processes ordered by this medium can also become self-referential. Self-referentiality at this level of communicative processes will be termed *reflexivity*. Assuming that this special phenomenon becomes sufficiently isolated, then one can postulate that love is only to be motivated by love, i.e. love refers to love, seeks love, and grows to the extent that it finds love and can fulfil itself as love.

Only once the reflexivity of the process has been established (or to be more exact, once the semantic codification of the process has become reflexive) does the medium become completely accessible and differentiated. The problem of inclusion and 'equality of opportunity' can only be solved after this form has been attained. As long as love had to do primarily with rare characteristics of the beloved, with wealth and youth, beauty and virtue, enhancement revolved round the value of these rarities and tried to find affirmation in them. This view, predominant in the seventeenth, and even in the eighteenth century, if taken literally, would have necessarily led to insoluble problems of distribution. For who would have stood a chance in love if only unusual characteristics were the basic premise of everything, when there were actually only very few really beautiful and virtuous ladies and gentlemen?[25] Developments have forced an increasing neutralization of the role played by such preconditions of love as do not reside within love itself. This neutralization takes the form of reflexivity and its function is to pave the way for the medium's universal accessability in terms of its self-regulation free of external intervention.[26] On the basis of this secured reflexivity, the characteristics necessary in order to love or be loved can be trivialized and made contingent on historical or biographical coincidence.

It is not difficult to find parallels in other media. Art takes objects which are ugly, part of everyday life and not in themselves suited to artistic treatment, and makes them worth depicting in art. Law is no longer simply an elaboration and adaptation of what is by nature 'law', but includes everything which has been made Law by judicial processes. Equally, political power, by subjecting every form of power to another power, is universally sensitive to all topics to the extent that they can be politicized; any person, therefore, has access to it as long as they take part in political elections. Important trends in modern society promote such constructs of the universalization and specification of reflexivity, and the medium for intimate relationships is no exception, despite its being tailored to extreme particularization in each individual case.

Codification becomes reflected in the semantics of love at a much earlier stage than in other media of communication as a direct consequence of printing. Even the early parodies of the novel themselves play a role in this context. Already by the seventeenth century it was common knowledge that the lady had read novels and therefore knew the code. This enhanced her attentiveness. She was forewarned – and endangered precisely by that very fact. Somewhat later, the sensitive male also became a victim of the novel.[27] Everyone else had also read of the clichés and gestures which were all part of the art of seduction. One cannot help but assume that the woman could see through them, but also knew that they would still be effective. The code thus not only regulated behaviour, but also documented its own recurrence in the very area of behaviour it regulated. Neither the code of power nor that of money would have been able to tolerate such a degree of transparency at that time. Only in love did the printing of books effect such a split; and precisely here one can fortunately rely on interests which ensured that love functioned in spite of this.

One must, after all, bear in mind that none of the generalized symbolic media of communication do not, quasi-automatically, form specialized social systems of this type. Media have a selective effect in socio-cultural evolution, but are not necessarily also a stabilizing factor. It is very usual for media to form systems that only stabilize in opposition to socially typical pressures, as well as prevailing attitudes and expectations. In early modern times this problem became more acute to the extent that, with the invention of the printed word, greater, more improbable demands were made of communicative media. Symbols cropped up within the media codes which had pointedly 'unsocial', or at least metamoral connotations – for example *raison d'état* in the sphere of power, profit in the sphere of property and money or even quasi-pathological passion in the field of love. This also shows that the means with which to form social systems did not stem from society in general, from some moral conformity or social strata, but had to be created from scratch. This was accomplished in some fields with the aid of organization – a particular type of corporative systems formation developed specifically for that purpose. The communicative field of love could not avail itself of this possibility.[28] What did it make use of instead?

Initially, it appears, love relied on a clearly defined awareness of the problem and at a later stage, on demands made in connection with marriage. Thus, in the following historical analyses of the semantics of love it must always be borne in mind that the love code's representational world also has the function of providing a defence against impositions and thus not infrequently appears somewhat extravagant. Life in older, locally denser social systems was characterized by complex networks of relationships which blocked both any self-exclusion by individuals, but also a 'private life' or any retreat into pair relationships. One was expected to share one's life with others within a framework easily understood by all that society's members. Intimacy restricted to two people was hardly possible, or at any rate not encouraged, but rather discouraged as far as possible.[29] We will therefore first have to isolate the systemic conditions for intimacy from prevailing opinions and emotions;[30] and this will probably be complicated by the fact that not all age groups were equally interested in availing themselves of this opportunity.[31] Pair relationships which are not anchored in society would also seem by nature to be rare and problematical. As sociometric research has shown, 'choosing each other' on the basis of reciprocal projection seldom occurs and usually only short-term relationships result from it.[32]

These conditions make it clear that the codification of (sexually based) intimacy commenced initially outside the established order and that this capacity had to be paid for with 'concessions' in the semantics used: especially in the form of an admission that such relationships were irrational, insane and unstable. Only after people had become acclimatized to such a programme was it possible to embark seriously on the task of building social reflexivity into the semantics and thus to attempt to create a stable code system in the process – one whose success is still disputed nowadays. Love based on marriage is the result of that endeavour and the increased opportunities for divorce the corrective to it. In other words, it is left up to marriage whether love will persist or not.

3

The Evolution of
Communicative Capacities

A further chapter is necessary in order to provide the appropriate theoretical background for the subsequent historical studies. First an understanding must be gained of how evolutionary changes in cultural resources are actually converted into communication. This cannot be adequately achieved solely by means of an analysis of their linguistic and epistemological history; and the transition to functional differentiation[1] and a differentiation of the corresponding communicative media proposed by a study of the social structures is too abstract for such a purpose. In addition to all this, one must have recourse to a more precise analysis of the communicative process that is grounded in the causal basis and continuous reproduction of intimate relationships.

This theoretical analysis will be guided by two initial hypotheses:

1 In order for intimate communication to take place, the persons involved must be individualized to such an extent that their behaviour can be 'read' in a specific way: on the basis of a difference. And this difference is that of their own immediate interests and/or habits and what is done out of consideration for the other person or the relationship to that person.

2 The difference between acting and observing plays a greater role in intimate relationships than in many other forms of relationships. Ego is observed as the actor by alter with respect to the difference formulated above. The acting may take the shape of and be intended as communication, but it may also be acting of a different type or, of course, also be one of those aspects of communicative acting which are not intended as communication. As has been established by empirical

research, this gradual division between acting and observing tends to create a discrepancy in the attributes the partners ascribe to each other and ultimately can become a conflict of attribution. In other words, the actor judges his acting to have been called for by the particular circumstances of the situation, whereas the observer in contrast tends to attribute the acting to the characteristics of the actor's personality.[2] Accordingly, both parties start from different points of departure when searching for the causes of action, and this in itself leads to conflict.

Both these hypotheses are founded on the assumptions of attribution theory. They avoid any form of theory which would explain love in terms of empathy or sympathy and end up with a (descriptively supplemented) tautology.[3] The basic question to be asked is, to which 'actual' causes the observer attributes behaviour. Subsequently, one must ask how this attribution is then used by the observer to weigh up the attitude of the partner in terms of the rules of the code for intimate relationships. Lastly, the question must be raised of how the partner can use the expectation of such observation, in combination with the attribution informing it, to adjust his behaviour a priori.

The above conditions make the reproduction of intimacy difficult – or even, as has often been claimed, improbable. Marriages are made in heaven and fall apart in the automobile. For the person sitting at the wheel acts according to the situation and is doing so to the best of his ability; but the person sitting next to him and observing him feels manipulated by his way of driving and attributes this to the driver's personality characteristics. This person can only act in one way, namely by commenting and criticizing; and it is not very probable that this will find the driver's approval. In a taxi one would have little reason (other than in extreme cases) to communicate about this. In intimate relationships, however, it is precisely such a situation that becomes a test of the question: is your partner acting in a way which is based on your (and not his) world? And how could you fail to attempt to clarify things by communicating, in the presence of doubt, if the other alternative were to become resigned and silently tell yourself and the other person that you do not want to risk putting this to the test?

This example can serve as a guideline in the search for

generalizations. It shows us firstly that a very high degree of situational knowledge – and which both partners are aware of having in common – i.e. a high degree of cultural preformation, must be presumed to exist from the outset. This has nothing to do with individuality or love, but can be used to outline the contours of nuances in behaviour which can then serve as the matter of attribution. (He's 'taking the bends too sharply, even though he knows I don't like that'; she 'won't get out of the middle lane, even though she knows that I am a stickler for the letter of the law'.) In this sense one used to regard sociability and social polish and even the finely stylized details of behaviour as the precondition, or at least as a possible opportunity, for observing and sizing up beforehand prospective partners whom one had in mind for a closer relationship. Not least of all, these forms of behaviour served as the condition that allowed freedom to be made visible and attributable – despite all etiquette. The festivities in the 'world of grandeur' provided an opportunity for this.[4]

Lotte doesn't dance, she cuts black bread.[5] This, too, can satiate a sensitive soul; only, of course, that is if the sensibility in question can draw on anything in the world in order to experience love and suffering. This, however, would overstep the bounds of the capacity to communicate. The dialogue of seduction, resistance and submission, which until then it was thought one had to get by with, is torn apart by this, and the actual experience of love retreats – from Werther to Lucinde – into the loving subject who is no longer able to communicate adequately or, what is more important, to communicate with a sufficient degree of success. When emphasizing the importance of communication today, one should know by now what this means, what one is letting oneself in for, how to limit oneself and how narrow and dangerous the bridges are which one is building.

Our initial hypotheses allow us to define the problem of intimate communication more precisely. Regardless of the topics and observations involved, such communication is always a matter of reproducing excessive clusters of meaning that permit the observer to conclude that one's love still continues. 'Appearing in the other's world and being able to act accordingly' is something which has to be reactualized continuously. This means that the actor has to make himself observable as someone who goes beyond the normal bounds of his habits and interests. Wanting this must not, in turn, become reduced to a habit like expecting a greeting, a present, or a goodbye kiss; it has to be repeated without assuming the qualities of repetition; or – since this almost invariably fails – at least this must be understood to be its intention. The strenuous observation of the other person for any sign that he (intentionally or not) may give as an indication to which one can in return signal one's love is one of the most important rules of the classical semantics of love,[6] the underlying insight being that only continuous attention and a permanent willingness to act with the other person in mind are truly capable of symbolizing love.

Attitudes such as love must find expression in actions, for more is involved than some mere assertion or the fact that one has simply been impressed; it must be possible to read these attitudes in the actions, but they must not themselves be part of the act of acting. In this context, attribution theorists speak of attribution to a stable, temporally and factually (but not socially!) generalized disposition.[7] The moment of the action must thus hold a promise of permanence.[8] This is achieved if the actor uses his identity, i.e. uses the meaning of his action in such a way that the observer in turn thinks he can perceive the actor 'identifying' with his action. Over and above all the nuances of sincerity and insincerity, and despite the frequent lack of clarity on precisely which of the two is involved, the interconnection of action and individual being-as-self is the key to the question of generalization – and this is why only factual and temporal, but not social (i.e. universally valid) generalization concerns us here.

This in itself sounds like quite a complicated task, and yet it is still not adequate in one essential respect – as one's identity has to be put at risk as a dynamic rather than static guarantor of permanence, i.e. not as 'this is the way it always is' but as 'growing through love'. Referring to one's own identity, however, initially gives clear contours to one's independence both from extraneous circumstances and from the influence of others. Thus, the semantic properties of such reference have to be erased and/or replaced: by a concept of identity-in-transformation. This means, among other things, that one testifies to the beloved (who also knows herself to be permanent) that one develops one's own Self both through her and through one's love for her. In other words, identity must be treated as a concept of stability and equally as one of enhancement.

Finally, an identity of this type must then be introduced into situations characterized by the difference in perspective of actor and observer outlined above. Owing to the exceptional demands on the partners made by intimate relationships, this difference is more likely to grow than diminish, since alter as the observer screens the acting of the ego for special signs of love, whereas ego is inevitably also occupied with the demands of the situation. To alleviate this, a frequent switch of positions from ego to alter, or vice versa, is resorted to by means of an intensification of interaction. And by possibly blocking such switches, certain structures or situations become a problem, whether this takes the form of rigid role differentiation (the woman cooks, the man waits for his meal), or technical requirements (driving a car). The interaction of the lovers has to be differentiated in terms of special contingencies which are all favourable for them. In addition to physical contact, conversations are also particularly suited to this purpose. The density in this case becomes so intense that both partners can observe and act on the different levels at the same time: at the level of two individuals participating, and at that of the social system constituted by the two of them.[9]

As is always the case with improbable demands, an occasional, if not frequent breakdown in communication is probable. This is particularly true of the ever-possible divergence of the attributive perspectives afforded by either observing and acting. What is more, the hopes raised in relation to both love and the lovers' behaviour can potentially be dashed. The individuality guiding the attributive process amounts to a demand that stubbornly exclusive views of the world and of self-estimation be recognized, and thus becomes an imposition. The lover may (be willing to) accept this imposition, and indeed may wish to provoke it in the hope of finding happiness in responding to it. But for how long? And with what solutions in hand for the foreseeable conflicts between two mutually exclusive notions of individuality?

It has been known for a long time that an ever-increasing degree of individualization endangers marriages and generally places heavy demands on intimate relationships which can only be met with the greatest difficulty. This is true not least of all because the person-oriented communicative medium virtually invites all conflicts to be attributed to the persons involved, i.e. does not treat them as mere conflicts of behaviour or roles.[10] Love is also – and particularly – tested in terms of the behaviour manifested in conflict under (as is in the nature of things) less than favourable conditions. With the gradual personalization of social relationships, love itself can no longer function as a regulator of conflicts stemming from expectations based on behaviour and role; for love itself is affected by conflict.[11]

In light of such considerations, one is led to ask whether the semantics of intimately binding love had not promised too much, had not held up the prospect of something which was all too improbable. The typical answer to this question points to the temporal limitations: the flame of love is fated to flicker out and must be replaced by more moderate forms of behaviour adjusted to accommodate each other. This may be an insight as correct as it is old. However, it does not answer the question of why – if one knows this – one ever embarks, even if only for a while, on such a painstaking and difficult undertaking.

The motives involved cannot be explained in anthropological terms (and certainly not by some crude reference to the need for sexual satisfaction). Motives do not arise independently of a semantics, for the latter describes how they can exist and how they are to be presented and comprehended. Motives are themselves a product of the evolution of generalized symbolic communicative media, i.e. an artefact of socio-cultural evolution. Taking a chance on love and the correspondingly complicated, demanding reorientation of everyday life is only possible if one has cultural traditions, literary texts, convincingly evocative linguistic patterns and situational images – in short, if one can fall back on a timeworn structure of semantics. Such a semantics must thus accommodate a 'corresponding degree of complexity'. And yet, such a semantics can only be reproduced in perpetually new variations if a particular interest already exists in it, one that ever since the invention of the printing press has been of a general nature, namely the interest in reading. This brings us up against a problem of self-referential genesis, i.e. the development of forms that – in terms of their adaptive capacity – are at the

same time the precondition for themselves. The theory of socio-
cultural evolution can provide us with an explanation for such
problems.

The approach this study adopts thus draws on both theoretical
and historical perspectives. In theoretical terms, it combines the
concept of the generalized symbolic communicative medium
with premises taken from social theory, evolutionary theory,
communications theory and attribution theory. This theoretical
corpus is then coupled with investigations into the evolution of
ideas, that is to say, into evolution in the context of an historical
semantics which, depending on the adaptive capacity afforded by
the development of social structures, reacts in communication to
experiences it has made with its respective conceptual resources.

4

The Evolution of the Semantics of Love

It is possible within the context of an overall theory of generalized symbolic media of communication to outline the specific requirements which a special medium for love has to fulfil. The need for such specification is clear if we presuppose that there is an everyday awareness of the difference of highly personal, intimate social relations and those of an impersonal, externally motivated nature. The experience of this difference stabilizes the need for forms of communication suited to it and reproduces the search for them. Such an experience is, however, only possible if love has already taken the shape of a symbolic medium that differentiates special forms of suitable communication. The experience of difference, which enables the institutionalization of a medium to come about in the first place, is only possible with the aid of the medium. Only by opening itself to self-referentiality can the medium differentiate social systems and be realized as a code for them. This confronts us with the question of how such a medium could arise if the experience of the difference of personal and impersonal social relations – which had to be produced in the first place – was not yet possible. In other words, how could the synchrony of self-referentiality become historically diachronic, i.e. transformed into sequential development? Or to put it more precisely, how can *new* self-referential formations even come about if their structure is such that they can only mobilize the conditions for their stability once they already exist?

It is certainly not possible to answer this question by citing some anthropological need for love. Aside from the fact that it would probably be almost impossible to prove the existence of affective properties or emotions independent of communicative forms, the root of our problem lies within the communicative

forms themselves. Although it is obvious that a basic anthropological predisposition (such as sexuality) must be presupposed as
part of the environmental basis for the differentiation of forms
within the social system, this assumption does not lead us further
methodologically at the level of the social system and its evolution.
Instead, the key to an explanation from the vantage point of a
theory of evolution must be sought in the differentiation that
occurs at the level of semantic processing, a level which we shall
term 'cultivated semantics'. At this level, evolutionary transitions
can be inferred with some provisional plausibility and retained
for a while, even though they cannot yet be used in the context of
the final function that they will have.

This method of approaching the problem and its basis in
evolutionary theory go some way toward providing an understanding of the fact that no clear caesuras separate historical
epochs, either in the totality of real life or in their semantic
processing. If this were not the case, then the processing of
information in semantic terms could never be self-referential. In
other words, there does not appear to be any instance of historical
processes which can be distinguished from one another according
to some new innovation, as changes are much too strongly
dependent on stable structures and enduring ideational resources
for this to be possible. Nevertheless, distinct differences do exist,
which, once they have asserted themselves, give past things a new
value and make future things accessible in a new way. What
characterizes an epoch need not therefore necessarily be 'new' in
the sense of appearing for the first time. Epochal signification
may very well be connected with famous figures who are only
now being moved into the centre of the historical stage. And
what is so characteristic of the deeply rooted structural shifts of
early Modern times is that they drew on a stock of quotable ideas
from a long-standing tradition, the only difference to that past
being an increase in the accessability, adaptability and selectivity
of the particles of meaning.

If, taking this consideration as a guiding principle, we no longer
search for epochal thresholds, but rather for central elements of
interpretation, then distinct shifts in emphasis within the field of
the semantics of love that develop parallel to an increasing
differentiation of intimate relations become discernible. The
major concern of Medieval love poems and particularly of courtly

love seems to have been to appear *not vulgar* – which is the reason why the references to sensuality were marginalized, giving way to idealization, sublimation, a closed form, and only then to a liberality which could set itself off from these. The much debated issue of whether or not the minnesingers could hope for fulfilment of their love is thus quite beside the point. The main thing was to be able to distance oneself from the vulgar, common, direct satisfaction of sensual needs in the face of an increasing aristocratization of the Medieval structure of stratification. In all of this the reference to stratification was of the utmost importance – and hardly the reference to individuality; and all that was required to bring this about was to shift love onto an ideal, an improbable plane, to transform it into something that could only be gained by special merit (and not by marriage!).

No innovation occurs in this context of thematic continuity – until early Modern times, when two main epochal differences are to be made out, the first in the latter half of the seventeenth century and the second around 1800. In what follows we differentiate accordingly between *amour passion* and Romantic love. In order to provide an admittedly very rough and schematic description of this interconnection of concentration and change, we will distinguish between four areas of meaning: the form of the code; the justification for love; the problem to which the change reacts by attempting to incorporate it; and the anthropological viewpoint to which the code can be assigned.

The *form of the code* indicates the principle according to which the code, despite its internal differences, still forms a unity within the field it regulates. The form determines what can be communicated within the code, and therefore also determines the transformations of such capacities for communication and thus also the meaning each respective epoch views as being of central importance. Without the differentiation of a semantics that codifies intimate relations there would be no such form and thus no evolution in this particular area of study. The form of the code changes in the second half of the seventeenth century from *idealization* to *paradoxicalization*. This in turn changes in the course of the transition to Romantic love around 1800 into a form of *reflexion of autonomy*, or, *self-referentiality*. The code's unity thus initially represents an ideal, then a paradox and finally a function, namely that of causing reflexion on autonomy. Once this sequence of changes has taken place, it becomes the code's function to allow for *problem orientation* in everyday life.

The different vantage points from which *love can be justified* vary accordingly. As long as love was thought of as an ideal, a *knowledge of the object's characteristics* was essential.[1] In the field of paradoxical codification, love justified itself by means of *imagination.* Once the autonomy of intimate relations had finally been established and raised to the level of reflexion, it was possible to justify love simply by the inexplicable *fact that one loved.* As a self-referential context of communication, love was its own justification. The beauty of the beloved, for example, now no longer had to be in evidence, nor did it have to be imagined; this had ceased to be a reason for love, and rather was seen by the lovers as a consequence of their love. And finally love came to centre on recognizing and solving the problems of an intimate relationship together.

These transformations in the semantics of the medium, in its unifying concept and in the resulting leeway for its justification are all related to the gradual *inclusion of new problems* into the body of the code. I have in mind those problems which, in the course of the progressive differentiation of a special area for intimate relationships, had to be allocated to the code and treated by it. What is to be noted in the historical case studies is that a problem does not permeate the reorganization of the semantics, but rather, inversely, that the evolutionary changes of the code precede the problem and only then permit its inclusion and/or resolve the corresponding discrepancies.[2]

The code had already entered a process of systematization and refocusing by Medieval times, namely in the context of 'courtly love' and *fin amor.*[3] The old difference of domestic reproduction and outside love affairs was not dispensed with, but transformed into the idea of a great love for one and only one woman, whose favour one had to earn but could not win either by fighting for it or by trying to force it upon her. Eroticism became directed towards something which one could obtain from only one particular woman (and not from every woman), thus forcing the knight to fall to his knees. At the same time, within this framework the highest ideals inexorably take on erotic connotations. Consequently, there is at least one highly stylized area in which the normally clear-cut difference between rationality and sensuality no longer applies and in which people can no longer neatly separate what they have in common with the heavenly kingdom from what they have in common with the animal kingdom.

In the seventeenth century the code went beyond this first concentration of love and sexuality. The ideal now became an empty, meaningless phrase. A paradoxicalization of the semantics of love completed the gradual dissolution of the old contrast between 'higher' and 'sensual' love and initiated the incorporation of *sexuality* into the code as an essential component of love. The special sphere accorded to love relations makes it clear that here *the code is 'only a code' and that love is an emotion preformed, and indeed prescribed, in literature*, and no longer directed by social institutions such as the family or religion. Yet, by virtue of the freedom it offers, love is all the more bound to its own semantics and to its inherent clandestine goal: sexual enjoyment. An awareness of these problems is clearly manifest in the literature and literary discussions of the seventeenth century, where it finds expression in the form of suspicion, exposure or candid frivolity.[4] However, it is not until the code has been restructured that such an awareness is taken up into great, enduring literary forms. It is the Romantics who first sanctify the coupling of sexuality and love, and it is not until the nineteenth century that the notion of love as being nothing other than the ideal expression and systematization of the sexual drive is fully elaborated.[5]

All this ultimately has repercussions for the question of *how people participate in love*. The media code creates an anthropology specially tailored to the human being. As long as love remained an ideal, human beings were characterized by their *reason*. Passion and *plaisir* were subject to its control or were at least conceived of as differing from reason. The paradoxicalization of the code leaves the way open for an anthropology which revalues passion and *plaisir* and accords central importance to the difference between them. The eighteenth century in turn retains this semantics and elaborates it in a conception that emphasizes the independence of *emotions* and differentiates between genuine emotions and *goût, esprit* and *délicatesse*. It is the former that are held to be the minimum prerequisite for access to sexual realization, for this is primarily what is now involved. A problem arises in this context, namely the incommunicability of genuineness.[6] But it becomes less significant to the extent that Romanticism proceeds to relocate the code's unity in the self-referentiality of love itself. This step makes it necessary to use a different anthropology – an anthropology that no longer draws up rules for love but rather exists by virtue of its reference to love. The ratio of independent and dependent variables is inverted, so to speak. Love seems to come from nowhere, arises with the aid of copied patterns, copied emotions, copied existences and may perhaps create a conscious awareness of this second-hand character in its failure. The difference then becomes one between *love*, on the one hand, and on the other, *the discourse on love* between lovers and the novelist who always knows in advance the way things should really be.[7]

It must finally be mentioned that inclusion places certain demands on the code. Those extravagancies of the code which initiate and promote the process of differentiation do not apply to all members of society. They initially remain – like all the noblest forms of behaviour – the prerogative of the upper classes, i.e. of the aristocracy. In contrast, overall social evolution in the transition from a stratified to a functional mode of differentiation calls for the greatest maximum inclusion of all segments of the population in all functional areas.[8] Here we again have to do with a case of evolution with contradictory demands which we can assume thus became part of the semantics, in that, on the one hand, there must be a special capacity for making the improbable possible, and yet, on the other, precisely this has to be within everyone's reach. In other words, whereas society needs stratification in order to both introduce the improbable and rearrange itself in line with the differentiation of functional systems, it is at the same time this rearrangement that undermines the need and capacity for stratification. The task of semantics, and in our case, of the semantics of love, would seem to be to sublate these contradictions, to reveal them in controversies, to relate them to one another and to mediate between them.

Understandably, the demands raised by inclusion only call attention to themselves once the new forms have been put down on paper. They go hand in hand with a tendency towards relevelling and normalization, but they can adapt selectively to cultural innovations. The paradoxical codification of *amour passion* is followed by an insistence on *moral feelings*, which takes account of and incorporates the bourgeois reading public. Love is trimmed back to signify friendship, but the psychological refinement first developed in the context of a tactful galantry is retained. What had originally been developed as the art of observation, seduction and adopting someone else's point of view outlives the critique of galantry and is now used in order to enable one to immerse oneself in the intimate partner's individuality. After the synthesis of all these pursuits had come to be formulated as *Romantic love* and this in turn had been taken as the prerequisite for marriage, various new attempts at inclusion were made. The code is described as 'ideology' (Destutt de Tracy), as a sign system that guides the imagination which, in turn, steers society's reproduction process. And this makes it possible for anyone to at times become intoxicated with love and to lead an existence as '*homme-copie*',[9] regardless of whether and in what manner only a select few experience the highs and lows of the passion of love. Thus, according to the code's final version everyone leads a copied existence, this being the precondition for one to be able to enjoy passionate love and make it one's own.

At this stage the above rough outline must suffice to preview the detailed studies in the following chapters. Some aspects look more complex and interwoven when viewed close up rather than within the framework of a theoretical overview. Broad, sweeping strokes highlight best the degree to which the transformations in semantics correspond to the parallels to the increasing differentiation of intimate relationships that we expect to find, namely, a relaxation of the overall social morality with regard to what is considered correct, appropriate behaviour in intimate relationships and a reaction to the attendant problems of autonomy, interpretation and the capacity for being a person.[10] History itself paints a far more complex picture, in that it never fails to come up with a host of redundancies, of surpluses, and with tradition and variation. Even so, the basic pattern of a transformation of society and its semantics set in motion by evolution can still be traced. The following investigations, which go into greater historical detail, will enable us to document the existence of such a change, although this will entail us resorting to numerous qualifications, extrapolations, modifications and additional explanations.

5

Freedom to Love

From the Ideal to the Paradox

Decisive elements in the formation of a special code for passionate love (*amour passion*) arose, particularly in France, during the seventeenth century, and were consciously codified from about 1650 onwards.[1] There are naturally a great many forerunners of this code: classical and Arabian love poetry, the Medieval *Minnesang*, and the wealth of love literature in the Italian Renaissance. To the extent that this literature searches for a genuine and viable semantics of love set apart from everyday knowledge, affairs and sensual consummation, it makes use of the simple means of *idealization*. Its code fixes ideals. Love finds its own justification in the *perfection of the object* which attracts it (just as, according to old teachings, every endeavour is determined by the particular object it pursues).[2] In this sense, love is an idea of perfection derived from the perfection of its object, is almost forcibly brought into existence and *in this respect* is 'passion'.

Perfection, of course, does not signify that enhancement can only be achieved in one dimension. Love is clearly experienced as being saturated in contradiction,[3] and is portrayed as bittersweet love (*amare amaro*) especially in sonnets of the Renaissance period.[4] This is an important point of origin for the ideational resources which were later to be transformed into the element of playful paradox. The idea informing love here is the unity desired by the lovers, the main problem being the difference of the lovers, which was also experienced and suffered as physical difference. The attitude towards sensual love varies from one author to another, but the common basis for including the physical was still the goal of finding redemption in some higher form of love. Sexual love is thus preformed through spiritual love.[5] Love is accordingly also forever kept under the spell of its enhancement by supernatural objects. The great love semantics of the Middle Ages focused on the *difference* between loving God and loving a woman with respect to make a distinction in view of the mystical unity promised *in both cases.*[6] Sublime love therefore presents itself to its addressee in a way which incorporates a religious content – and not just as something which allows satisfaction and non-satisfaction to be distinguished from one another in relation to the addresser's own autonomous desire. Such love thereby presupposes an adequate *knowledge* of its addressee.[7] Thus, it runs parallel to both the social hierarchy of the time[8] and the idea of a moral order, i.e. an order which regulates the conditions of esteem, and of disregard for esteem. In other words, such love takes no risks at the level of the prevalent formalized semantics (even if one must always assume that the interest in love is also fed by other sources). The *theory* of love coincides with the *lovers' own notion* of it, or at least claims that such a coincidence prevails.

In the seventeenth century all this still functioned as an example to be followed. Ever since the Medieval *Minnesang* (if not before), in addition to the tradition of *amicitia* and *caritas*, another idea had been cultivated, namely, that courting love depended on not only winning the beloved's recognition, but also on an advancement of the lover's self-esteem and self-control. This provides the basis from which all social reflexivity of the semantics of love could proceed. Furthermore, the semantics of love well into the seventeenth century drew on a concept of 'service' that combined duty and enthusiasm and could be applied to aristocratic behaviour as a whole. This concept was used to portray the ability to overcome self-centredness and in this sense was moral in nature.

Nevertheless, at least one important aspect changed during the seventeenth century: the unattainability of the woman worshipped was shifted by virtue of being transformed into a decision made by the woman herself. During the Middle Ages she was shielded by class differences.[9] In Italy it was possible, or at least so it is claimed in seventeenth-century French literature, to presuppose the existence of effective external controls.[10] Attracting the attention of the beloved, encountering her, catching her eye were all difficult tasks in themselves.[11] In France, on the other hand, care was taken to ensure that the social status of women was endowed with greater freedom and with the possibility of the woman deciding things for herself. This led to the distinction between the '*précieuses*' and the '*coquettes*': the former always said no and the latter always said yes. It comes as no surprise that the *précieuses* were the more worthy objects of pursuit.[12] In any case, freedom of decision was assumed to exist: 'La liberté est de l'essence de l'amour.'[13] If this is true, however, the lover for his part could also make demands based on a self-determination of his own desire; he could not justify his love solely by referring to his desire. The persons one loves are divested of any immanent perfection; the cult of perfection starts to collapse and the figure of the *cavaliere servente* loses its credibility. And desire itself bathes its object in a beautiful semblance which it then adores. The freedom to choose the object of one's love became established with the help of self-fabricated illusions, and these fictions were in turn always seen through. It is only by virtue of this initial situation that the need arises for a code which not only provides forms to be used to glorify one's own emotions, but is also designed to regulate communication between two partners. The differentiation of a 'double contingency' – the freedom each partner has to decide whether or not to become involved in a love relationship – stimulates the development of a special semantics to which, if social relationships become unstable, one can cling *instead*.[14]

It cannot be emphasized enough that the freedom to choose someone to love applies to the *extra-marital* relationships of *married* persons. Unmarried daughters were protected quite effectively against seduction, and seducing them would have hardly added to the '*gloire*' of the hero. Freedom thus began with marriage.[15] In terms of its significance for the evolution of love semantics, this meant above all the elision of an important proof of love, namely the willingness to marry. The persons involved no longer made such a choice available, were no longer able to marry, and for precisely this reason had to wrack their imaginations for forms with which they could prove their love and/or ascertain whether the love offered was sincere or not.

As a result, the essentially old and cultivated ethics of love became highly complex by the mid-seventeenth century. Many different impulses intertwined with the end result that a new code for *amour passion* emerged.[16] During the decisive decades[17] a control of passionate love was admittedly still thought possible, but already considered problematic. Such a control was only possible in the form of a (moral) self-esteem and a willingness to allow oneself to be caught up in the rules of loving. Our discussion will consequently focus on these rules.

Over these decades an ambivalent situation developed, especially within the context of the precious view of love, which consisted of mastery on the one side and ridiculousness on the other, with both sides being completely inseparable.[18] The over-exaggerated, 'involutively'[19] developed and superlative linguistic forms were increasingly seen through by a psychological acuity that provided the only means of documenting and calculating one's freedom of decision. At the same time, the combined impact of *salon* conversation and book printing dissolved the unequivocal orientation towards rules. Maxims which cropped up in light, galant conversation were convincing, but, when put into print, sounded like rules which one had to distance oneself from in order not to appear subordinate. A rhetoric injected with new impulses blossomed forth only to be already outdated from the outset by the printing press. The result was an intolerable pedantry of strong words – and mockery. Against this background the form of utmost perfection, in which all cultivated semantics had up till then been couched, collapsed.

Laying claim to freedom in this manner can no longer be used within the old semantics, and more importantly, neither can the concession of freedom. Granting the beloved the freedom to decide what he feels should suitably happen and according to his own emotions renders the regulating process based on *ideals* quite ineffective. To take this into account, the adaptive capacity for enhancement is shifted and relocated in the *imagination*.[20] The imagination allows one to avail oneself of the other's freedom, blends it into one's own wishes, and overlaps with the double contingency at the metalevel at which what one's own ego projects is attributed to both one's own ego and that of the beloved. But where does imagination come from, how does it create the space and time for itself? The answer, as we will show in more detail, lies in its focusing on the last and final favour to be granted –

and the deferral of such gratification. Idealization is replaced by a temporalization of the semantics of love.

Furthermore, incorporating the other's freedom into the reflexion of the social relationship necessarily undermines the erstwhile orientation toward the *specific characteristics* of the partner. Rather, this orientation is replaced by one toward the partner's *love*. The beloved can in turn identify with the other's picture of himself – precisely because it is offered voluntarily. This notion of only love breeding love is a very old one; nevertheless, it is much more difficult to refrain from going into the partner's characteristics than it is to render the ideals paradoxical. It is almost impossible for real behaviour to be geared to such an approach, and at any rate this stance is not yet absorbed into the code during the period under consideration here.[21] With regard to this question, at this point one typically comes across blatant contradictions or mediating considerations in the literature examined. In La Fontaine's version of the legend of Amor and Psyche, love is expected to be able to persist despite certain, not all too grievous failings of virtue (Psyche's curiosity) and even faults in beauty (a temporary blackening of her skin), because it is thereby made less dependent on time and chance.[22] Le Boulanger[23] stresses that love can only be won through love, that alone love is of itself the prize of love; but he goes on to add that love is insufficient: it must be supplemented by the perfection of the lover's character, and one of the five sources of this state is in turn love itself, as *passion dominante*.[24] The act of loving is not yet autonomous, it is not yet able to rely exclusively on its own devices, but is still made a part of normal social appraisal of the aristocracy (in the case of Le Boulanger especially the pursuit of *gloire*). It is not until the nineteenth century that this can safely be put into words: 'La beauté détrônée par l'amour'.[25]

There is one isolated example which is particularly well suited to illustrate the shift to the imagination thus set in motion. In the Middle Ages the notion, derived from Antiquity, that the passion of love was a type of disease was still understood in completely medical terms, a symptomology had been developed and forms of therapy (such as coitus) were suggested as treatment. Sexuality was looked upon as normal physical behaviour, whereas passion was considered a disease.[26] By the seventeenth century all that remained of this view was the metaphor, the rhetorical device;

hardly enough to make one consult a physician! Nor would it be quite in keeping with the presupposed freedom of choice in love for one to want to curry the favour of a woman as if this were a medicine available on prescription. The figure of speech persists – but only as a metaphor seen through by both sides.

In other words, freedom asserts itself, but it would be a mistake to conclude from this that freedom automatically amounts to individuality.[27] As can already be seen from the type opposites of *précieuses* and *coquettes*, freedom was of interest as the localization of effort and resistance. As a form of freedom it thus had only one dimension, so to speak. This eased the way for a new semantic development and simplified further differentiation. Accordingly, relatively impersonal sources of ideational development are to be found in which the persons, regardless of their sex, appear to be interchangeable, for example, the pastoral novel and especially the monumental novel *L'Astrée*,[28] the copied love letter written in the form of a rhetorical formula;[29] the *salon* conversation touching on love themes, particularly the parlour game of '*questions d'amour*' and its literary counterparts.[30] Both court of law (*cour d'amour*) and school (*école d'amour*) are used as metaphors to express the ability to judge and teach behaviour in matters of love.[31] The novel was thus often more a description of galantry than a plausible tale.[32] In other words, printed literature would appear to bear out the assumption of the time that the proper attitudes and modes of behaviour could be codified. The lists of prescriptions for love were written as if there were such a thing as a fail-safe means of seduction, despite the fact that the freedom to say 'yes' or 'no' was taken for granted. Whatever one would have to concede in terms of individuality was dressed in the costume of rhetorical exaggeration and thus again standardized.

In all these forms guided by the rules of the art of loving a process of discovery is set into motion, one therefore particularly interested in the typical, and not in the individual.[33] The novels introduce persons with a rank and a name – this being deemed sufficient characterization – and accordingly, their actions are judged in terms of generally valid criteria. There is a discussion, for example, over whether or not it was right for the Princesse de Clèves in her situation to make her famous confession.[34] The individual case is only manifest as an application of a general principle, which is precisely why one can copy phrases and compliments without having to be afraid that the addressee will take this as a sign of awkwardness or tactlessness. An individual element is nevertheless manifested in conversation to the extent that topics are never taken up without consideration for those present, and special love topics, in particular, are never discussed without drawing the ladies present into the conversation.[35] Failing to make mention of those present was strongly disapproved of. This in itself, however, also means that nobody can present themselves or be treated in an overly individual manner, as this would infringe on the general rights of the others.

The differentiation of a semantics for love is naturally founded in the isolation of the interaction among lovers. The code is developed in direct relation to this delineation. Nevertheless, the isolation of interactional processes remains strangely ambivalent. As in the Middle Ages, lovers are advised to keep their relationships secret; but they find themselves being continually observed and talked about, and there seem to be people who make this their primary occupation.[36] Apparently, keeping love secret is a both suitable and unsuitable form for socially valid differentiation to take. This problem cannot be solved at the level of interaction, but only at that of the semantics of the code of love.

Initially, therefore, we have to do with views on morality and maxims for behaviour that are in general reserved for the members of a certain strata of society. It is this stratified social life and the accompanying sense of security which not only makes its possible to differentiate love relationships, but also forms the basis for this process and with it the referential framework in which the code can then be differentiated. In *L'Astrée* this situation takes the form of leisure. Even at a later period, nobility and especially wealth are considered almost indispensable prerequisites for love,[37] and their absence can only be made up for, if at all, by virtue – and then only with the greatest of effort – and hardly by the individual uniqueness of personal traits. To this extent, the behavioural model of love is firmly wedged in the jamb of class-bound social differentiation. At the same time, features appear within semantic formulation that go beyond these conditions, namely paradoxes, consciously fabricated illusions, formulae which can be evaluated in diametrically opposed ways – in short, strategic ambivalences which mediate the transition to a different kind of social composition.[38] However surprising this may sound, the fact remains that *paradoxicalization* proves to be a technique with a strong drive toward *systematization*, as we will demonstrate below; and systematization is also the form in which stability can be acquired for improbable demands on behaviour.

Before going into the details, a few words on paradoxical codification would not be out of place. Generally speaking, codes of generalized symbolic communicative media function to secure an adequate degree of probability for the reception of improbable expectations. In the end, it is always *this* socio-structural paradox which is transposed into the semantics and then expressed as an inherent paradox (in the essence of religion, of insight, of love). The enhancement and discovery of the basic paradox that gives rise to the differentiation of communicative media results in the formulation of other paradoxes which on the one hand cover up this basic paradox and, on the other, enable it to operate in certain areas of communication.

Paradoxicalization must not be interpreted to signify an inability to act. Nor does it imply a need for selection and decision. Lovers are not confronted with 'forced choice' patterns or with incompatible alternatives. Rather, the paradox refers to the level of expectations made of one's partner in an intimate relationship; and love symbolizes that it is nevertheless possible for all these expectations to be fulfilled. All normal expectations are filtered out by paradoxicalization (and not, as before, by idealization); and the stage is set for love to make its entrance.

In a culture which held rationality in high esteem and viewed logic as a sign of good health, paradoxical motivation was understood in terms of pathological considerations – the one exception being Pascal.[39] According to a currently widely held opinion, it produces schizophrenia[40] or at least the compulsive repetition of pathological behaviour.[41] Yet, it also gives free licence for any and every behaviour. On the one hand, paradoxical communication destroys personality; and on the other, it has the effect of destroying the social system. Psychiatry has pointed to the consequences in the former case, and the discussion of the concept of Romantic love, for example, has pointed to those of the latter. It will come as no surprise to sociologists that any transformation of the improbable into the probable is up against precisely such risks. The real question is thus whether it is possible to provide a more accurate indication of the conditions which lead to such a pathological state.

If we raise this question with reference to all symbolic media of communication, we can at first in many cases isolate them from the process of communication itself.[42] For example, Gödel's improvabilities are of no practical relevance for research in this area. The same is true of master/servant paradoxes and the practice of successful or unsuccessful political communication.[43] As for the economy, a change in course is clearly to be found in Adam Smith's work, where no solution to the general moral paradox of altruistic self-interest is provided in terms of moral theory, but rather in terms of economic theory, in that the paradox is held to no longer influence behaviour negatively. It is precisely this undisturbed pursuit of one's own goals which automatically has an ordering effect then celebrated as the creation of order out of disorder.

This way of treating the problem, i.e. by sealing off the level of interaction from paradox by isolating ongoing communication from paradox – despite concomitantly recognizing the para-doxical constitution of the system – is a solution which cannot be applied in the case of love. Love regulates intimate communication, and thus intimate communication does not constitute a system beyond the level of interaction. At this point such types of differentiation of paradoxical macrosystems and regulated interaction as are based on an illusionary conception of modern society as a specifically rational society (Max Weber) cease to function. When in love, the partners have to put up with the paradoxical nature of intimate communication; indeed, they have to use it expressively. This is where any flight into false rationality fails.

The reasons for this become apparent if one considers which specific structural problems of intimate communication are solved by means of paradoxicalization. The problems involved derive in different ways from the dependence on free decision, which excludes the rules being made in such a manner that they could directly condition behaviour. If, in contrast, the code is rendered paradoxical, all behaviour oriented toward it can claim to have a designated meaning and an assigned place, and at the same time, to be free. Moreover, the form of the paradoxy helps not to solve, but rather to dissolve, the problems of causal attribution. A clear-cut attribution of duties and responsibilities (as in the contemporary literature on family and household) is then no longer possible. Intimacy is also not understood to be a relationship based on exchange. Reasons for everything that happens are to be found in the other person or in oneself, and every act of directing attribution to either the ego or the alter in itself constitutes a violation of the code. We shall return to this point in the next chapter with regard to the suspension of the difference of passive and active.

But how does the paradox become a semantically viable reality? There is no lack of suggestive answers to this question. Classical literature, as we shall see in a moment, came forward with the rationality of a cultivated irrationality, whereas Romanticism relied on the concept of irony and the idea of the enhancing value of insincerity. However, these forms were too taxing (and in any case, their application was restricted to certain social strata). Rather, it appears that a certain trivialization of paradox had eventually asserted itself: the semantics of love was able to supply everyone with the words and emotions they wished to call up. It allowed for flexible behaviour that did not owe its consistency to the code which guided it, but instead, if at all, to consideration for the partner and the history of the system of interaction. This form of solution might be adequate if what is often assumed today were actually true: namely, that precisely under the conditions of modern life people have a spontaneous need for personal relationships and intimate communication, so that no great barriers of improbability have to be overcome. But is this in fact the case?

6

The Rhetoric of Excess and the Experience of Instability

Presenting statements on love by giving them the form of paradoxy is not a specific invention of the seventeenth century but was handed down from Antiquity and the Middle Ages.[1] A *casuistry of love* resulted because paradoxy can only be solved on a case by case basis and by the actions of the lovers themselves.[2] This is why love is so well suited to narrative portrayal; for it is the subject *par excellence* of novels. Although at the level of the images, formulae and metaphors used, it is difficult, as it is elsewhere, to assess what real innovations are new,[3] if one views the code as a whole, an apparent change in trend would seem to be discernible. Whereas the Middle Ages clung to an all-encompassing mystical unity (*unio*) beyond all semantic contradictions, in the seventeenth century, paradoxy started to be related to itself, made available for its own sake, and thus precisely this came to be regarded as the unity of the code of love. As a consequence, paradoxy became the final shape of the code and therefore provides legitimation both for instability and psychological refinement. The 'casuistic' solution of paradoxy was shifted from the level of the *exemplary* to that of the *individual* and this in turn meant that a different paradoxical construction was required. In the seventeenth century predominantly temporal problems take the place of the paradoxical relation of courtly distance and a passion that overcomes everything.

A comparison of La Fontaine's tale *Les Amours de Psyché et de Cupidon*[4] and its Roman predecessor by Apuleius reveals this new focus on paradoxy. The oracle at the beginning of the story is transformed: the normal meaning attributed to it is changed into themes that emphasize the paradoxy of love. The central theme of hubris is refashioned as the (justified) desire for fulfilment of the last, still outstanding wish. That no fulfilment of this wish is (initially) forthcoming is not a result of some numinous presence, but is purely a whim and therefore also an actual element in the affairs of love itself. The tale is rewritten, at least in part and to the extent that the material allows, in terms of the typical psychological process of love, and the paradox of the oracle (a 'monster' brings about the greatest happiness; mourning is worn on the path to love) becomes a natural law that elevates the status of love.

Love in particular is exceptionally well suited as a topic to demonstrate this alteration in the positioning of the paradox, because it is an appropriate vehicle with which to proclaim the unstable stable. Hylas in *L'Astrée* (which still follows the idea of the mystical *unio*) or Don Juan provide corresponding models of behaviour – that both possess a deeper core than their subsequent moralization would like us to believe. Inconstancy now becomes necessity. Even if one can no longer always love the same object, so it now goes, one must believe that one will always be in love.[5] In each individual case the lover is supposed, against his better knowledge, to allow his actions to be guided by the fictitious belief that love will endure: 'Il doit agir comme si son amour ne pouvait jamais finir.'[6] And the answer to the question as to its duration is rendered in the style of the *questions/maximes d'amour*: 'Il n'y en a que dans l'idée et dans les promesses des Amans.'[7] A class can formulate such a proposition as long as it is fully confident of its position. But once paradoxy and illusions come to be taken seriously and can be formulated in terms of a code, then a certain stability is also created at the semantic level for the unstable, a stability that can outlast its initial preconditions.

The thematic structure of *amour passion* contains a wealth of material that can be used to describe this transformational effect in detail. At the same time, this structure also shows how this transformation fuses the code of the medium of love into a unity. In the following, the most important elements involved will be taken up in order to prove that these historical and semantic relations held true.

A solution to perhaps the most important problems that had arisen with regard to the differentiation and special treatment of love and also the internal order of a corresponding code was provided by the concept of passion. Essentially, this concept afforded one the opportunity to conduct oneself in affairs of the heart free of social and moral responsibility. 'Passion' originally signified a mental state in which one suffered passively instead of actively doing something. This did not in itself exonerate one of the need to justify actions which had originated in passion. If a hunter shot a cow, he could hardly use passion as an excuse. This situation changed, however, once passion came to be recognized as a sort of social institution and as an expected precondition for the formation of social systems. In other words, things changed once an expectation, if not a demand, was aired that one submit to passion – for which one is not accountable – when entering into a close relationship of love. In this case the semantics of passion was used to shield institutionalized freedoms, i.e. to protect and at the same time mask them. Passion thus became freedom of action and neither it nor its consequences needed to be justified; activity became disguised as passivity, freedom as compulsion.[8] And the semantics of passivity was exploited rhetorically in order to urge the woman to fulfil the man's love; for, after all, it was her beauty that had given rise to the man's love and he accordingly suffered through no fault of his own, unless, that is, some respite was forthcoming.

This was in no way the original meaning of 'passion'. In the Middle Ages, the concept had been accorded a central role both theoretically and theologically. The notion was used to demonstrate how one should deal with the general difference of the physical and the non-physical. Passion was held to be the sensitive self-activation of the human body. If one accepted St. Augustine's strict division of body and soul, then only the soul could be considered the bearer of higher qualities. The body was left at the mercy of its drives. If, on the other hand, one accepted the consubstantiality of body and soul (St. Thomas Aquinas), then it was precisely passion, the self-activation of the body, which became the 'subject' of the virtues,[9] or at least the arena where one could overcome temptation, where the higher and baser instincts did battle. 'Passion' in this manner had to bear the whole ballast of problems which arose for anthropology from the difference of *res corporales* and *res incorporales* which was so central to ancient European thought. What happened to the concept thus ultimately depended on whether more emphasis would be placed on difference or on unity.

With the gradual disintegration of the above setting, in which the concept had originally been utterly bound up, it was possible to now use 'passion' in a completely different context. The meanings with which the concept was loaded could now be emphasized differently, tailored to meet new needs. Both the sense of drama and of wrestling with oneself continued to inhere in it, as did the carefully described passivity of the self-activation of the body. Consequently, in the seventeenth century the concept of love as passion still remained linked to the older conception of a 'passive' passion. Thus, passion continued to involve the anguished toleration of the impression that the other person conveyed. Desire itself was still conceived of in the old manner as passive, as a *faculté appetitive*, and was expressed only as a consequence of the impression made by the desired object's qualities. Thus, we can still speak of virtue (*virtus, vertu*) taking passion as a suitable vehicle for itself. 'La passion est la reception de la vertue de l'agent; comme quand de beaux yeux donnent de l'amour.'[10] But since this is the case for both partners, action and passion overlap on both sides. 'Bien souvent l'agent pâtit en agissant, et le patient agit sur son agent.'[11] 'L'Amant et l'Amante sont agents et patiens à la fois.'[12] The *'puissance passive'* and *'puissance active'* of love were differentiated and yet precisely in so doing were regarded as two forms of one and the same thing.[13] We can see here that, owing to social interaction, action and passion became welded into a unity new in the history of ideas; passion was activated, so to speak, into becoming the motive for passionate action.[14]

This activation of passion led, in the second half of the seventeenth century, to a positive re-evaluation of the concept. It became possible, for example, to abandon the stark contrast between passion and *honnêteté*, Chevalier de Méré's basic starting point, and to re-evaluate passion in anthropological and class-specific terms. The transition from a passive to an (equally) active concept of passion is moreover the first stage in any possible individualization, for only action, and not inner experience, can be attributed to individuality. What proved to be the decisive thrust in the rearrangement of the semantics of love from ideal to paradoxical behavioural expectations was, in our opinion, both the concept of active passion that was adopted once the reflexive social conditions of love had been accepted and the fact that the lover's role, once activated, became instilled with personal characteristics. Whatever the case, this point highlights the manner in which socio-structural conditions both trigger off transformations in semantics and promote differentiation within a code.

Love can now be depicted as a sort of superpassion which engages all else in its service, or simply as the quintessence of all passions.[15] It becomes elevated to the principle of activity, and the fact that this principle is called passion now signifies only that no explanation, reason, or excuse can be provided for one's activity. In the case of love it can be shown how this passion press-gangs opposites into its service: presence and absence of the beloved, hope and despair, daring and fear, anger and respect now all serve solely to strengthen love.[16] The unity of love becomes the framework in which paradoxy that has a practical function in life can be portrayed.

This emphasis on passion appears at first glance to indicate that love takes place outside the arena of rational control. One might thus expect deliberated behaviour and all skilled con- versation to be deprived of any room for development. The opposite, however, holds true: precisely the irrationality of passion makes it improbable that two people are seized by it at the same time with respect to one another. Cupid does not, after all, shoot off two arrows at once; love may well occur by coincidence, but normally not as a double coincidence. One has to help it on its way, not least of all because one's own feelings stabilize in the course of wooing and seduction. Being utterly exposed to one's own passion as well as refinement with respect to the other person become caught up in a spiral of enhancement – i.e. the more passion there was, the more discreet and premeditated one's behaviour. This occurs to both parties to the extent that both are unsure of the passion of the other and thus experience the situation as asymmetrical. In other words, the initial impression of the incompatibility of the semantic designations involved is not to be trusted. Because the projected social relationship is subject to double contingencies, the combination of the diametrically opposite is not only made possible, but becomes necessary. Love as a communicative medium refers not to the psychic but to the social system.

In this manner the *ars-armandi* tradition is continued. When leafing through the extensive descriptions, tracts and handbooks on the art of seduction one must not just skim the surface, for although these may be presented as secret knowledge, they were in fact published openly and also discussed in the *salons*, leading one to conclude that they functioned, at least in the cases of ladies, as a warning.[17] Yet the warning itself embodied a danger, and husbands were actually advised not to warn their wives about seduction,[18] as this might arouse the latter's interest and attention and would really expose them (as is the case with all forms of resistance) to the full brunt of love. Regardless of how it is used, skilled conversation alone can be no grounds for feeling secure.

Once it has been taken up in literature and formed into a doctrine, seduction becomes a game with two players, at which point it can only be a game which both parties see through, i.e. in which you take part only because you wish to take part. You agree to subject yourself to the code and its rules and allow yourself to be seduced or at least play for a while with fire, whereby the game's fascination lies in this quality of its conceivably getting out of control – from the points of view of both players.

The fusion of activity and passivity on the part of both lover and beloved in a new concept of passion does not mean to say that the asymmetry in the relation of the sexes to one another is overcome. However, it has to be reconstructed in terms of this unity of action and passion, by means of *two opposing asymmetries*. On the one hand, love is characterized as a *battle*, as the woman being besieged and conquered.[19] On the other hand, love presents itself and 'pleases' in the form of *unconditional submission* to the wishes of the beloved.[20] This absolute surrender involves complete renunciation of personal characteristics. The Medieval mystical tradition[21] and the platonism of the Italian Renaissance[22] still set an example in this context. *L'Astrée* is also governed by this principle of self-renunciation, annihilation and rebirth in the other person.[23]

This demand clearly corresponds to the old 'passive' concept of passion, according to which love culminated in a *loss of identity* and not, as one would think nowadays, in a *gain in identity*. Even the self-sacrificing lover felt justified in urging that his love be requited and was prepared to demand that it be paid to him, as if it were a duty owed. But this really has to do with him wanting to 'preserve' his life, with *'cibo per conservar se'*, as Nobili puts it.[24] This approach also leads one to the principle of *vivendevole amore*, although this must be seen against the background of a feeling of imminent downfall rather than as an attempt to create real humanity. French Classicism recollects this imaginary world from a distance – particularly with the aid of *L'Astrée* – but imbuing it in contrast with clearly more mundane characteristics. In the second half of the century love can thus still be defined as *self-alienation*.[25]

In other words, love fuses together what appear to be diametrical opposites: conquest and self-renunciation. This is possible, but only under the further condition that one does not yield to the resistance the woman puts up,[26] for this would amount to sinning against the holy spirit of love. In this context, such unconditionality is also a symbol for differentiation. In that it is excessive – and not just 'pure' love – love makes no allowances for anyone's interests.[27] Even love's development in time has a law of its own, whereas interests subject to love would draw in problems alien to it in an attempt to resolve them.[28]

Conquest and self-subjugation can be combined because of another important element in the thematic structure of the code, namely, the fact that in the lover's opinion the beloved only has positive qualities.[29] This enables both the acts of pressing for something and of demurring to be enhanced. This combination is reproduced in the corresponding metaphor of blindness and vision, where on the one hand love is deemed to blind the lovers and yet on the other give them superb vision. Love is said to govern one's sight, to make use of eye-language, and in so doing even allows negative qualities to be perceived – but these are judged to not be impressive.[30]

Similar paradoxes could be mentioned here, all of which strengthen the impression that the most important thing in this context is for contradiction to force something to occur which would otherwise be impossible. For example, love is often termed a prison from which one does not want to escape, or an illness which is preferred to good health,[31] or an injury for which the

injured person has to pay the price.[32] Clearly we have to do here
with the attempt to specify something which contrasts with
normality, i.e. an unusual situation which makes unusual
behaviour appear understandable and acceptable. And in such
phrases as 'les Amants aiment mieux leurs maux que tout les
biens,'[33] or 'l'Amante la plus misérable ne voudroit pas ne point
aimer,'[34] or 'la plus grande douceur est un secret martyre,'[35] or 'les
plaisirs d'Amour sont des maux qui se font désirer'[36] evidence the
differentiation of a classificatory system for love. Even its negative
value is part of love in such a way that it cannot be outbid by
values of a different order.[37] The position of suffering as a
semantic part of love changes (as does its religious interpretability)
by virtue of becoming incorporated into the paradoxical code.
One now no longer suffers because love is sensual and arouses
earthly desires; one suffers because love has not been fulfilled or
because its fulfilment is not what it promised to be. The hierarchy
of a person's different relations to the world are replaced by the
entelechy and temporal structure of a relatively autonomous area
of life and experience. This purely self-referential causal
grounding – including personal suffering – had in former times
been reserved for the characterization of God.

This form of argumentation is explicitly adopted whenever this
paradoxy itself becomes the topic of discussion. In one of
d'Aubignac's novels[38] a woman is so naive as to doubt 'que le
martyre, la tyrannie, les feux, les fers soient des choses fort
plaisantes' and demands an explanation of the paradoxy. In the
answer the following differences are made: love is not desire, but
by its very nature it creates the desire to be loved, and this desire
in turn, to the extent that it remains unfulfilled, creates all the
lover's joy and suffering. Although paradoxicalization is thus
tacitly indicated to originate in sociality, it is nevertheless still
attributed explicitly to the heart in the sense of *volonté parfaite
d'être aymé*. And what is concluded from this is that one must not
therefore doubt the truth of the paradoxy, 'il ne faut donc pas
s'opiniâtrer dans la contradiction d'une verité si publique.'

Furthermore, as the quality of the code changes, so does the
degree to which behaviour in affairs of the heart can be taught. It
is proposed and denied at one and the same time that such a
capacity for instruction exists. In the instructional text, *L'escole
d'amour,*[39] love is paraphrased[40] as 'un ie ne sçay quoy, qui venoit

de ie ne sçay où, et qui s'en alloit ie ne sçay comment'[41] and further defined as follows: 'et par ces termes qui ne nous apprennent rien, ils nous apprennent tout ce qui s'en peut sçavoir.' In other words, we are concerned here with a didactic, but actually meaningless phrase! Only in this manner is it possible to initiate someone in a code, the unity of which has to be expressed in the form of paradoxy.

The contradictions of love were shown in two different, typical descriptions of it, namely, hopeful and dashed love. Alongside the Latin sources, Guilleragues's *Lettres portugaises* are representative for the latter case. Fulfilled, happy love is thought of as free of contradictions; it resolves all contradictions and is the point of reference guaranteeing the unity of the semantic paradoxes, but is of no lasting duration. The resulting unhappy love, especially as portrayed in the *Lettres portugaises*, illustrates the deep suffering one then experiences – in the manner prescribed by the code. The most intensive forms of self-alienation rely on forms made specifically for this purpose. Love remains genuinely felt, seduction remains the affair of the seducer – and both remain in the final instance the product of the code.[43]

The replacement of idealization by paradoxicalization as the form of the code has consequences for the conscious attitude adopted. The ideal is retained[44] as the *desired form* and in this capacity provides protection against pure licentiousness. Yet at the same time paradoxicalization makes possible a new form of distantiation from regulations, techniques and even from received attitudes. One could distance oneself from ideals only be referring to the unsatisfactory nature of fulfilment, whereas paradoxical forms invite self-distantiation and self-preservation in the process of distantiation.[45] The mystifications of love are now treated as a refinement. Accordingly, one finds that retranslations go hand in hand with the development of the code and the great gestures it requires – be these translations into the ironic or simply into the rhetorical. A famous example of this is the typology of the sigh in the *Dictionnaire des Précieuses*.[46] The incorporation of the 'merely rhetorical' into self-portrayal is equally prevalent, as is the forms' consciously transparent treatment as forms, as exaggerated exaggerations. And this is then reintegrated into the thematic body of the code.[47]

Paradoxicalization and particularly the incorporation of effort, worry and pain into love further result in a differentiation of love and interest, i.e. love and economy (in the broadest sense, i.e. including the household economy). In contrast to what is true of one's interests, it is imposssible in love to calculate the costs or weigh up the accounts, because both one's profits and one's losses are enjoyed; indeed, they serve to make one aware of love and to keep it alive. Admittedly, it is possible to exploit love in the pursuit of certain interests, but not to transform interests into love: 'C'est que l'amour sert de beaucoup à l'interest, mais l'interest ne sert iamais de rien à l'amour.'[48]

The various paradoxes (conquering self-subjugation, desired suffering, vision in blindness, a preference for illness, for imprisonment, and sweet martyrdom) converge in what the code proposes is central to love, namely: *immoderateness, excessiveness.*[49] Regardless of the great importance attached to moderate behaviour, in the case of love this counts as a decisive error. Excessiveness itself becomes the measure of all behaviour. As with all communicative media, the code here has to create within itself an exception for itself, in that an institutional framework for the code requires the presence of negative self-referentiality. As a consequence, both the semantics of love and the external presentation of love involve a more or less pronounced distancing from *raison* or *prudence*. Showing that one could control one's passion would be a poor way of showing passion.[50] The imperative of excessiveness in turn symbolizes differentiation, i.e. the transcendence of behavioural limits set predominantly by the family.[51] Furthermore, excess differentiates love from the laws of conversational sociability. The differences are consciously formulated, which does not exclude that this may also have been the task of the *salon*. In the final instance it is precisely the excessiveness of passion which lends clearer contours to its social forms and characteristics. In keeping with the title of an ethnological investigation, one can speak of 'Excess and Restraint – Social Control Among Paris Mountain People'.[52]

In semantics, extreme values function to render normal regulations ineffective. Only excessiveness can justify the woman's submission.[53] This is also the case both for institutionalized role expectations and interwoven complexes of rights and duties, and for *ius* in the main sense it had then. Thus, the notions of justice are abandoned that played such an important role in the Medieval semantics of love and allowed for legal recognition and judgement based on efforts, services, worthiness, as well as rewards for these, are abandoned. Any distancing from the codex of rights and duties also involves differentiating love from the legal form and regulation of marriage. Love only comes into being when one exceeds what can be demanded and prevents a legal entitlement to love from ever coming about.[54] This difference to institutionalized love is what makes it possible to discover and formulate something which has, ever since, belonged to the entelechy of love and as such could only become part of an updated conception of marriage at a much later stage: 'Je ne sçay rien qui ressemble moins à l'amour que le devoir.'[55]

'Excess' clearly is not taken to mean that only extreme behavioural positions are adopted. Thus the man's unconditional 'surrender' to the woman is simultaneously an appeal to the woman's generosity, and the woman worshipped would be considered cruel if she did not reciprocate. The semantics of immoderation brings new forms of freedom into being that must be lent substance and redefined by the history of love – and no longer by society itself.

Taking excess as the measure of love provided the basis for a new set of considerations. Above all, love totalizes. It makes everything that has something to do with the beloved, even trifling,[56] appear relevant, and thus bestows a value on everything that enters its field of vision. The totality of the beloved's inner experience and activities demand continuous observation and assessment in terms of stereotyped oppositions such as love/indifference or sincere/insincere love. Thus, a new form of universalism came into being which broke with the old difference of essential and inessential characteristics.

Love was accordingly also depicted as a closed circle, all elements of which served to reinforce each other and from which there is no escape.[57] Love could thus not afford to allow even the slightest negligence. To this extent the code tyrannizes without being compelling.[58] Faults (*manquements*) in one's treatment of the beloved were unpardonable precisely because they affect the heart of the matter, i.e. the imperative of excessiveness and the claim to totality.[59]

Excessiveness provided a point in which hatred and love could converge in excessiveness or at least easily overlap with each other. The older, Idealist tradition treated love and hatred as clear opposites and was only able to conceive of hatred as a reaction to injustice, as hurt feelings – for hatred was not inherently perfect.[60] In contrast, the relationship of love to hatred was now pardoxicalized. We have to do here with different expressions of a basically uniform passion:

> Quand le dépit vient d'un Amour extrême,
> On dit qu'on hait, et l'on sent que l'on aime.[61]

The 'scientific' discussion on the theory of affects develops in a similar, parallel direction.[62] Hatred accordingly belonged to the code of love, in that whoever found their love unrequited should hate their beloved; the question was solely whether they were able to do so.[63] In this manner love and hatred became dependent on one another and together described a relationship which differed from friendship.[64]

The imperative of excessiveness furthermore created problems for any regulation of the code of love, for, as a consequence of it, the code's unity was set at a level above all codes of behaviour. One was thus unable to ascertain from rules whether one's own behaviour was correct or not: following rules meant not to follow the beloved.[65] It is against this background that we must understand statements which emphasize the self-referentiality of love and thus appear to anticipate something first brought into being by Romanticism. However, it was only making oneself dependent on rules and regulations that was thus rejected.[66] And yet, an art of seduction clearly existed, i.e. a technique of excessiveness based on experience that can be taught and learned.[67] The code remained, despite all reservations with regard to a dependence on regulations, essentially an orientation that could be translated into various operations. Whereas an orientation towards rules would be subalternate in effect, a means – end orientation adopted for the effect it had was nevertheless possible because the beloved could not very well deny the fact that she was the end all the efforts were aimed at. All attention to effects (side-effects, opportunity costs) other than the achievement of this end were considered to be in bad taste; here we encounter an aspect of specific totalization, in that the end exerts absolute dominance over everything else.[68]

Last but not least, corresponding to this imperative, all the justifications given for love failed in the final instance. To give some definite reason would be to contradict the spirit of love. Ineffability was itself the reason.[69] The proofs (*épreuves*) of love took the place of further reasons. They did not refer to their causality, but to their facticity. Numerous portrayals of this were elaborated up to and including de Callieres's attempt to subject the proof of love to the rules of logic.[70] The dilemma is obvious: the desire to receive a final proof of the woman's love was in itself no sure proof of the man's love.[71] The gradual verbalization of this problem (already effected in *L'Astrée*), i.e. one talks, insists, writes, required a formulated code. And the codification of forms of expression inversely furthered doubts as to the genuineness of feelings. Emotions functioned as a continual catalyst against which formulations separate out without this actually solving the problem. True love or false love – this question became of central importance not only because of the difference between code and behaviour, but also owing to the temporal deferral in achievement of the end.[72] What happened at this point, at least initially, was that the question was referred back to stratification, in that the ability to differentiate between true and false passion was reserved for the *honestes gens*.[73]

Were there any limits placed on excessiveness? Because it obtained to no negative form, excessiveness possessed internally no limits and there was thus no curb on pushiness, desire or expectations. It was quite clearly not assumed that what was suited to the individuality of a personality, or what could be expected or demanded of a particular person (in contrast to all others) itself amounted to a limit. Yet, this love, limitless in all factual and social respects, was at the same time limited in another respect, namely temporally. Love inevitably ends, *and indeed faster than does beauty*, in other words, *faster than nature*; its end is not accorded a place in the general decline of the cosmos, but is self-determined. Love lasts only a short time, and its end compensates for the absence of all other limits. The essence of love itself, excessiveness, is the very reason for its end, and inversely 'en amour, il n'y a guères d'autre raison de ne s'aimer plus que de s'être trop aimés.'[74] The moment of fulfilment itself almost comprised the end, and one therefore almost had to fear such a point, defer it or attempt to avoid it: as inevitability it cannot be repeated. 'Si la possession est sans trouble, les desires

ne sont plus qu'une habitude tiede.'[75] Precisely for this reason one
had to hold resistance, detours or obstacles to one's love in high
regard, because only through them does love endure. The word
served as the medium for this duration, in that words divide more
clearly than do bodies, turning difference into information and
thus also into the cause for continued communication. In this
manner the code of communication itself created the verbalization
necessary for its own genesis.[76] Love, however, only existed as the
'not yet'; the moment of happiness and the eternity of suffering
mutually determine each other, are identical.[77] Accordingly,
nothing would be further from the mark than to think of marriage
when thinking of love. Love ends in indifference and with the
tactical problem of 'cooling out',[78] or, in Madeleine de Scudéry's
view, with feigned continuation 'par générosité'.[79] Georges
Mongrédien formulated the principle involved as 'se donner avec
passion et se reprendre avec prudence'.[80]

Love could also be seen as a process hitched as it were between
beginning and end. Its extension in time and its filling out of time
by instilling the latter with a history were also important features
in earlier literature, but in the seventeenth century what fills time
and goes to fulfil events became more differentiated. The
Medieval knight had to prove himself by overcoming danger,
through heroic deeds and by realizing the ideals of knighthood.[81]
In the seventeenth century, in contrast, the lover was called upon
to prove his love in his role as lover and social demands now only
provided the general background, i.e. in such concepts as
honnêteté, or *bienséance* and in the verbal forms of galantry.
Thus the process of love was switched over to autodrive, and had
to continually recharge its own batteries.[82]

The process of love was first accorded a dynamic of its own in
the image of it being driven by a self-propelling *plaisir*, by its own
need to constantly change forms and continually devour
something new.[83] However, experience of the nature of love
affairs soon led to the introduction of a more tactically oriented
element. Unlike the demands made by *plaisir* or love, activities
and events were now judged in terms of what they may possibly
imply for the future. The woman had to weigh up whether she
could allow herself to accept letters or even answer them, receive
visitors, express wishes or lend out her coaches, as such acts
might have led to the conclusion being drawn that her intentions

allowed for more.[84] Conversely, the tactics of seduction centred precisely on exploiting such signs as the basis for something more. A sensibility for these nuances increased the intensity of such pointers to a temporal horizon of events. Occurrences became self-referential in time, in that one had now to consider both the fact that one was later to come back to them in the course of more intensified expectations, as well as the manner in which this was to occur. And all of this was shot through with social reflexivity. The lady, having granted the first signs of favour, could ward off further heightened pushiness. But she could now no longer treat more open wooing as a complete surprise or as effrontery. The seducer could now bank on her considering the fact that she encouraged his further efforts; and what counted were not her actual intentions but what could be construed as a sign of them and thus no longer negated at this level.[85]

The process of love was consequently self-referential in time. The lovers started – and their history was already programmed for them by the code. The process of love was thus accorded a time of its own, and the beginning, just like the end, had its own particular characteristics, that are atypical for love. Here one could still make a rational choice. One knew the code and thus loved, as it were, before actually falling in love, but at first one still had control over oneself. Frequently, the decision to embark on a love affair was depicted as an act of will by means of which one satisfied the rules laid down by a social game.[86] The importance of making the right choice at this point, before one lost control over oneself, was continually reiterated.[87] Even Cupid had to operate 'incognito' at this stage.[88]

In the initial phase, characterized more by 'complaisance' than by love, one will believe that one is in love without actually loving, or one will play with love which will then burst into flame once the first hurdles are encountered. Indeed, these 'obstacles' served both to make one conscious of passion and to heighten it.[89] The first favour shown by the beloved thus also possessed a particular quality of its own: it could not be demanded, but once it had been granted, it served as a launching board to greater things.[90] In other words, once the process had been set into motion, it became subject to its own special code, and only once it grew stale did normal, common sense modes of behaviour again assert themselves.

This creation of a temporality unique to each love affair was the precondition for a process of enhancement that found expression in the constant mention of a concept of *hope* (and accordant fears).[91] This enhancing effect was comparable with what economists refer to as *credit*, and was based on indirectness, circuitousness, 'deferred gratification' and functionally specific guarantees that the continuity of the process was nonetheless uninterrupted. The beloved could initially finance the game by offering hope and thus postpone offering himself. The lover would then be all the more inclined to value the chase more than the spoils. This extension of the time-span involved aided intensification, verbalization and sublimation and formed the common, latent interest in love. And last but not least this was – seen from the viewpoint of semantics – the form in which the precious (for example Madame de Scudéry) and the libertine (e.g. Bussy-Rabutin) converged: in agreement on the value of the game as a game.[92]

Hope also meant that cashing the cheque in on the future would be more expensive than one had expected. Side costs which one had not anticipated now played a role and they could no longer be compensated for by passion. This discrepancy was then heightened by the reflexive structure of the lovers' expectations, i.e. the common inclination to overinterpret, which had originally served to build up the relationship, and the comparison of hope and reality both now accelerated its decline.[93] The relationship was not up to coping with its own temporality and dissolved.

By laying claim to time, love destroys itself. It dissolves the characteristics which had lent wings to the imagination and replaces it with familiarity. A real beauty appears less beautiful the second time round and an ugly person seems less so.[94] In other words, the code's switch from a natural to an imaginary basis[95] exposes love to temporal corrosion, an erosion that is actually faster than the natural decline of beauty would be. Subjectification and temporalization go hand in hand.

This form of processing temporality in connection with subjectification and social reflexivity is particularly noticeable when compared with other models of the linkage of temporality and sociality. Whereas temporality is only woven into conversational theory as the need for continual change, the concept of friendship deems constancy and calmness to be the characteristics of a perfect relationship. In the seventeenth century the problem of time was thus still predominantly thematized as the difference of change and constancy, and not as a process that built itself up and tore itself down. It was only in the semantics of love that the former view was surpassed – here the connection of temporality and social reflexivity was rendered dynamic by being accorded the form of a special process with its own history. This is an important indicator that work was under way on the differentiation and autonomization of a specific functional area.

The explosiveness of this theme of temporality and brevity, if not the momentariness, of love can also be seen from the fact that it receives a fixed location in the generalized symbolic code of the medium of love and is subsequently treated as certain knowledge, as a generally known fact. The literature of the seventeenth century still attempts to show that this is the case; in the novels and plays of the eighteenth century the same theme is presented as the knowledge of particular persons, thus becoming a component in the structure of motives of love.[96] The impossibility of its lasting makes love difficult, especially for the women. They have to become unhappy, whether they *nevertheless* decide in favour of love or against it *for the very same reason.*[97] Literature reflects the effects of literature just as novels reappear in novels. This makes it possible to move the moral themes into the foreground of pure rhetoric and to let the thematics of time dominate the proceedings. What is available as a 'virtue' is in truth an interest in permanence, in calmness – as it were, almost in salvation.[98]

This complicated character of the relationship of literature to literature, of temporality to morals and of the reflection of this complication in the social reflexivity of the intimate relationship could clearly no longer be common knowledge. Here, the codification came up against the barriers to its success posed by communication in society. A Marivaux could become a successful author in the opinion of both his contemporaries and later readers, whereas Crébillon could not.[99]

This theme warrants an investigation of its own. Be this as it may, the temporal structure given to the process of love certainly facilitated the differentiation of the code formed for it. Above all, it forced a distinction – previously only a matter of frequent discussion – to be made between love and marriage.[100] Love and marriage were contrasted so pointedly[101] that it would be fairly safe to assume that more than anything else this *difference* between passion and the socially prescribed, family-bound marriage brought about a consciousness of the differentiation of relations of love.[102] One statement on the subject, for example, claimed that the God of Love in a fit of madness forced the lovers into marriage and thus into disaster.[103] Entering into marriage, Bussy Rabutin maintained, was an honourable way to break with a lover.[104] What remained true despite all its exquisite qualities was that 'il suffit d'etre marié pour ne plus aimer.'[105] Or: whoever wants to marry his lover wants to hate her.[106] In Cotin's works one finds the following verse with the title of 'Amour sans example': 'Iris, je pourrois vous aimer, quand mesme vous seriez ma femme.'[107] And in a letter Le Pays[108] speaks of death and marriage as two forms of misfortune which he had managed to avoid despite a fever and parental pressures, thus saving his life. These were not arguments against the institution of marriage (although such do exist within the feminist movement), but rather arguments that differentiation be made within the code of love, and it is the problem of time – of duration – that became the pivot of all difference.

7

From Galantry to Friendship

The temporal reference of love makes it possible for the theme to be treated in narrative, i.e. for 'love stories' to be told, and thus allows for the production of a kind of functionally specific surrogate for myths.[1] Both the beginning and the end of love remain adaptive, be it to other love affairs or for whatever else one may have yet to do. Likewise, the elision of reason and judgement also symbolizes the differentiation of the special treatment accorded to love. One would expect reasoned judgements to arrive at the same conclusions in all cases; it is precisely the irrationality of 'inclination' that keeps this from happening, ensuring a more even distribution of the chances of love coming into being.[2]

However, in addition to the separating off of intimate relationships and the particular type of distribution problem these involve in temporal and social terms, differentiation also requires concepts linking them to other environments. In the context of a society still structured in terms of stratification, this necessitates above all a link being made to the generally valid forms of upper-class social interaction. The concept of 'galantry'[3] serves this purpose for a certain transitional period. Under the guise of galantry, courting can take place – and to a certain extent, without obligation – in the presence of third parties. Galant behaviour provides adaptive links both to intimacy as well as to sociability[4] and can bridge differences in rank. It seeks only to please, without by so doing implicating oneself and the others.[5] Galantry is possible in a social setting and yet at the same time appears to be an indispensable ingredient of love,[6] essential if love is to have a civilizing, educating, socializing effect. In the things it implies and the linguistic forms it takes, galantry retains a novelistic, idealistic semantics – suited for any purpose, thus providing a socially binding style both for deceptive and seductive behaviour as well as for truly loving courtship. As a consequence of this dual purpose, it becomes difficult to decipher what a person's behaviour signifies and to know true love. This further gives rise to an interest in unmasking the real intent of behaviour, a process in which the art of love is both taught and exposed.

Under the imperative of this socially fixed form, *précieuses* and libertines alike contribute – in spite of all their radical differences – to the emergence of the code of *amour passion*.[7] Both groups share a common purpose, namely, to avoid marriage.[8] Given this basis, it is precisely the heterogeneity of their sources and intentions which furthers the genesis of a new synthesis of the paradoxies of *amour passion* – leaving aside how the more conventional forms of mere galantry are overcome in the form of paradoxy. In other words, the libertines, and this must be said to prevent them from being misunderstood, also took pains to establish a semantics worthy of preservation, the difference being that they were interested only in a stronger moral autonomy specially tailored to love. However, literature that consisted solely of barbed remarks can in this context contribute nothing to an understanding of our topic,[9] and will therefore not be considered.

One can assume, furthermore, that the idealization hitherto at the centre of the semantics of love (as the only conceivable form of a normative code) continued to form the basis for the innovations of *amour passion* that were replacing it.[10] This is well documented in a work entitled 'La justification de l'amour' which was published in the *Recueil de Sercy*.[11] Love is depicted as being *amour raisonnable*, as something necessary, reasonable and good, which automatically includes a justification of *plaisir*. Everything reads smoothly and beyond moral reproach, laced with clever little precautions: love should be kept secret to preserve honour from being damaged, for all great things in the world are, by nature, secret.[12] And, because following humankind's fall from grace sin has become unavoidable, it is best to commit one's inevitable sins in love, where they are the 'douce offense, la plus naturelle et la plus agréable'.[13]

The use of the semantic form of idealization already appears somewhat out of place in these riders; but apparently it is still indispensable as a means of persuasion, for many new elements thrive on the traditional premises. But to the extent that the semantics of *amour passion* becomes a self-contained system and begins to have a functioning framework, the necessity of referring to the ideal recedes, at which point the rhetorical tirades, the copied feelings, the periodic sighs and repeated genuflections start to seem ridiculous. The psychologically refined elements of the new semantics encourage the demand for a 'return to the natural'!

The genetic basis for an idealization still held up as an example and for an as yet incomplete differentiation are rendered obsolete by the semantic developments themselves. Galantry – the connecting link to the generally valid forms of social life – is rapidly superseded as the demands for an individual stylization of love increase and as the bourgeoisie begins to usurp the behavioural models of the nobility. Galantry, having fulfilled its transitional function, is subject to rejection and ridicule, and the function of reintegrating love and society devolves to a new figure: the moral legitimation of emotion.

It is also noticeable in other respects – and specifically, always in direct relation to the problems of differentiation – that the efforts made in the *salons* and literature of French Classicism to cast and formulate a code for the communicative medium love rapidly pass their zenith. One has the impression that love ages with the king. Whereas it was fresh, easygoing, imaginative, daring and even frivolous around 1660, by 1690 it again falls subject to moral controls. What was once paradoxy, lightness or even frivolity is now distorted into something cynical, and soon becomes an object of rejection.[14] And at the same time, a new literature on women emerges in which passionate love is not even mentioned;[15] the novel also moves in this direction. In view of the devastating '*désordres de l'amour*', the novel advises its readers to follow the example of the Princesse de Clèves and opt for renunciation and abstinence as a moral achievement – and as pleasure![16]

The return to a form of religious and moral judgement is only possible because the problem of intimate personal relationships has not yet presented itself. A text by Bourdaloue serves well to demonstrate this point, showing it to have occurred toward the end of the seventeenth century.[17] The new, mundane model of a friendship that considers itself absolute is reprimanded for ultimately being based in egotism, for failing to have the salvation of the friend at heart and, in the final instance, for actually being indifferent toward him.[18] *Caritas*, whereby one strives to love God in the other person, is the opposite of such a secular human friendship. The bizarre, disturbing characteristics of the other person present no obstacle to this endeavour, his positive characteristics are not the reason for loving him, nor does the rule of *aimer ceux qui nous aiment* apply.[19] In other words, *caritas* is also indifferent to the other person; it is not concerned with his destiny or characteristics, but only with his salvation. The difference between the two forms of loving a friend is the difference between two forms of indifference. If one chooses to make the difference the point of orientation, any orientation towards the individuality of the other person is already excluded from the outset by that very choice. In an era when a need for orientation toward individuality is already being created at the level of socio-structural changes, this means that religion and morals become superficial. *Caritas*, with its reference to God, is taken to be 'easy and practicable' – precisely because it can disregard the characteristics of individuals.[20]

One of the forms which expresses this reversion to morals is the revival of a milder, more general ideal of friendship.[21] Around 1660 the decline of the ethos of friendship was lamented and considered inevitable (perhaps under the impact of political conflict and court intrigues). Toward the turn of the century, however, the notion began to regain ground. The '*sûreté*' and '*douceur*' of friendship were celebrated, as were both the superfluousness of all extravagance and the possibility of going beyond mere short-lived pair relationships. In still another respect, a check was placed on the code for intimacy being clearly differentiated, in that friendships were at the same time self-characterizations vis-à-vis the outside world.[22] It is no wonder that from this point of view the decline of galantry – of the old forms of reintegration – was lamented.[23] At the same time, at least initially, the strict contradistinction between friendship and love was upheld.[24] An analogous development was under way in England at about this time: the severeness of the Puritanical concept of marriage was relaxed by resorting to both psychological refinements and a stronger person-related concept of friendship.[25] Love as duty is transformed into love as a liking for another, and thus brought closer into line with the ideal of friendship. This had the overall effect of weakening the asymmetry of domestic order, for the old demand that no person should be forced to marry against his decided will was given a new foundation in considerations of reason and morals.

This effort to adjust the code for intimacy to one of 'close' friendship permeated the entire eighteenth century,[26] signalling the conclusion of the initial steps toward rendering marriage intimate – not on the basis of love, but on the basis of a friendship that can only be induced by love.[27] In this manner, love in marriage could once again be emphasized more strongly, provided, however, that it was not *fol amour* which determined the choice of a mate and that love remained rational.[28] But the *raisonnable* was now a person who was happy and gay, carefree and discreet – and, accordingly, the attempt was made to purify love of all the exaggerations that enthusiasts and dissatisfied husbands and wives had come up with.[29] Loving friendship nearly effaced the difference between the sexes, *la mollesse ayant tout feminisé*; it was not heroic feats, but *petits soins* which won the women's hearts, and excess was only heard of in the form of an echo: 'Il est de la nature de l'amour de ne point vouloir de reserve, mais sa principale substance est le sentiment.'[30]

Seen from a more strictly theoretical angle and taking the tradition of practical philosophy into account, it would seem above all to have been the alignment to reflexive sociability which changed the conceptual relationship between love and friendship (in addition to the superficial prescription of friendship as a solution to problems in marriage). The traditional conceptual hierarchy had favoured love over friendship; love had been viewed as a quality, whereas friendship was only a relationship. Moreover, love was possible in relation to God and oneself, whereas friendship was only possible in relation to other people. Thus, friendship remained (as it had in the development of the *Nichomachean Ethics*) an addendum to the treatment of questions of ethics. Around 1700, however, this seems to change, to the extent that social reflexivity was taken as the point of departure for a new treatment of issues of natural law and ethics, and for a time it appeared as if it were possible to fuse love and friendship – were it not for the obstructive factor of sexuality, which made it necessary to nevertheless distinguish between the two. In any case, both concepts now competed with each other for the right to shape the code for intimate relationships.

The signs that sociality is understood to have a deeper thrust are scattered and covert. Thus, for example, Goussault[31] criticizes the aristocratic principle of generosity – which was not only more or less a self-portrayal of one's *own* virtue, but on its transposition into bourgeois conditions was also to become a principle of exploitation – with the remark that friendship included both granting *and denying* one's friend loans; for a true friend could hardly deny his friend the freedom of being able to say no. It was a test of true friendship to have understanding for this even if one was oneself affected by it.

English literature on courtship provides another example. Importance is attached here not to some impassioned and impulsive insistence, but to quite the opposite, namely to the *seeming inadvertency* of behaviour when making acquaintance with somebody.[32] 'Carefully careless', a form of behaviour invented on Bond Street, or so Stendhal surmised.[33] Even if – and indeed precisely when – such a stance is seen through, it affords the partner an opportunity to immerse himself voluntarily in the game at hand and at the same time has the advantage of not (as yet) overinvolving the player. The intentional portrayal of inadvertency is a technical refinement that can only be understood in the context of social reflexivity and that can be practised without any risk of disappointment, because it fulfils its function even when seen through.[34]

In such cases, social reflexivity is not yet raised to the status of a principle and is not elaborated systematically; but the idea is already present, and begins to transform the casuistry of both friendship and love, and becomes visible here and there in the course of the argumentation. And it is hardly coincidental that it appears at those points where the transfer of values from the aristocracy to the bourgeoisie cannot be affected.

Viewed as a whole, it is nevertheless love and not friendship which has won the race and ultimately determined the code for intimacy. Why? It is not easy to pinpoint or verify the reasons for this, but one can, however, assume that despite all privatization of and distinction between everyday and special friendship (Thomasius), it proved impossible to delimit friendship, i.e. to differentiate within it. The obsession with virtue within the cult of friendship, relying as it did on a generally recognized set of morals, would seem to bear this out. Furthermore, once social reflexivity had become the very maxim of interaction,[35] such a preoccupation alone no longer sufficed as a means of shaping the contours of a special code for intimate relationships. Last but not least, one must bear in mind that the symbiotic mechanism of sexuality that underpinned differentiation at the level of inter-active relationships was not at the disposal of friendship, for this was precisely what distinguished the latter from love.

Generally speaking, it can be said that around 1700 nature and morals again came to play an increasing role in semantics, signalling a tendency towards retrogressive differentiation, towards a relevelling of semantic innovation. However, this trend never really asserted itself. Galantry was sacrificed, but love was not. Perhaps the love behaviour of the upper classes was too ill-suited to being packaged under moral labels. Above all, however, changes in the semantics itself indicate that the budding interest in individual love relationships outside the domain of strict social control could not be stemmed. Love's reinstatement as self-love,[36] which had at first been considered problematic, now became normalized.[37] Activated passion became perfectly adapted to accommodate emotions and instilled with the functions of individualization. This saved the semantic instruments of the code for *amour passion* from collapse and it is precisely in the search for unity in paradoxicalization and ambivalence that these instruments showed themselves to be viable.[38] The form they found bore within it the chance of a linkage to more strongly individualizing interpretations, without, however, proclaiming this programmatically.

This analysis confirms a supposition which can be formulated in more general terms within the framework of a theory of the evolution of ideas. Variations in the ideational resources, which, because of their plausibility at a given time, were able to achieve success (in our cases, that is, to be convincing in the *salons*), acquired stability and could be handed down because they were systematized. In other words, they were brought into a context in which they reciprocally affirmed each other.[39] Then, in the course of their continuing reproduction, they again allowed variations to arise which, however, were compelled to conform to the prevalent semantics and were thus only able to transform this complex very slowly. In this sense, we can say that the classical code of *amour passion* changed into Romantic love while upholding the notion that a uniform idea was involved. The unity was not logically grounded; but on the contrary, and, what is more, just as effectively, it came to be guaranteed by paradoxicalization. This form of guaranteeing unity and coherency served perhaps to enhance the lovers' emotions, and at any rate ameliorated the problems of portrayal besetting those who wrote about love. It held the medium together for nearly two centuries and only became problematic once love was called for as the basis for matrimony; for it is then that the semantics of love raise the question of whether marriage can also be understood as a paradoxical institution.

8

Plaisir and *Amour*

The Primary Difference

Before tracing the points at which the code of passionate love
begins to provide adaptive links for individualization any further,
let us turn our attention to two theoretical complexes that we
have already touched on. The first has to do with the fact that the
code belongs to a special generalized symbolic medium of
communication. Such a code has to be able to fulfil a function
which we shall designate *the generation of information*. It has to
be able to render all the actions and inner experiences that fall
within its scope identifiable as information and to provide them
with an adaptive value connecting them to further experiences
and actions.

Information is, according to Gregory Bateson's oft-cited dictum
'a difference that makes a difference'.[1] Regardless of what one
thinks of their ontological and metaphysical status, or their
incarnation as 'script' (Derrida), or similar approaches, differences
direct the sensibilities which make one receptive to information.
Information processing can only take place if, beyond its pure
facticity, something has been experienced as 'this way and only
this way', which means that it has been localized in a framework
of differences. The difference functions as a unity to the extent
that it generates information, but it does not determine which
pieces of information are called for and which patterns of
selection they trigger off. Differences, in other words, do not
delimit a system; they specify and extend its capacity for self-
delimitation. Semantic codes specify the differences which form
the basis for something being comprehended as information.

However, they only have a reality within the process of information processing itself and only affect the system by means of this process. From the perspective of a theory of evolution, the social system can be said to refine its preparedness to process information by differentiating differences that are both tailored to particular functions or interactive constellations and further specify the other possible occurrences in comparison to which certain events gain in informative value.[2] The differentiation of a semantic code for love is a good example of this.

These general theoretical assumptions make it clear that the differentiation of a communicative medium occurs *by means of their reduction to a basic semantic difference* compared to which everything that happens within the scope of the medium can be regarded as selection and thus as information. With respect to its function the unity of a communicative medium becomes all the more pronounced the more it succeeds in reducing numerous relevant oppositions to one central difference that renders all the variances and contrasts understandable. By means of such a reduction it is possible to achieve seemingly diametrically opposed objectives. On the one hand, the communicative field and the pattern of information acquisition dominant in it are pinpointed, and, on the other, the degree of freedom from regulation within the code is augmented, so that there is a greater capacity for adaptation both to particular circumstances and to specific intentions and inclinations.

There are a number of communicative media which give their primary difference the form of a binary opposition. One need only think of the logical structure of the code for truth or of the difference between legal and illegal behaviour. This has the advantage of creating a wide-ranging 'technicalizability' of information processing within the code's scope. In other cases an 'open' duality of value terms exercises the same function, for example the difference of progressive and conservative options in the code for politics.[3] One would scan the code of empassioned love in vain for an exact analogy to this. François de Callieres's attempt to derive such a code from a logical structure[4] appears as pedantic and out of place even in the context of its own time. The form taken by the central difference that generates information is dissimilar, but functionally, however, completely equivalent. It consists of the difference between *plaisir* and *amour*.[5]

What becomes particularly evident when viewed from the standpoint of the functions codes have is that in the seventeenth century the semantics of love does indeed change fundamentally, becomes more unified and simultaneously more sharply differentiated. The numerous distinctions which play a role in love relationships, e.g. the distinction between the sexes, between young and old, and that of the beloved from all other people are all semantically subsumed under this primary difference of *plaisir* and *amour* and, as a consequence, are permeated by new contingencies. The distinction between *plaisir* and *amour* creates a need for information specific to this communicative field and at the same time bestows a specific structure on information acquisition. It creates and reinforces a sensibility, valid only within this area, for differences that would find no use in other contexts. It thus instils numerous occurrences or actions with an informative value – for instance as symptoms or signs of love as opposed to *plaisir*, whereas they would either be ignored or accorded a different value if applied in other contexts.

How is this centring on a difference accomplished? And what semantic tools serve this function?

What meets the eye above all is that, compared to the traditional code, *plaisir* is now introduced as an anthropological concept and thus precedes any moral judgement. As a result, almost being forced to court a woman as part of normal social intercourse and the necessity of love affairs for one's existence as '*honnête homme*',[6] and the subsequent distinction between true and false love are all reduced to one common denominator and anchored firmly in statements on mankind in general. Human beings are at any rate held to seek *plaisir*, both for themselves and for the others by means of galant or interested forms of wooing, by true or feigned love. *Plaisir* becomes the guiding principle of life, and unlike the 'good life' promulgated in the traditional code (εὐ ζῆν), is based on a subjective facticity devoid of any immanent criteria of measurement. By virtue of *plaisir* human beings are subjects. This means that the reality of *plaisir*, like that of thought, is an established fact, regardless of whether it makes use of correct or incorrect presuppositions or operates with honest or dishonest means. *Plaisir* is *plaisir*. If someone claims to feel *plaisir* there is no point in claiming the contrary. In the case of *plaisir* the subject requires no criteria to make certain it is experiencing *plaisir*, but rather can be sure of itself in a sort of self-referentiality bare of evaluative criteria.[7] In other words, here there is none of that fateful duality of authentic and merely feigned love which otherwise had been such an intriguing topic of social intercourse with regard to the behaviour of *others*. In the 'Discours sur les passions de l'amour'[8] already cited this is made utterly clear: 'Un plaisir vrai ou faux peut remplir également l'esprit; car qu'importe que ce plaisir soit faux, pourvu que l'on soit persuadé qu'il est vrai?'[9]

Not only do other people lack any criteria by which to control this self-referentiality, but so does the subject, who is not even able to question the *plaisir* experienced, cannot discriminate with regard to it or get rid of it, that is unless such efforts in turn were the source of *plaisir*. Even Stendhal still maintains, in a crucial passage: 'L'homme n'est pas libre de ne pas faire ce qui lui fait plus de plaisir que toutes les autres actions possibles.'[10] There is thus in the final instance no freedom vis-à-vis one's own *plaisir* and accordingly the subject can also not be reduced to freedom. But one can enjoy pain, can attempt to eradicate *plaisirs* by means of thriftiness or even suicide – with *plaisir*; and to this extent *amour passion* comes into close contact with pleasure in suffering. It is only logical that masochistic figures subsequently appear on the scene, ensuring the totality of the principle of self-referentiality. One replaces, as it were, the freedom towards oneself, which is no longer attainable, with self-torment.

Every occasion where *plaisir* manifests this immediacy of self-referentiality has far-reaching consequences for social relations. Feelings may arise without criteria as to their 'correctness' and thus appear to not be correctable. Statements on these feelings can, however, only originate within the context of another self-referential system, a social system, and can therefore not relate this 'unquestionability' to themselves,[11] for they *can* err, *can* deceive and *can* be disputed. Above all, precisely the unreflectedness of *plaisir* stimulates reflected social usage, namely, in relation to the inner experiences and actions of people in one's social environment. It is especially easy to observe and size up people who are in a state of *plaisir*, because they open up – their joy makes them strut – and they are thus exceptionally exposed to the eagle eye of others.[12] *Plaisir* makes its subject defenceless in the face of observation and treatment by others. The *art de plaire* becomes a technique of experimentation and observation, a strategy for reconnoitring the dangerous terrain of mundane relationships.[13] Nurturing *plaisir* is, from this point of view, quite the opposite of passionate love, and is rather something which requires that one keep cool and take a reflected approach.[14] The basis of calculation lies precisely in the distinct indisputability of *plaisir*.

This indisputability of self-experienced *plaisir* is carried over into social behaviour when it involves trying to please others. The intentions or techniques directed toward achieving this are, therefore, not questioned.[15] It is *here* that the social regulation of the *art de plaire* – just as important as the orientation towards *raison*[16] in the second half of the seventeenth century – *came into force*, but with reference to the subject experiencing *plaisir*, and not to a set of morals to be applied and also no longer to self-realization within the context of honour and fame. As a result of this, once religious and moral behavioural regulations fade, and specifically in the context of love(!), anthropological certainty can be recoined as social behaviour. One can be sure – irrespective of all uncertainty with regard to love – that one's efforts to please are enjoyed and themselves create the criteria by which they are judged. The addressee of the efforts remains sovereign with respect to *what* pleases him, but *how* he can be pleased can nonetheless be learned.

This extension in society is countered by the temporal curtailment of *plaisir*. *Plaisir* exists only momentarily and only for the moment in which it is experienced. The passage of time is experienced in the moment of *plaisir* as the necessity of change: 'Chaque plaisir est passager, il le faut prendre à son passage.'[17] This now means more than simply '*carpe diem*'. Self-certainty is itself now temporalized and can be cast into doubt as the 'not yet' or the 'no longer'. Against this background the lasting nature of love, as noted above,[18] inevitably becomes a contrafactual assertion: an eternal oath that only counts for a moment, but which is necessary in that moment in order to contradict one's awareness of inconstancy.

In other words, *plaisir* will always be one's starting point and *plaire* accordingly becomes the (honest or dishonest) means of acquiring (true or false) love. The unity of the semantics of *plaisir/plaire* disguises the fact that the anthropological argument of a facticity devoid of evaluative criteria cannot (at least not readily) be applied to social systems.[19] This tension between anthropological basis and social regulation appears in the conceptuality of *plaisir/plaire* as the necessary unity of nature and art. Each subject is highly regarded as an expert and receives fulfilment from the knowledge that his expertise pleases as nature. However, precisely the *procédé de la galanterie*, which attempts to please, arouses suspicion as to its motives by virtue of its being socially oriented intentional behaviour and thus triggers off the search for criteria with which to distinguish between sincere and insincere behaviour. Here coquetry branches off as the capacity to maximize the number of admirers without simultaneously losing oneself in love.[20] Coquetry expects to be disappointed and reacts to this with pretence – all in the opaque medium of *plaisanterie* on the basis of equally indisputable, mutual interest. But it can happen that in the process one unintentionally crosses the threshold of love,[21] this being the start of the ensuing tragedy.

Taken on its own, *plaisir* is not actually a medium of communication because it is not affected by the problem of acceptance or rejection. The *art de plaire* is accordingly an undifferentiated, universally applicable social technique that cannot be easily thrown off balance. It gives behaviour social cover, and protected by it, one's operations cannot be repelled and one can close on love. Precisely for this reason, if one wishes to cross the threshold into love, one cannot let things be at this point; and the compulsion to please, by dint of its being a form of social relations, destroys itself by its own exaggeration.[22] How completely unlike love! Love, in order to be distinguished from the communication in which it may be disguised, must be able to take on the function of a generalized symbolic medium and as a consequence becomes subject to a further set of conditions, in the context of which efforts to please can only figure as foreplay.

Things become even more complex if the distinction between true and feigned love is refined in such a manner that one differentiates the latter form in terms of its simulation or dissimulation. A double disguise must then be considered: the simulation of (not experienced) love and the dissimulation of (experienced) love.[23] Both can, particularly if working in tandem, throw up sufficient 'obstacles' to set off a love affair.

Irrespective of all the differences between *plaisir* and *amour*, it is *plaisir* which in the final instance keeps a firm hand on the pattern of things. It determines how long love lasts. Love ends when it no longer gives *plaisir*. According to one of the Marquis de M.'s letters 'l'amour ne lie qu'autant qu'il plaît.'[24] All mannerisms which feign permanence become intolerable to the person who still loves. Even sincere love is powerless once the well of *plaisir* dries up. It would then have to transform love into duty – and that would contradict the code since the latter differentiates between love and marriage.

The code consequently relies on a highly complicated semantic architecture. The difference between true and false love, which is to be distinguished from the communication that may disguise it, is based on the difference between *amour* and *plaisir* which in turn serves to formulate an increasing differentiation between anthropological self-referentiality on the one hand and social realization on the other. Or inversely: the socio-structurally determined need for a clearer separation of personal and social reflexivity is expressed in the distinction between *plaisir* and *amour*, which in turn enables, with reference to *plaisir*, genuine and inauthentic modes of behaviour to be detected in *amour*, a distinction which then informs each person's concrete sensibility for information in factual love affairs. The interconnectedness of this series of switches serves to lend semantic expression to the basic socio-structural conditions. This makes it possible to read information in terms of such conditions, without, however, at the same time having to thematize the social structure itself – which tends towards a stronger individualization of fate – and thus expose it to negation.

If information is generated in the context of a semantically fixed difference, this initially has the effect of providing a causal basis for the illusionary, the fictitious and the negative. Something can act to trigger off behaviour, although, or rather precisely because it is not present. The system extends into the negative the degree to which it can be stimulated (which of course presupposes internally the existence of self-referential structures and processes). Similarly, pure unchangeability is instilled with an informative value and causality if the pattern of differences allows one to expect or hope for change. The mere *duration* of the beloved's *absence* in the final instance allows conclusions to be made as to his love, and sets off reactions if such a reading is informed by an expectation of love or indifference.[25] Indeed, one is able particularly in affairs of the heart to allow one's behaviour to be determined by illusions and may expect the same of one's partner, even if one knows that these are illusions. 'Excessiveness', exaggeration and a one-sided stance are themselves rendered transparent and yet both taken as the reason to acquire corresponding information (positive or negative) and allow one to be motivated by it. The difference between illusion and reality itself then becomes reality and precisely this legitimates the code as love, a love that goes beyond mere *plaisir*.

Perhaps the most important immediate consequence of this particular grouping of semantic differences is the *temporalization* of love already treated in the previous chapter. The temporal difference between a momentary present, on the one hand, and the past and future, on the other, makes the difference of illusion and reality seem plausible. Accordingly, the unity of love in the form of the unity of moment and duration, the paradox of momentariness is called upon to provide an eternally lasting value.[26] Here the paradox also fuses the difference, which has to function as a difference, into a unity only by formulating it. The paradox nevertheless remains dependent on the fact that love is a process and that it bestows a temporal status on all information.

Each love has its own history (which need not in this context signify an individual, unique, incomparable history). It has a beginning and an end and between these a process of waxing and waning within which the relevance of the pattern of differences changes. It is thus often suggested in the literature that the beginning of a love affair, before the love has been granted any social certainty, depends above all on *plaire*.[27] However, precisely this forces the difference of true and false love; one is compelled to scan one's efforts to please for information that refers to this second difference until, at a later point, the ebbing of one's efforts offer the first signs that true love is starting to wane.[28] The love relationship gradually becomes inauthentic – one that can only barely be kept going, and the partners are constantly on the look-out for information indicating that the end is in sight. The fact that the beginning of a relationship is determined by a more or less conventional form of *art de plaire* (which is therefore hard to interpret) also means that one can embark on love without knowing that it is love.[29] Particularly in its verbal regulation galantry takes on a form that is not only oriented towards *plaire*, but also embraces both true and false love; yet at the same time it also contains a secret meaning *if* it is true love. In this context obstacles assume the function of making love conscious, and any further obstacles one of testing love. One may start with a somewhat conventional friendship and the exchange of pleasantries only to notice after a certain time – when it is already too late – that it is love. One can fall in love while in the process of feigning love, get caught up in one's own galantry and then miss the right time for withdrawal. One fears coquetry above all because it can quickly lend the relationship the form of feigned love. That the process ends in indifference also means that the difference between true and false love is now used to access completely different information, i.e. in order to cool out the relationship and to avoid affective reactions which would no longer be suitable.

This and the many similar observations that can be made not only describe the history of a typical process of love, but also – and to my mind for the first time, historically speaking – show how the process itself alters the conditions under which information is accessed and then has to be interpreted. What is more, they demonstrate that the specific pattern of differences which have to be activated to access particular information depends on the phase reached in the process. At first, hope and anxiety, the alternative to true and false love, arise in the transition from *plaire* to *amour*. The one difference releases the other from within itself without thereby disappearing.[30] The overall structure of the semantics of love unfolds in time, and as a consequence there can be no claim made of the code that does not itself have a value and place in time. The process remains sovereign and decides on the difference it employs to access information.

Precisely for this reason, the code of passionate love does not need a moral foundation, an anchorage in the lasting guarantors of the social order. It is grounded, if I may be permitted to use the phrase, in the shortness of life,[31] not in eternal life. The selections chosen justify themselves by the difference between the moment and the before and after, and not with regard to a stability still to be achieved. The selective function is relieved of any stabilizing tasks to a greater degree than at almost any other time, and something of this is retained when love in the passionate sense of

Romanticism is later seen as the precondition for entering into marriage.

It must also be remarked at this point that such daring semantic innovations tend towards renormalization.[32] They are still quite improbable and therefore their return to some simply cognitive or moral difference is probable. Furthermore, referring back to the class characteristics of the '*honnestes gens*' as a solution to the problem of difficulties in differentiation,[33] still possible around 1660, probably became less and less convincing after 1700. Thus in 1715 an anonymous text (signed 'L.B.D.P.') appeared[34] presenting the opposites of true and false love once more as if these simply amounted to a difference in objective qualities. It was then possible for the author to couple this with a request to avoid false love. Pure love, he or she contended, although always true, was disfigured by the corruptness of the heart, by malformations which had to be exposed and countered, an undertaking in which the author proceeded to engage extensively. What becomes apparent here is not only that this actually created a list of malformations which could then be confessed to, but that at the same time the complex differentiated structure of a set of morals specific to love that had been gained in social and temporal terms was again lost.

9

Love versus Reason

Now that the necessary analyses have been made of the structure underlying the attempt to codify intimate relationships by means of an application of the difference between *plaisir* and *amour*, we can turn our attention to a second, equally fundamental question: the differentiation of this code. In so doing our enquiry will remain at the level of historical semantics and will refer to a short text which is particularly revealing in this context, namely, a 'Dialogue de l'amour et de la Raison'.[1]

The Dialogue should be read bearing in mind the traditional ideal of a love ordered by reason.[2] This ideal is now broken down into the opposing principles of love and reason, and thus no longer permits hierarchical and domesticating solution, but instead only a kind of socially reflexive mirroring of the lover's opposing interests in the beloved. In order to be able to depict this, the personifications of love and reason are allowed to speak in the course of the narrative, thus remaining – in terms of form – at the level of allegory.[3] The Dialogue comprises a debate in the *salon* of a lady to whom the author assigns an extraordinarily good knowledge of Love and Reason. In the Dialogue – and this is the crucial point – Reason represents society to the extent that society is embodied in its structural demands. This is particularly true for the two main issues which Reason has to defend: the parental (paternal) choice of a matrimonial partner for the son or daughter; and the occlusion of inter-class marriage or intimate relationships. It seems only self-evident to Reason, and actually to Love as well, that these are reasonable demands. If they were not adhered to, society would be inconceivable, and Reason therefore has good reasons to complain about the irrational impulses with which Love disturbs society. This is why Reason has the impression that Love withdraws from all forms of control subject to Reason so as to play its irresponsible game in the sphere of the irrational.

Love counters this reproach by citing her *own reasonable grounds*. These are essentially based on asserting that she inhabits a domain of her own, i.e. that she possesses her own claim to power. Parents make a mistake if they do not consult Love before deciding on the marriage of their children. And as far as differences in social standing and the fatal consequences of a love bridging such boundaries are concerned, Love's crucial argument is that she levels the lovers and thus suspends these social differences: 'A mon égard je les rend toûjours égaux, quoy qu'ils ne le paroissent pas aux yeux de ceux qui ignorent mon pouvoir et mes mystères'.[4] Based on the particularity of her realm and of her power, Love is able to show that she possesses a rationality of her own (whereas at the end of the Dialogue, Reason's capacity for love remains a mere wish galantly addressed to the lady of the house).

Love remains fully aware of the fact that she cannot compete with Reason, for the latter must be universally applicable, and Love cannot relieve her of this task. However – and this is the crunch – this is precisely why Reason cannot claim absolute power. Universality and absolutism are mutually exclusive. 'Et c'est ce qui rend mon empire bien different du vostre; car vous ne scauriez rien ordonner en Maitresse absolue, puis que vous estes obligees de rendre raison de toutes choses. Mais pour moy j'agis en Souverain, et ne sens raison que quand il me plaist.'[5] Reason sees this argument only as an invitation to violent conflict and indignantly breaks off the discourse.

The Dialogue can easily be translated into the language of sociological theory. Society has to renounce the 'reasonable' (i.e. the self-referential justificatory) control over intimate relationships, without its existence as a society thereby being at stake or even being undermined.[6] When conditions become more complex, claims to universality and to totality must be disengaged from one another. Any claim to having the only valid interpretation of the world can only be made in special circumstances, and in love, as we know from other sources, it can only be achieved for a brief moment. On the other hand, it is precisely under this condition of disengaging universal applicability from its totalizing impulse that the increase of expectations and fulfilments – so crucial to love – is possible.

Love demands priority for her reasons, a priority asserted in the style of the sovereign statement: 'because I like it that way'.[7] This is reflected in the numerous paradoxies inherent in the codification – paradoxies that are mentioned not owing to some sort of logical embarrassment, but rather as a form consciously selected by the speaker. However, this does not mean that Love manoeuvres herself out of society in order to function as she sees fit, i.e. lawlessly. Rather she herself cites Reason as an authority. 'L'Amour a des raisons qui valent mieux que celles de la Raison mesme.'[8] Love only insists on her sovereignty when pushed into a corner. If left to her own devices, she functions according to her own laws, as are formulated in the code *amour passion*.

Finally, it becomes noticeable that Reason is old, Love is young and that Love not only has the stronger arguments but also a better overview of the conflict. Reason can only attempt to deflate Love's arguments, by characterizing them as hair-splitting or subtleties; and she, not Love, eventually resorts to conflict. After Reason as the representative of the class structure of society becomes a party to the dispute, there is no longer any neutral authority to turn to for settlement of the conflict; indeed, one is forced to ask oneself whether such an authority will ever again bear the title of Reason.

Nonetheless, all in all, the seventeenth-century dialogue between Love and Reason centres on the issue of establishing territorial rights, one's own logic and sovereign rule over the way people behave. Love demands to be recognized, demands a moral status of her own. In a sense she wants to be left in peace as the source of unrest. It is not until about 1760 that the case for this demand is argued in an increasingly aggressive way. Moral conventions as such come under attack. At the same time, Love expands her repertoire: to include *ménage à trois*, role exchanges, free rein over one's own body, and incest – everything that meets with the partner's approval goes; and all that Reason can prohibit is that which harms another person.

10

En Route to Individualization

A State of Ferment in the Eighteenth Century

Let us return from our digressions into semantic structures and the differentiation of a special code for *amour passion* to address the question of whether, and to what extent, the latter development can be correlated with a greater reliance on the individual characteristics of the parties concerned. One of the most obvious hallmarks of the semantics of love (in contrast to notions of friendship) is its *exclusivity*, in that it is generally regarded – and there is a broad consensus on this point[1] – that one can only love one person at any one time. It is additionally sometimes claimed that this can only happen once in a lifetime, although on the whole this assumption is rejected as being incompatible with the imperative to continually be in love.

As long as love was still understood to form a mystical losing of oneself in the other person, the demand for exclusivity had a clear place in the code, because how was someone supposed to be able to lose himself in more than one person without having to multiply himself? In the face of the shifts in the code of intimacy, this idea nonetheless loses ground. Indeed, the hallmarks of the code, and above all the imperative of excessiveness, the obligation to continually be in love and beauty's function as stimulation now all go against the grain of this claim for exclusiveness. Nonetheless, the logical consequences of this were ignored.[2] Regardless of the contralogical form in which it was often presented – d'Alibray speaks of a *'superstition religieuse'*![3] – the demand for exclusiveness fulfilled an important function in terms of system formation because it symbolized the demand for a new beginning to each love affair. Only thus could the code of intimacy act as a catalytic agent of the system, i.e. the breach of logic is not out of place for it has a functional purpose.

Nevertheless, this limitation of love to a pair relationship in the seventeenth century cannot be read as an expression of the individualization and personalization of love affairs, for it counts, as it did in Antiquity, as a *reduction* that permits an *enhancement* of emotion.[4] At a later date this connection between reduction and enhancement is then used to give greater depth to the personal individualization of love affairs. At this point in the code's development, however, one was concerned only with enhancing the perfection of love itself.

In French Classicism the claim to individuality was part of the world of appearances inhabited by the lovers. In this respect love was also dependent on self-deception and in the end even this proves to have been an illusion. The Duc de Nemours's breach of secrecy finally led the Princesse de Clèves to realize that she, too, had loved a man just like any other and had been treated by him like just any woman: he boasts of her love for him (!): 'J'ai eu tort de croire qu'il y eût un homme capable de cacher ce qui flatte sa gloire. C'est pourtant pour cet homme, que *j'ai cru si différent du reste des hommes*, que je me trouve *comme les autres femmes*, étant si eloignée de leur ressembler.'[5] And I would go so far as to suggest that this was her motive for not becoming united with the man in question, rather than some notion of loyalty until death. Love finds the motives for its decisions within itself and not in marriage. Its claim to completely individualized uniqueness can only give proof of itself in the exceptional, in the negative, in renunciation.

In other respects as well, one should not overestimate the extent to which individualization occurs in statements about people during French Classicism and in the period immediately succeeding it. The idea of love held by the *précieuses* was admittedly constructed around the woman's attempt to gain distance from herself and her own sensuous drives and to ensure that this *distance* in the form of words and gestures was *respected* by the man. Love thus no longer referred solely to an idealized person, but to that person's self-referentiality, i.e. freedom. This self-referentiality is, however, still conceived of in impersonal terms, and is characterized by *one* problem that *all* women have to deal with.

The characteristics that make a woman attractive are presented as general concepts. If one loves them in one woman, how is one to deny that they do not exist in other women? Cotin gives his lady some food for thought by pointing out 'i'ay trop de ioye à vous aimer, pour haïre ce qui vous ressemble.'[6] This is precisely why the constancy of love is to be found only in change, in inconstancy.

Last but not least, one must consider the fact that the psychology of the seventeenth century, which still worked with the old concepts of temperament and humour, allowed no room for personal development (which, of course, does not mean that people were not aware of the process of ageing).[7] Immediately behind this very imprecise and formal psychological conceptuality lay the opaque field of factual drives, affects, motives and self-related interests. As a consequence, scepticism predominated and the moderation that informed all social conduct decreed that caution was to be exercised when penetrating into the all too personal. This reserve was formulated not only with regard to general sociability, but also to more intimate relations (although here it was often outdone by ideal formulae).[8] For similar reasons nothing was further from people's minds than the thought that love influenced the development of the individual personality. Jaulnay explicitly denied that love could change the person experiencing it: 'elle ne peut changer nos humeurs.'[9] 'Les manières nouvelles dont, on se sert ne durent guères, et c'est ce qui fait tant d'inconstance.'[10] Such statements show quite clearly that love is *inconstant because* people *cannot be changed*. The constancy of the actors creates the inconstancy of their love – given the differences in their sex and characters. In keeping with the imagery of love one could also say that identity is consumed in the flames of love and can only save itself by being inconstant,[11] or so it would appear from the thematic structure of the code. This only changes in the course of the eighteenth century, at which point people are now conceived of as being changeable, capable of development, as still unperfected, and love therefore came to be regarded as something that would be lasting, indeed in the final instance as a viable basis of marriage. These variables are still linked in the same manner, only the signification is now reversed: the characters' indeterminacy and plasticity make it possible for love to be steadfast.

The efforts to reform the relationship between the sexes that commenced in England around 1685 and later spread to Germany were ushered in with the aid of a polemic on morality.[12] French served as a contrasting foil. The old two-pronged attack – praising virtues as well as satire – was taken up again in the form of drastic portrayals of contemporary moral degeneracy and a vivid picture of the good, the simple and the utilitarian in the lives of men and women. The effect of this in literature hinges on such contrasts being drawn, but these, however, increasingly became informed by a sharp psychological viewpoint. Literature of this period started to focus on the problem of marriage, considering 'mutual love' as the only solid foundation for a marriage in both a psychological and a moral sense. Marital love was emphasized, i.e. a love that neither took its cues from novels, nor was sexually based passion.[13] The woman – fragile, tender and weak, always on the verge of fainting (Pamela!) and with no sense of her own sexuality – found in marriage a human role and moral perfection for the first time. The basis for this was mutual understanding, respect, promoting the interests of the partner, and friendship, and use was made only hesitatingly of the expression 'love'. What counted was not dramatic gestures, but rather attention to details. All in all, then, of the old alternatives of love and friendship, the latter was clearly opted for as the basis for both intimacy and the special tasks assigned to the family in society. This choice made it possible, particularly with reference to the woman, to merge education, housekeeping and relationships to persons with whom the wife came into contact in a new synthesis.

Overall, the debates that arose in England and later also in the USA[14] remain in the realm of applied anthropology. The woman was discovered to be a human being,[15] the hierarchy in marriage was accordingly dispensed with,[16] and at the same time it was judicious to conform to society. Everyone was meant to be happy – with the aid of his or her partner. Any intimacy one could hope for was related to the household and thus took on sufficiently clear, comprehensible contours. To relate intimacy to 'society' would now – at a time when society was increasingly becoming understood as an economic entity – have seemed misleading (whereas the elaboration of the code of *amour passion* profited precisely from the fact that it did not centre on a well-defined household, but rather on a social behaviour freed of external regulation). The quite concrete elaboration of moral models of behaviour probably appeared meaningful for the domestic sphere, and was egged on by a critique of immorality and bad examples. But the social sphere remained steadfast, and the development of a code for intimacy, which had still to find its own limits, was therefore not necessary.

England conveyed these new ideas to Europe through Richardson's work. They had quite a diverse effect on the continent, and in France there was assuredly less emphasis on domestic details.[17] The portrayal of sexuality as nature and the questioning of all institutions went against the grain of English taste, and thus charged with morals, *amour sérieux* gained ascendance over *amour frivol*, for example in Marmontel's works, and even *amour frivol* itself now donned a moral quality, namely evil.

Any assessment of this reform movement must consequently also take note of the fact that well into the eighteenth century, despite all the shake-ups in morals and moral theory, the tradition that used *moral* categories to describe what made a *human being attractive as a human being* remained intact. Accordingly, the personal and moral effects of human beings on one another were presumed to form a unity. To relinquish such a view, to do without it, must have been an almost inconceivable innovation, for moral theory was supposed to state what was essential to human beings irrespective of all individual fate and without regard for social position. The theory formulated each person's individual responsibility for himself. How could it be otherwise, where ties, love and friendship between people were concerned? The new, individualized tailoring and the switch from rational to emotional perception of the other person, to emotions and sensibility did not by any means therefore break with the premise either that the moral qualities of the other person were at stake – or that what was involved was something which could not be realized exclusively by a particular person alone.

In the classical code of *amour passion* the precautions taken for individualization were invisible and only very indirect, and amounted to the fact that the code's thematic structure was systematized by means of paradoxies. An ideal code in contrast leaves practically no room for variants, and individualization is only possible as deviance. Only negative figures can be portrayed graphically, just as there is only one such thing as health, whereas there are many diseases which in turn determine numerous different individual fates. This block posed by a uniform ideality is broken when the code for intimate relations becomes rearranged in terms of paradoxies, for this creates a capacity for diametrically opposed solutions to the problems that arise – and thus for individual behavioural choices – despite all subsumption under the unity of the code. Literature at this time was full of such contradictions and the individual benefited by them. If excessiveness was meant to be a behavioural technique, then one could choose between a more technical approach which emphasized one's skilfulness or a mature idealist concept. One could, as a precautionary measure, withhold certain secrets (which follows from the maxim of a one-sided choice of the positive) or unreservedly trust everyone (which also accords with the imperative to completely adapt to love). Alternately, one can use one's own '*honnêteté*' as the point of attraction or also show that for the sake of love one was prepared to go beyond it. Some might try their luck on the flute of 'estime', others on the trumpet of 'inclination'. The uniqueness and incomparability of the lovers was not, as such, foreseen in the semantics of love. However, a preliminary stage for it was nevertheless reached precisely owing to the ambivalence inherent in the principle according to which the communicative medium was differentiated and systematized. At any rate, the causal structure of the medium no longer stood in the way of a stronger personalization.

A second change occurred that is both more difficult to discern and took longer to become established; it concerns the form in which a binary schematization of experience and action was codified. Classicism's answer to this question was strictly a matter of logic, i.e. analogous to thought and knowledge, and concentrated on, in other words, the distinction between loving and not loving, or on recognizing the difference between true and false love[18] – invariably in relation to two people. Whether or not these two people (truly) loved one another was the question, and both the mental calculations and the deliberate efforts were related to this. Needless to say, this problem of 'do they or don't they' remained important, but the impact of this schematism appears to have shifted in the course of the eighteenth century to the extent that what constituted a human being as a person and as an individual was reformulated. The decisive process that triggered this off was probably the transformation of the code into one based on the semantics of emotion, of an emotion which reappeared, was formed and confirmed in social affirmation, i.e. in requited love.

The strength with which this (in semantic terms completely unprocessed and somewhat lame) insistence on feelings asserted itself in the first half of the eighteenth century was above all attributable to reasons originating in the history of religion. The increasing differentiation and internal confessional differentiation within the institutional system of religion triggered off a series of counter movements – such as Puritanism, Jansenism and Pietism – which all emphasized individual religiosity as opposed to organized religion. The renunciation of the Church's role as an intermediary for the institutionalized relationship to God was the crucial point of difference, and as a consequence, within such movements the social aspect took a back seat compared to the relationship to God. More than ever before the individual was left to his own devices in this absolutely crucial awareness of himself as being entirely dependent only on his faith and God's mercy. For the sake of the difference to the institutionalized Church, the individual became isolated in social and religious terms.[19] But precisely the sharpness of this antithesis provoked a second difference, namely a feeling in favour of socializing that countered the notion of an isolated individual. It was Shaftesbury who really stimulated this development. The second difference gains favour on the basis of the first difference – without much extra semantic ado. Accordingly, one immersed oneself enthusiastically in feelings, in sensibility and in friendship and at first the problems appeared to stem only from those encountered in avoiding loneliness and selfish self-centredness. Little wonder that seducers were subsequently able to discover and exploit the extent to which the language of devotion was well-suited as a language of love.[20]

With the intensification of an understanding both of oneself as a person and of one's feelings, the code's schematism initially changed with respect to the interconnection of *plaisir* and *amour*.

Whereas in the seventeenth century *art de plaire* and galantry were viewed as essential elements for getting a love affair off the ground and maintaining it – components in all too fatal a way, open to both honest and dishonest use – the balance now shifted once more in the context of the new understanding of what constituted a person and his emotions. *Art de plaire* and galantry were now both considered as *tendentially dishonest*.[21] Whoever wanted to be honest in his dealings with the 'world' (i.e. with women) now had to imitate insincerity and exaggerate it in such a way that he was able to achieve a measure of individuality.[22] Having a bad reputation became the only path to success, and a person with a good reputation became a slave of it and could gain little attention.

Equally, women could no longer depend on their own uprightness. A woman defended herself with her 'virtue', not because she feared *its* loss, but because she was afraid of being made unhappy by the man's inconstant love. She thus not only found herself at the mercy of the difference of sincere and insincere love, but also became embroiled in a sort of self-seduction by defending the interests of her virtue and yet at the same time taking part in her seducer's game; in neither role could she be at peace with herself.[23] If surrendering oneself to love could only mean deceiving oneself and others, then the difference between upright and feigned passion no longer was of any real significance. The paradoxy of the code thus became the very form of its existence, and was psychologized. This meant that the presentation of the semantics of love was no longer possible in terms of a set of rules, i.e. *maximes d'amour* or the like, but could only be effected in the form of the novel.

This convergence of sincere and insincere behaviour results in the final instance from the *temporalization of social complexity*,[24] from the insertion of a reflexive consciousness of time into the process of love itself. The lovers find themselves faced by the necessity – or so their code instructs them – to distinguish between present future and future present. They take an oath on their love's duration – in the moment and for the moment. And they know that they are deceiving themselves. This problem cannot be eliminated by either normative or cognitive modes of expectation; and it is solved neither by demanding that promises be kept, thus making love an obligation, nor by relying on an ability to learn and adapt in future situations. The ethics of supra-temporal phronesis also collapses in this process. One can only surrender to love itself, and only live in the present and for the present: thus submitting inadvertently to the *difference* between sincerity and insincerity. All the same, this reference to the present remains relevant by virtue of the concept of passion.[25]

Nevertheless, two different attitudes ran parallel to one another, from Montaigne to Rousseau. The capacity for sincerity was already in doubt and attempts to be sincere had also already been exposed as pointless. And in the end one had to acknowledge that the experience of the ego, of genuineness, of being oneself, was incommunicable. Yet, a way out of this dilemma was continually being sought with the aid of the difference of naturalness and artificiality, of nature and civilization. The problem was reduced to a rhetorical *faux pas* and later to a particular historical situation, by insisting that it was only impossible to behave in a sincere manner in the present, cultured world, and that another mode of behaviour existed which was natural in origin. On the one hand, psychology now had the task of presenting the *paradoxes* of love as *nature* and thus as a *unity*. This naturally could not take the shape of a scientific doctrine, but could certainly be depicted in psychologizing literature, where genuine love (for which the difference of sincere and insincere love no longer obtains) appeared in part as 'witty, cruel, polished, brutal, dignified, and unprincipled';[26] the way in which these elements go together was shown in the novel. On the other, one now trusted again in the goodness of nature, which had, however, to unequivocally admit to its own sensuality: Rousseau! In the one case, what is indispensable to nature is in the final instance only refinement, spirit; in the other it is sensuality which legitimates itself by virtue of being nature.

The relation between these two versions allows us to observe, to put it somewhat pathetically, the death throes of Old European rhetoric, for which naturalness had been both nature and a rule to be followed,[27] and for which there had only been problems of insincerity and inelegant mannerisms. Modernity's problem with sincerity and its incommunicability only arises once the relation between the author and what he communicates is no longer conceived of as natural or as technically produced, but rather as a forgery of existence. At this point, declarations of love are no longer possible.

Once this stage has been reached there is no longer any sense in trying to test the difference between 'sincere' and 'insincere'. The difference can no longer be translated into operations, and cannot be refined further in a situation where refinement would lie precisely in treating sincerity and insincerity as a unity in practice. Furthermore, any reflexion on it would reduce the difference to the common denominator of insincerity, for one can neither know if one is, nor even claim to be sincere. The point is to accept this state (and with it the incommunicability of actual love), which means adopting an attitude that is in turn open to a new code-consciousness, to a form of loving in accordance with cultural prescription, to Romantic irony, and to a 'scientific' portrayal of love as the ideology of reproduction.

However, we must not jump the gun. Against the background of an incommunicability more inferred than formulated, any attempt to repel the desiring man by precious or galant verbal behaviour had to be abandoned once and for all.[28] The eighteenth century brought with it an end to all trust in physical gestures and an end to rhetoric. The collapse of utter trust in cognitive and moral schematism must be seen in this context – signalled by the superficiality of the new moral concepts, by the attempt to uncover, not sin, not narcissism, but mediocrity (de la Bruyère), and last but not least, by diagnosing the 'world' as turbulent (one need only think of the vogue words *tourbillon* and *torrent*) and as frivolous.

Consequently, some of the old problems took care of themselves. Above all, love and friendship could now no longer involve simply knowing a truth, because the person who sought knowledge participated in the genesis of the object. Emotion was – and this is what is new – no longer just activated passion, but rather, if it were to be able to solve deep problems of existential insincerity, now had to be conceived of as *capable of judgement with regard to itself* and thus as capable of judging with regard to love. No external instance and no pointer to the class-specific abilities of the *honnêtes gens* was required. The old problem of distinguishing between true and false love thus receded, for self-judging emotion now generated only true love – or failed. 'En amour', Chamfort maintained, 'tout est vrai, tout est faux; et c'est la seule chose sur laquelle on ne puisse pas dire une absurdité.'[29] The differentiation of love could hardly be formulated more succinctly. It was no longer just uncontrollable passion, it was the breakdown of the matrix of cognitive and moral differentiation in love that gave expression to the rules of love.

In about 1760 the seducer as a moral figure took his leave from the historical stage with one last magnificent gesture. Once mere success with women had become a matter of course and thus trivial, he overstepped the bounds of clear-sighted techniques and operated methodically according to the self-made logic of Evil; he destroyed for destruction's sake.[30] By assuming this negative form – stylized as a value in itself – the unformulatable expectation of a morality beyond morality arrived on the scene: a morality that gave free reign to love, but to nothing else!

Towards the turn of the century emotions ceased to be judged using the differential matrix, true/false, but came to be evaluated – at least in German literature – by a cognitive reference to the world. The idea that love is aimed at a particular view of the relation to the world, at a unique individual, and therefore at a uniquely seen world, spread and was rounded out to form a new concept of individuality.[31] This subject-related world no longer availed of any truth, it could only be taken on qua love and not qua knowledge (nor qua knowledge of love). The moment of one-sidedness already fixed in the classical code of *amour passion* and the totalization brought about by it both shift accordingly.[32] They are no longer related to any trifling matter, or to the positive qualities of the beloved 'object', or even to the deliberate oversight of that person's negative qualities. Both elements now refer to the unique, idiosyncratic relation the beloved has to the world, a relation that affords no basis for consensus. The *reduction* on which *totalization depends* is thereby differentiated more sharply and based more clearly on a social reflexivity of its own. Only once this has occurred can one take up Jean Paul's formulation of 'love for love's sake'.[33] This means, however, that the basis of love no longer resides in the other's *qualities*, but in his *love*.

This development in differentiation can also be seen in Marivaux's plays. The external circumstances and obstacles which handicap the lovers recede into the background. Love now handicaps itself until it finally finds its way happily to marriage.

And this is presented in a consciously programmatic fashion and is consciously used as an historical difference: 'Chez les comiques', Marivaux himself stated, 'jusqu' ici l'amour est en querelle avec ce qui l'environne et finit par être heureux malgré les opposants; chez moi, il n'est en querelle qu'avec lui seul et finit par être heureux malgré lui.'[34]

This new heightened differential semantics of *plaisir* (or *goût*) and *amour* may increase the leeway for information and communication, but the typifying style of the code's presentation is not disrupted. Paths to personal individualization are opened up, but left uncharted. Signposts, place names, warning signs and speed limits do not yet exist. The subjectivity of *plaisir* – as life itself – is everyone's prerogative, but this is not to be confused with individuality. Precisely *plaisir* is not context-free, but nevertheless is divisible, and thus contradicts all the conceptual characteristics of the notion of individuality prevalent at that time. And yet only the individual person can feel *plaisir* and *amour* and certify their genuineness. The integration of these concepts into a code for communicative behaviour, as a ground rule for communication itself, forms a basis for the self-centredness and wilfulness of those communicating. One can perhaps conclude that once this rule is accepted it is communication and its open processing of code-specific information which personalizes the subjects participating by allotting them respectively individual fates.

11

The Incorporation of Sexuality

The analysis undertaken in the preceding chapter relied heavily on the use of interpretation – and to a much greater extent than did the analysis of seventeenth-century literature. This step was necessitated by the fact that the literature examined consisted no longer of direct factual statements, but rather of the narrative of novels. Despite this shift in literary sources, there was very little development at the level of thematic discourse and official love semantics in the transition to the eighteenth century. On the contrary, these tended to stagnate. Forces of normalization set in, and – notably – had an effect in two ways (which can therefore be combined at a later date!). On the one hand, the semantics of *amour passion* was pushed into the sphere of the light, the pleasant, the frivolous, and the noncommital.[1] The problematic elements of libertine thought were purged – something to which one had by now grown accustomed. On the other hand, people become receptive to new, toned-down syntheses of feelings, virtues and religious elements.[2] The mainstream traditional concepts of reason, morality and religion were still indispensable, but hardly generate a greater capacity for differentiation. The progressive development lies in the enhancement of a psychological and social sensibility for the personal, which, however, had not yet crystallized out into an enduring semantics. Descriptions of ardent love still resorted to the code of *amour passion* for lack of another form of expression (even though the lovers had already seen through this code as a linguistic form, if not actually rejecting it).[3]

Owing to this absence of a rigorous, demanding semantics, one was able to love sin and virtue – each at its proper time – each existing alongside the other. One could choose between the thrilling and the harmonious – at least when it came to reading. The daring suggestion that one accept passion as the *principle of selection*, irrespective of the fact that it has no prospect of stability, and thus also lead a life in the unity of paradoxy, split up into the different strands it contained. The distinction between frivolous and sentimental love cannot function as a *difference* within any *one* code – as did that of *plaisir* and *amour*. Frivoliity can only be enjoyed as frivolity, feeling only as feeling, virtue only as virtue. There is no need for a greater literary form that would embrace all this.

However, we can assume that this two-track nature of love somewhat irritated all those who deal with love in literature, and that it did not suffice in the long run to negate virtue, ties or marriage by means of frivolity, nor conversely, to speak out in favour of virtuous love and against sin. But where is the opening for a recombination here? Charles Duclos found a provisional solution for his hero: after completely working through all (the possible) love relationships with all the different types of women, he was able to form an overall opinion, whereupon he steered for the haven of a marriage built on virtue and friendship.[4] But who manages to get that far? And is it not then possible to spare oneself the trials and tribulations of frivolous love and simply make the right decision straightaway – based on what one has learnt from reading?

If it is indeed possible to attempt a totalizing interpretation of the ensuing changes in the semantics of love, then this would probably reveal that the symbolization which expresses and legitimates differentiation in the area of the media was both retained and reinforced. The classical code's incorporation of *skilfulness*, *individual* seduction procedures and *social* galantry was abandoned – instead literary characters concentrated on those moments in the semantics which symbolize irresponsibility, and took advantage of the notion that a quite active approach to matters of love is still regarded as 'passion'.

As *frivolity*, love differentiates itself from *moral controls*; and as *feeling*, from controls imposed by *reason* (both of which always signify the participation of others). The fact that frivolity and feeling are diametrically opposed to one another does not keep them from having a common function, namely to advance the process of differentiation. This process makes use of two levers that can be applied alternately, depending on whether society attempts to keep lovers under control by means of morals or reason. Both approaches – a forced form of frivolity and the idealization of sentiment – are not up to the task of establishing a stable relationship with the everyday life of a marriage tied to a family – thus contributing to their destruction, irrespective of which of the two principles one opts for. Toward the middle of the eighteenth century the concept of nature permitted a common denominator to be found for sexuality, which was increasingly becoming a topic in its own right, and for passionate feelings. The concept simultaneously expressed the fact that love was gradually liberating itself from society's fetters and, as nature, had the right to do so. At this point the concept of nature also symbolized differentiation – and no longer perfection in its essential forms. It was possible to combine this with the notion that suggested passions were 'useful', regardless of whether their factual presence was subject to regulation or not, and that they should supposedly be judged on the basis of their effects. From about 1760 onward a great number of novels appear in which the heroes portray their passion as their nature and rebel in the name of nature against society's moral conventions. 'Free love' went one step further, becoming an attack on society,[5] by taking the form of incest – which was held to have been good originally and only to have become shameful once subjected to society's judgement.[6] Marriage was rejected for the constraints it placed on time and form, and free love reduced itself to the full enjoyment of sensuality, for this was the only way in which it could appear as natural.[7] And it thus overlooked the fact that 'nature' was also always a restrictive concept which excluded uniqueness – and thus, individualization.

The most significant changes which occur in the eighteenth century have to do with sexuality – not so much the practice of sexual intercourse as such,[8] but rather its treatment as a symbiotic mechanism in the semantics of love. The Christian and Barbarian's conquest – at least in Bertrand Russell's opinion[9] – initially destroyed the sexual culture of the ancient world, degrading sexual life to the level of animal instinct. However, while its semantic devaluation and repression persisted, from the sixteenth century tendencies toward stronger privatization and intimization developed, as for example in the sense of a growing reluctance to expose one's naked body in public.[10] Accordingly, communication provided discretion and indirectness; as prescribed by one of the *précieuses*, one was not allowed to speak about *faveur*, but certainly about *douleur*.[11] Thus, the stage was set for a codification of sexually based intimacy. Parallel to this, theory underwent a change. As nature, sexuality was on the one hand a part of man's corrupted being after the Fall, but on the other, was also God-given, and thus not something in itself despicable. At the beginning of the seventeenth century the problem was put in the following way: nature is good in and of itself, but tempted man to behave in a manner *which he himself could not condone*.[12]

This notion, that one must approve of one's *own* behaviour, dates back to the Middle Ages.[13] In keeping with this idea, individual behaviour was related to reflexive behaviour while also being subject to social conditioning (for the criterion by which one can either approve or disapprove of one's behaviour had a natural social origin). This conceptual model of the portrayal of the sexual drive as nature in need of control and consensus was still adhered to throughout the seventeenth century, and in fact for a time even asserted itself more strongly as the criteria of acceptance began to lose ground.[14] As shown in chapter 6, passion itself was in the final instance able to create the necessary inner consensus and thus to legitimate an involvement with sensual love. Toward the close of the seventeenth century, the form in which the reference to sexuality facilitated the generalization of the symbolic medium love was left open. The conceivable possibilities range from

1   *sublimation* by means of temporary or even definitive *exclusion of possible* sexual contact; or
2   moulding the course of love stories after the form of a *secret analogy to sexual intercourse* (contact – foreplay – climax – indifference and the need for separation); to
3   shifting the generalization to an *alternative in which sexual relations do not play a role* (friendship).

In all these variants the further development of a code for intimate relationships was left undecided.

In the eighteenth century, however, the increase in personal and social reflexivity began to change the premises on which an analysis of the phenomenon of sexuality had to be based; this increase filtered the reflexivity out of the prevailing complex of religious, and moral and political themes, thus making it possible to treat the phenomenon more openly.[15] The barriers erected to the consummation of sexual relations not only for, but precisely in, marriage[16] were dismantled and replaced by a revaluation of the concept of (physical) nature,[17] as well as by the proposition that love as such was a virtue in itself and required no further moral justification. It also appeared that, in general usage, the meaning of love or *amour* came to include sensuality.[18] As a result of all this, the alternation between either religious or pornographic currents in literature that had pervaded all previous discussion ceased and with it the oscillations between idealizing and sarcastic remarks on love and women particularly characteristic of French literature.[19] Acceptance of this underlying mechanism afforded the 'stubborn' insistence on love a new stability. The result was a (self-legitimating) interconnection of sensuality and refinement which could be set apart from mere sexuality on the one hand and from 'platonic' love on the other.[20]

Certain factors lend credence to the supposition that it was above all the transition to an enhanced social reflexivity that initiated the emancipation of sexuality. The novels of Claude Crébillon *fils* are structured in the form of dialogues that attempt to get as close as possible to the facts. '*Coeur*' becomes dispensable, but not '*esprit*'. Love 'is' no longer excess, but merely 'un désir que l'on se plaisoit à s'exagérer';[21] it is this transcendence of nature, this exaggeration, which causes unhappiness,[22] but it nevertheless appears to be necessary so as to provide for some sort of mediation between the sexes. Advances toward a potential lover are improvised in a daring, frivolous, casual manner and as called for by the given situation. They are made with an eye to achieving the desired effect, but are never vulgar, and allow themselves to be borne by a sophistry which does not have to worry about being seen through, for this has instead been taken into the calculations as the grounds for the next move. In this way, the ineffability of the last piece of clothing may then prevent the undressing from continuing for a while – or leave it to the reader's imagination. With regard to the semantic form, all this involved a radical breakdown of the subject of love into discreet moments in time and into differing perspectives – a temporal and social punctilism to which behaviour had to adjust.[23]

It is likely that the lifting of social controls on sexual relations among the upper classes of France, particularly in the second half of the eighteenth century, had gone too far – too far in terms of a possible integration of sexuality and love.[24] Other countries and other literatures, at any rate, began to react negatively to French models. Strangely and remarkably enough, the English interest in sexuality blossomed and then suddenly became inhibited. More than ever before sexual problems became the focus of attention in England, once heroics went out of fashion; but at the same time, the norms for dealing discreetly with such problems became more stringent and the area as a whole was pushed into a zone of incommunicability. 'Victorian' prudishness is a misnomer – it is actually a product of the eighteenth century.[25] We can assume that this interest in sexuality was omnipresent – which is precisely why it is stamped down with such resolve. While this can hardly be considered an after-effect of Puritanical moral austerity, it was certainly an after-effect of the latter's shortcomings. In France, as we have shown at some length, a highly complex code for matters of love had been devised based on the case of extra-marital relationships; in this respect, England was unprepared. Thus, in France it was possible to work the revaluation of sexuality into the traditional semantic context; in England it had to first be completed and then repressed. This reveals the extent to which the evolution of ideas depends upon adaptive capacity, on self-selection from the material available. The connection between love and marriage, first proclaimed in England, may have made an impression on the continent, but it had one crucial, fatal weakness: the woman had to be chaste in order to marry. This would not have been a requirement for love. This discrepancy is the fatal stumbling block to integration, both psychological and semantic. It was a demand, but one which could not be met without hypocrisy: falling in love before marriage, but without this including the sexual experience until marriage. If it had not been possible to accord the man a different capacity to learn, greater knowledge and accordingly a double standard of morality, not even the novel would have been able to attain some semblance of plausibility.

It is also worth comparing the developments in France up to that date with those of German literature (both were exposed to English sentimentalism). In eighteenth-century Germany any interest in sexuality was still rejected out of hand.[26] Rather there was still a much stronger attachment to the traditional conceptual framework and, drawing on Thomasius and Leibniz, a distinction was made between two types of affection for others (*amor concupiscentiae/amor benevolentiae*),[27] later to become an interest in a union of the flesh and an interest in human perfection, respectively), whereby the issue in question continued to be formulated in the framework of the general distinction between the human and animal kingdoms. This apparently has something to do with the fact that elements of the old *amor rationalis* continued to be retained in the concept of a 'love based on reason',[28] reason being that which distinguishes man from other species. 'Sensibility' and even 'tenderness' were the concepts in German literature that referred to the objective moral qualities of the loved person,[29] whereas emotion was still an organ for the perception of moral qualities. The concepts involved in sentimentality therefore continued to characterize reason's control of one's passions and were still bound up with the old European notion that the object specified the abilities in question, so that there was no place for sexuality other than among the animal drives. This comparison reveals the extent to which the revaluation of sexuality is tied to the differentiation of a special semantics for love and to the dissipation of the old European terminology.

It is easy to test the factual dissemination of this climate of opinion. One need only read the multitude of ecstatic formulations, including references to the body, in the religious and secular cult of love as friendship. How friends lavish each other with a thousand kisses; fall into each other's arms (and this inside a secluded wanderers' hut!) and that they lie on each other's bosom (like Johannes Christo); that they have no qualms at all talking about 'gushing from the heart' (*Herzensergüsse*) – all of this could never have been written in this way if the writers had had to fear being accused that the thought of their own bodies had led them to take pen in hand. Rather it seems that the relationship to the body was apparently still oriented to the old semantic difference of *res corporales* and *res incorporales*, with the emphasis on the non-physical, spiritual side of this difference. It was not until the last third of the century that the stability of these preconditions was upturned (a change that naturally does not stem from the galantry and art of seduction of the French and certainly not from Wieland).

The exclusion of sexuality presumably also bore a hidden relation to the stratified social system. The unreserved blending of sexual attraction into the code of love would have left the door wide open to promiscuity by all the classes. The Marquise de M. stressed in her letters that she did not need to rely on her virtue to defend herself against bourgeois admirers; all that was required in such cases being good taste.[30] In England the *mésalliance* with a woman one rung higher on the social ladder was rejected above all because she allowed her sexual interest in a man to be seen too blatantly[31] (and, as depicted in novels, women were expected to exist with no awareness of sexuality whatsoever). Such attitudes again underscore the primacy of stratified over functional differentiation, and also indicate that it was easier to overcome virtue than the barriers posed by questions of good taste. And even so, one is led to wonder how secure this taste still was – for example, in light of the attractiveness of an *arlequin* or a valet in the plays of Marivaux. A late piece of evidence suddenly illuminates the situation (and also documents how narrow the concept of sexual attractiveness was if symbolized by beauty and youth). Humboldt noted in his diary (July, 1789)[32] how his 'wanton desire' was stimulated by the 'sight of women doing hard physical labour – preferably lower-class women' – and founded his marriage on other considerations. Be that as it may: the new formation of a code especially designed for intimate relationships that included the sexual component as an essential element was – via the reinforcement of functional differentiation – also to foster a neutralization of class differences. But this was not possible until after July 1789, until Romanticism.

I would guess that, via the revaluation of sexuality, it was subsequently possible for the competition of 'love' and 'friendship' as the basic formulae for the codification of intimacy to be decided, with love the winner. At the beginning of the eighteenth century, both formulae started with differing chances of success. Even Rousseau cannot decide – the strength of his portrayal of love contradicts his option in favour of friendship. Friendship had the decisive advantage of being easier to generalize in temporal and social terms. It could feign permanence and was also possible between persons who could not or did not want to enter into sexual relations.[33] It was the only option capable of realizing social reflexivity at the now necessary level of individuality, whereas the increasing expectations of individuality were only able to push love further and further into unhappiness.[34] Should one not follow the example of the Marquise de Lambert and base the prognosis of superiority on the higher degree of generalizability of the notion of friendship? The English sentimental novel was essentially saying the same thing when it emphasized the role of love in marriage.[35] And would not the increasing degree of psychological reflexion also tend to favour friendship rather than love? It seems that the eighteenth-century cult of friendship initially thrived on these plausibilities. It is no coincidence that, above all, German literature manifested a receptivity to this idea, whence it progressed to seeing marriages as intimate.[36] Love, on the other hand, profited ever more from the revaluation of sexuality.

Although the theoretical inclination toward a strict separation of (spiritual) friendship and (sensual) love was kept, friendship was now availed of predominantly in order to revaluate sexuality. 'But love only serves a function when friendship beats with it in the same breast.'[37] Love between the sexes was now an indispensable basis for enhancement (but one rejected as mere sensuality). Deprived of this basis, it would not be possible to set the process of ennoblement into motion, the 'inclination of souls' would not be able to make it on its own. 'Love is not *aroused* by the inclination of souls; only *ennobled* if otherwise present.'[38] Marriage provided a constant and permanent form for this ennobling process – and it is touching to discover that the same tendencies toward sexually based marriages of love are to be found in the lower classes as well.

This development cancelled out – parallel to and in harmony with reflexivity – the orientation toward the aesthetic and moral qualities of the beloved. Mauvillon, for example, still used the term 'moral love', but in a sense that had changed fundamentally. He explained: 'I would be misunderstood if one were to think that this is the ability to be moved to love by the object because of the moral characteristics. Nothing could be further from the truth. It is nothing more, at least in the case of our sex, than a very specific guidance of the sexual drive toward a single object.'[39] At first glance this change of heart is somewhat perplexing: morality as directed sexuality? But the explanation makes sense: bliss (in marriage) thus becomes dependent on the 'emotional disposition of one's other half.'[40]

The result of the competition between friendship and marriage confirms a theory which asserts that symbiotic mechanisms are of the utmost significance if one is to be able to differentiate generalized symbolic communicative media. This theory, however, must be defined very precisely and refined. Above all: it does not state that friendships were not possible or sufficiently probable; nor does it by any means suggest that sexual intercourse was an indispensable condition for intimate, highly personal communication. The all-important aspect is a negative one, and this is equally true of all other media and symbiotic mechanisms.

An unregulated capacity to make use of exceptionally plastic organic processes sensitive to cultural formation would render the functional specification of communicative interaction difficult and exclude greater expectations in this respect. In this manner, capital-intensive budgeting presupposes an adequate satisfaction of the overall population's primary needs as well as a 'containment' of physical violence as a condition for political order. Indeed, this appears to be the reason why, if the partners are free to choose to enter into sexual relations with *other* persons, highly personal relationships can only with difficulty – if at all – become more intense, intertwined and escalated into the improbable as a result of intrapersonal interpenetration and an adoption of the partner's world view. The intimate content of human relationships transmitted via sexuality is so great that it cannot be ignored simply by adopting a different form of relationship, one that is only 'friendly'. The pressure exerted by other possibilities of intimacy would, at any rate, be difficult to bear, and the reciprocal awareness of this problem, if only one side were to react to it, would make this difficulty all the greater. It is therefore logical to incorporate sexual relations into the model of intimate communication so as to prevent them from becoming a source of irritation; as the relation to the environment of one of the intimate partners, they would become a permanent source of disturbance.

Just as physical violence is contained by the state, the containment of sexuality in marriage also appears as a precondition for all higher development. It may be that marriage in the upper classes of the seventeenth and eighteenth centuries had indirectly provided a reservoire of experience on these questions. The upper strata of society had reacted to the trend toward stronger individualization and a decidedly individual determination of action by liberalizing their view of marriage; they were able to release individuals, but not marriages, from the code's control, since this segment of society relied on marriage (and not, as today, on careers) for its reproduction. This meant that the code of *amour passion* was developed for extra-marital relations. 'Un bon mariage, s'il en est, refuse la compagnie et conditions de l'amour,' says Montaigne.[41] Marriage was a channel for diverting excess sensuality, but its essence was mutual understanding and not passion.[42] Courting one's own wife would have appeared highly ridiculous as would have any expenditure of passion in order to gain access to one's own conjugal bed – which certainly did not mean that respect and love (in its traditional sense) and above all a considerate treatment of one's own wife were to be excluded.[43] This semantic and institutional rule had to block marriage from developing into an intimately personal relationship – at least in the upper echelons of society. And from this one can tell that sexuality and intimacy contradicted one another in a way which could not be suspended in the given order. Liberated sexual relations prevented marriage from being transformed into an intimate relationship, and most likely similar experiences were made with regard to friendships.

The search for a new unifying formula for love, sexuality and marriage and the location of this in the idea of personal self-realization ultimately had consequences for the area of pornography and the obscene. What could be rejected in the name of these concepts now had to be restricted and accordingly is weighed down with complications which could then once again stimulate a desire to attempt to balance on the border between them and love. It was no longer possible for the interest in and the portrayal of sexuality in themselves to suffice as a reproach; however, it was not yet possible to draw a line separating sensuality and the soul if the unity of both is required for love and marriage. The obscene discounted itself owing to the fact that it occluded an interest in the person, or more precisely, owing to the exchangeability of the persons involved.[44] At the same time, this also entailed an awareness of the unity of sexual interest (however culturally and socially formed this will have been), so that love took liberties, including the possibility of being obscene (be it momentarily, in the form of expectation or memory or for others). The orientation towards the individuality of the partner was enhanced by means of this *difference* and at the same time came up against the limits of what could be preprogrammed by cultural codification.

In all this one recognizes clear tendencies, even prior to Romanticism, toward a new synthesis that goes beyond the old differences (sensuous/spiritual, love/friendship, *plaisir/amour*) and can in principle (despite certain differences) apply for all classes of society. Intimacy is viewed as marital bliss, and it requires that sensuality be integrated into a process of the reciprocal formation of spiritual and mental forms. With demands such as these the semantics of love remains sufficiently open and rich to enable it to spur on further developments. The systematics of paradoxy elaborated by French Classicism conveys the impression that this orientational area provides both a plausible context and a form that is not arbitrary, and is neither replaced nor surpassed in this function. However, such a systematics does allow for variations with which the store of themes of *amour passion* can be adapted to new conditions, and which enable the semantics of love to find a form that has since become a tradition known as 'Romanticism'.

12

The Discovery of Incommunicability

It is difficult to summarize complex intricate analyses such as those as were necessary for the investigation of the eighteenth-century semantics of love. Any generalization at the level of semantic morphology would ravage the historical material. This is especially the case if one endeavours to establish which ideas are actually new in the belief that such an inquiry will reveal the essence of an epoch. And yet, in retrospect, the eighteenth century left a discovery to posterity which is worthy of consideration: the discovery of *incommunicability*.

During the seventeenth century the great heroic adventures and their happy or tragic outcomes – particularly with respect to love – had already started to be internalized. One of Madame de Villedieu's heroines finds herself in a castle at the end of the story: 'Nous la laisserons former ses regrets en liberté, et se preparer à recevoir sans repugnance le poison qui luy fut apporté quelque temps apres.' The murder by poisoning, the other ensuing forms of murder and atrocities as well as the downfall of empires are all not worthy of treatment, because that would be to 'tomber dans un Recit Tragique que j'ay toûjours soigneusement évité.'[1] In the following century, morality switched its techniques of disclosure over to disclosing mediocrity, and literature undertook to do the same in its narrative technique. Both began to take an interest in normal people. Virtue became a defensive formula, which could be dispensed with in the case of a pronounced sensibility and normal people could be expected to understand this. Great demands were no longer made of one's will power and dramatics was shifted into the sphere of communicative problems. It was not possible to fully convey the complex psychic reality of the participants within a message, for this involved '(de) ces choses dont on ne peut dire que la moitié de ce qu'elles sont,' as Marivaux's Marianne put it.[2] Incommunicability, it would seem, was invented in order to take the banality out of mediocrity. It was incommunicability that enabled normal people in the literature at hand to come up with a story which others could find interesting.

Incommunicability no longer just meant that passion set rhetoric off stuttering, upset the most eloquent speech and thus betrayed itself. It no longer just involves psychic and situationally determined disturbances that were themselves suitable for passionate communication. Rather, categorical barriers to communication now began to emerge. It was not the failure of skilfulness that is the problem, but the lack of a capacity for sincerity.

This was at first quite generally the case. The experience of incommunicability cropped up wherever morals were embraced in concepts that had a contra-intentional effect when communicated, concepts that had to rely on authenticity, i.e. naturalness, genuineness, sensitivity and originality; and the moral codex of the eighteenth century was tuned into precisely such concepts.[3] This experience also blocked the expression of individuality in the sense of uniqueness (if indeed politeness did not already forbid one to emphasize one's own particularity in comparison with others). Whoever stressed their own incomparability was, in effect, setting up a comparison; even being aware of this would in itself have amounted to cancelling out that very incomparability.[4]

This discovery is above all else the most important factor affecting the codification of intimate relations. Codification involves a communicative medium and therefore seeks to enhance the effectiveness of actually improbable communication, and precisely thus seemingly presents a barrier to experience.

The differentiation of intimate relations is admittedly only possible with the aid of communication. This presumes the existence of special codification and a familiarity with highly demanding semantic forms. It leads to the formation of (as always, only temporary) social systems that reproduce the interaction of two people. The social system functions to intensify such interaction, and this intensification is also the process that creates an awareness of the incisive barriers to communicability. The experience of incommunicability is one aspect of the different-iation of social systems for intimacy. It does not contradict intimacy, but corresponds to it; and it is an inevitable part of the differentiation of such systems.

Incommunicability is not adequately grasped if one only thinks of it in terms of the limitations on the linguistic capacity for expression. It is also not simply a question of the fact that communication takes time and that events happen more quickly than communication, so that, for example, one would always and inexorably lag behind while writing one's own biography if it were supposed to include everything that happens to one. And of course it is no longer a question of the old doctrine according to which certain things are of their very nature secret and thus cannot be revealed.[5] Even the insight that there are forms of information on one's own moods, one's speculations and particularly one's views about the other person which the other person could not bear to hear, does not get to the heart of our problem. The problem in question is far more radical and centres on whether there is not meaning – especially in intimate relationships – that is destroyed by virtue of being made the object of an utterance.

All communication rests on a clearly localized difference, namely that between information and utterance. Without the protection afforded by this difference, the recipient of an utterance would be confronted directly by the factual contents of the world, as is the case in the course of quite normal perceptions. Communication and acceptance or rejection of the selections it conveys only occur if the recipient can distinguish between the selectivity of the information and the selection contained in the utterance. This also means that one has to react to *both*, and in certain cases *can react to both in different ways*. One may judge the utterance to be genuine and sincere, but the information to be false; or may be thankful for unpleasant news, or may hold the facts given to be irrelevant and the utterance to be annoying ('Your tie is crooked'). If it is true that this difference of utterance and information is constitutive for the unity of communication, and that any acquisition of information depends on this ability to distinguish in a like manner, then the question as to the immanent barriers of communication must be related to precisely this difference.

In light of this we can state that there can be such a thing as experiencing a meaning which cannot be communicated, because the assertion of difference between utterance and information destroys itself in relation to the meaning in question. Metaphorically speaking, the utterance cannot keep cool if the information is too hot. Bearing in mind the treatment of intimacy from the viewpoint of attribution theory in chapter 3, one will hardly be astounded by the fact that the above situation is typical precisely for the differentiation of highly individualized intimate relationships, and that it was precisely intimate relationships that led to the discovery of such states. All behaviour, even the behaviour involved in transmitting the utterance, is used here to recognize, test and reproduce the partner's dispositions with reference to the intimate relationship. The utterance itself, owing to the information it provides, becomes information for the attributive process. It allows conclusions to be drawn as to how the other thinks of himself as someone who loves or no longer loves, as someone hoping for love, expecting or demanding it; how he overcomes his doubts in the chances for a lasting relationship; how he assumes the partner to have such doubts or attributes them to her in order to exonerate himself; how he exploits the fact that the partner knows, but cannot say, that she is no longer loved; and how he manipulates situations in which both know that both know that non-communication has more advantages for one than the other.

Precisely this oblique evaluation of all utterances is predictable in intimate relationships and comes to block communication. One knows from the outset how things will go and then hesitates to set something in motion that will be difficult to control once part of the communication. Under the conditions of intimacy each communication refers to a person and holds the expectation that both sides perceive this, make allowances for it and share the responsibility for it. An attempt to evade this would, like all else, still be abiding by the iron law of attribution. Certainly, some may be able to manoeuvre more skilfully than others, and it may be hard to catch them at it. But then one also knows, without being able to communicate this knowledge, that such behaviour does not measure up to a relationship defined as love according to the code of intimacy.

The eighteenth century witnessed the end of rhetoric, i.e. the end of a technical faith in communication. This failure of gestures only destroyed false, but not true love.[6] All the same, what went on between two people was initially still regarded as an entirely communicative relationship. Social relationships were already conceived of as thoroughly reflexive, and precisely this brought communication up against the barriers of the possible. Never again was there to be such an abundant repertoire of efforts to manage such situations. The consciously playful manipulation of the forms was one possibility; others made use of paradoxicalization, irony and cynicism. In other words, the communicative error was noticed and then adopted as the form of communication. In order to avoid it, it was committed deliberately. In this manner one at least ensured that one was not reproached for not knowing what one was doing or for not having an adequate grasp of the means at hand. It was this form that fitted so well into the Enlightenment's programme. The concentration of all intimate communication on access to sexual relations also fitted into this context. This topic at least contained an indisputable, indissoluble reference to reality. Lastly, coquetry with loneliness, a somewhat German variant, also formed part of this reaction to incommunicability. One accepted what one had to learn – not within the social relationship, but as an alternative to it.

We have chosen a literary form, the epistolary novel, to describe this phenomenon in detail. This form of novel, so popular in the eighteenth century, is especially well suited to illustrate the communicative situation in interpenetrating relations, for it itself was never completely (but almost) topicalized by communication. A letter may describe (or conceal by describing) the reasons for which it was written, and thus may fuel an affair that it was in fact designated to curb. Crébillon's correspondent wrote that she rejected love, but the very fact that she wrote the letter brought her closer to the matter at hand and, in the course of the correspondence that ensued, the relationship progressively changed, as did the motifs used to describe it. The novel's author was also able to arrange things in such a way that the reader (and the reader of the letters in the novel) could see this more readily than the writer of the letters, i.e. things were more evident to the observer than to the actor.[7] The obviousness of things for the reader (at both levels) included the fact that things were not obvious to the writer. The latter could thus remain naive (or take advantage of the opportunity to appear naive and, from this vantage point of feigned naivety control the amount of insight the reader (in the novel) gains. Thus, the novel provided both the course of the story (e.g. the hopes and fears reproduced in the story) and the superiority of the novel reader's insight at one and the same time, without having to write down or be a mouthpiece for the observer's knowledge, which functioned as both a driving force and a vehicle of insight. The form's unity derived from the instances of incommunicability that were produced in the communicative process; and it also managed to make the incommunicable into a source of insight, without its having to be communicated – which would only have destroyed it.

When the ways of life that tried to find an answer to incommunicability came to an end in the bourgeois criticism of the courtly world's 'moral decadence' the problem went down with them. Attention was drawn to the aristocracy's frivolity, to the frequency of adultery among them and to Versac's[8] figure of 'libertinage de tête'.[9] What was forgotten, however, was that such forms had not been chosen whimsically or practised for their own sake, and their portrayal had been anything but complacency with the way things were: none of this can be remembered or passed on to subsequent generations. The Romantics still had some knowledge of this, particularly Friedrich Schlegel perhaps – which is partly why Lucinde sparked off such a scandal. On the whole, the above forms were replaced by a humanism both highbrow and unviable, both demanding and trite. This was above all a result of the need to now establish a solidarity of love and marriage. Indeed, up to the present day all attempts to recover a sense of bitterness at being alone within intimacy have failed. Neither a communicative medium nor an elaborated semantics have been of any help, because symbolic generalizations of this sort are specialized in rendering improbable communications possible. There was therefore nothing in tradition that could be taken as the basis for an experience of incommunicability. It refused to allow itself to be canonized as some *maxime d'amour*.

Against this background people grew accustomed to the new model provided by *Pamela*. The maxim was 'to remain a virgin, immaculate until the night of one's marriage'. This maxim expressed the unity of love, marriage and sexual relations and has a place, at least as a component part, within the code. Love was thus taken to be that curious excitement which one experienced on noticing that one had decided to marry. This was in keeping with the image of a woman who lived before marriage without any sense of sexuality; instead, she remained virtuous.

But a sense of one's own virtue is, of course, a sense of one's own sexuality. And the refusal to engage in any sexually oriented relationship prior to marriage can also be conceived of as a subtle push or a tactical move in the direction of matrimony. This model consequently nullified the old distinction between *prudes* and *coquettes*, which required much too strong an awareness of sexuality on the part of married women. The old distinction between *sincere* and *insincere* love was also abrogated, to be replaced by a *new sort of difference of conscious and unconscious, proclivities, drives and aims*. The woman was officially desexualized in order to safeguard this difference and a sense of virtue attributed to her. She was unconscious, or rather had to remain unconscious, of the fact that she wanted to use this to get married and often indeed to marry into a better social station.[10] All behaviour remained ambivalent, for even this difference between the conscious and the unconscious was not allowed to be conscious *to her*.

And this in turn meant nothing other than incommunicability. No consciously pursued understanding could be reached of the 'true motives' involved;[11] the physical behaviour that went with this was to faint. The man had also to allow himself to be infected by the woman's virtues and to eventually marry *because of them*; he certainly would not permit himself to be seduced or even blackmailed into marriage. Only the reader of the novel could read the story in terms of the difference of the conscious and the unconscious, and it was made plausible *to the reader* (in other words, it was communicated after all) that there were incommunicable things within such relationships. This implies in effect that the detour via literature, via novels, was a necessary one, necessary if the intimate code were to be comprehended.

We shall return at a later stage to the subsequent developments of the communicative medium of love, to how the hurdles of incommunicability are cleared and especially to the simple reception of sincerity and 'self-disclosure'. No trend towards a normalization of the problem of incommunicability would appear to arise. Nevertheless, forms will have to be found for it, for with the intensification that follows from the differentiation and codification of intimate relations, human interpenetration also transcends the possibilities afforded by communication. The language of love with its words, eye-language and body-language creates a transparency of its own; it creates ties that grow beyond it. Interpenetration cannot be intended, conveyed, demanded, reached by pact or ended. Human interpenetration means precisely that the other person, conceived of as the horizon representing his own experiences and actions, enables the lover to lead his life as a self which could not be realized in the absence of love. This presentation of a horizon embodied in inter-penetration glides along with all communication – and yet cannot be grasped by it – and having to accept an experience of it can make one bitter or happy, depending on the state of one's love.

It is no coincidence that the experience of incommunicability is followed by Romanticism. Whatever the main principle or principles this new movement involved, one of its characteristics was that the author (or artist) staged something which he knew the reader (observer) did not believe. The 'realistic' style is abandoned for a while, only to be reintroduced with a great deal of fuss (as a style!) in the second third of the nineteenth century. Romanticism itself is based on the author and reader presuming of each other (and knowing that they presumed it of each other) that the staging – intended to signify the world – was not to be taken seriously. Precisely this became the basis of mutual understanding, the fascination all works of art exert, and can be interpreted to be the indication of something inaccessible to direct communication. The incommunicable is accessed via distantiation; and this no longer had to do only with the ambiguity of feelings, the mixture of motives, the one-sidedness and falsification of meaning by communication in dialogue; rather the problem was generalized and sublated within a notion of the world that transcended all means of expression. The exploration of the world was complete and now became enigmatic in itself: all ideas now had opaque sides to them. Their transformation into ideologies and later into trivialities was the next step along the way.

13

Romantic Love

Although we have found that the experience of incommunicability was the eighteenth century's main new insight, it was certainly at no point celebrated as an accomplishment, nor was it absorbed into the code of passionate love. In spite of all the progress made in integrating a view of sexuality, and in spite of all the favouritism shown to feeling and all the enthusiasm for intimacy, the development of a medium for intimate relationships stagnated in the eighteenth century; or at least it did not, as yet, absorb the important changes that were beginning to take shape.

For one thing, it failed to take notice of those tendencies which called for love not only in the old sense of solidarity with one's spouse, but rather also proclaimed passionate love to be the very principle upon which the *choice* of a spouse should be based – in other words, a love match. This idea is by and large still rejected in the eighteenth century.[1] More attention was paid only to the *inability to love each other* as a reason for *refusing* to marry (which in itself, of course, represents an important breakthrough). This question can hardly be inferred from some difference in viewpoint between the aristocracy and the bourgeoisie;[2] it probably had more to do with the fact that the family was still seen as a unity that survived the change of generations, so that marriage did not signify the freedom to found a new family, but rather had to be controlled as the means of reproducing one and the same family.[3] This is why, well into the eighteenth century, all the bourgeoisie had to set against the 'depravity' of the upper social strata was an insistence on the man's dominance in the marriage and family affairs and on the woman's subordination.[4] The view on conjugal love had an essentially rational basis, in that they rested on an acceptance of one's assigned role in life. A case in point is the fact that fear and love were not seen as incompatible, much less contradictory; man's relationship to God was taken as the model for one's relationship to one's master and thus for the woman's relationship to the master of the house.[5] What was considered important is not living out one's own passions, but rather a voluntarily (and not compulsorily or slavishly) developed solidarity within a given order. And the master was thought of as someone who loved his property, i.e. his house and home, wife and children.[6]

The first inroads into this common European structure of male domination in the home were made in England. England was the site of these changes not because the woman's social role, but because the woman's domestic role in relation to the religious and hierarchical domination of the man became topicalized. In the first drives for reformation, entirely rationalistic and psychologically sensitive analyses were used as a basis for constructing a principle of matrimonial equality and for founding marriage in love, reason and mutual respect.[7]

'Love and peace' is Milton's formula for this.[8] A 'healthy' family was, in his view, a prerequisite for any reform in government. This, and not the mere physical reproduction of humankind, was to be aimed for; and this polemical difference at first precluded there being a need to explain the formula of 'love and peace' in greater depth. Although Milton's thought already contained egalitarian elements, these were ahead of their time (and, for the same reason, suggestions that restrictions on divorce be relaxed also had little chance of success).

This specifically English development must also be seen in relation to the fact that a monetary economy was increasingly asserting itself, particularly with the incorporation of landed property and work into the integrative framework of the monetary system. In the process, the old and actually quite natural idea of loving what was one's own became less plausible. It was not necessary to dispute the emotional content of the old love of property (which embraced house and home, wife and children). The point was that it became ever more difficult to thus combine personal ties and notions of property in the course of the increasing functional differentiation of both areas and ultimately such an undertaking lost any semantic credibility. This, too, was a phenomenon that embraced both the aristocracy and bourgeoisie, and was by no means either specifically bourgeois or limited to the gentry.[9] Nor did this, judging by what we know today, have anything to do with 'industrialization' as such. Domestic intimate ties as well as interests in economic survival and profit must be seen as different forms of commitments, and must be assigned to different semantic codes; and this distinction had already been made by the time industrialization got underway.

The call for an intimate personal family life, which first asserted itself in England,[10] was linked to a new kind of moral sentimentalism. In both respects, the difference that had given rise to the topic was the rejection both of a structural subordination of women, and of the transference of a political hierarchy into the family. For its part, the stronger *structural differentiation* of family and political rule generated the *semantic difference* that accelerated the evolution of the code for intimate relationships. In any case, the intensity and literary success of the new semantics of feeling can only be understood when seen against this institutional background. This does not mean that individuality had fully asserted itself yet. One might grant the individual the wish to enjoy his love, to express his feelings, to seek and find happiness – in a relationship with another person; but founding institutions such as marriage, the family or education on this principle was a different matter altogether.[11]

Another obstacle was posed by the view taken of the individual personality. Although literature on the subject of love and friendship in the early eighteenth century already emphasized that the people who sought their fortune in such relationships were individuals, this initially meant little more than negating the relevance of one's social standing. One was an individual in so far as it was of little or no consequence in socially intimate relationships whether one was from a bourgeois or an aristocratic family. The galantry practised only in the upper social strata declined, as did the terminology that had been used – as a prerequisite for friendship and love – to pinpoint class-specific attributes. Forthrightness took the place of *honnêteté*. However, the characterizations involved remained generalizations for the casualness with which friends were sought out by letter-writing, and the speed with which the closest of friendships developed, attest to the fact that personal characteristics were not all that important. Friendships were not founded on characteristics associated with only the one friend as distinguished from all others.

Only in the course of the century did the semantic void left by this abstract idea of an individual no longer tied to his social standing become filled out and enriched with content. There was only a gradual growth of insight into the formative influences of environment, milieu, education, travel, and friendships, and it was not until the turn of the century (and actually only in German philosophy) that the radical formulae were found with which to assert both the ego as 'being in the world' and the subjectivity of views of the world.[12] It was only by virtue of this philosophical anthropology and the Romantic literature influenced by it that the *concreteness* and *uniqueness* of the individual could be raised to the level of a *universalistic* principle. Two souls were now regarded as constituting two (different) worlds. Madame de Staël came to similar conclusions; she too found love to enhance *everything* of *consequence* by referring them to *one* other person.[13] German Romanticism of the time, however, progressed from seeing the world only in relation *to* another person to a revaluation of the world *through* that other person.[14] Having refined characters and how they were treated only in psychological terms, Romanticism now moved on to a kind of subjective conception of the world. The world of objects, (i.e.) nature, became the sounding board of love. If one compares novels of the early eighteenth century with those of the nineteenth century, one finds that the lovers' dialogue recedes into the background; it was either supplemented or virtually replaced by the enchantment of the objects through which the lovers experience their love in relation to the other.[15] If love thrived to such an extent on its own sphere of experience, to which the lovers submitted themselves – and that is precisely what love now *was* – then love could no longer be connected to a theory of state or economics; rather the concept corresponded precisely to what was to be expected in terms of the other's love, as his unreserved acceptance of the *uniqueness* of the *world* (and not merely its characteristics).

The subject matter that could be associated with love was thus expanded and at the same time reduced to a central principle. Love was no longer exclusively dependent on an exhibition of physical and moral qualities. 'Anything goes' – in spite of the preference in bourgeois literature for a bready semantics,[16] domestic life, the garden, etc. The change lay not only in the situations, images or opportunities which now allowed for love to be observed and described; it also lay in their expansion and reduction. The complications incurred when love came to be understood in terms of social reflexivity now had to be outmanoeuvred once again. Only thus did one arrive at Romanticism, whose love semantics referred to a relationship between the individual subject and the world.

What is new here can best be shown by a comparison with the principle of individuation in Leibniz's philosophy.[17] Leibniz had also defined individuality in terms of a correspondence to the world, but had related this correspondence to representativity in the *factual dimension* (taking the mirror as a metaphor). It was only in the course of the eighteenth century – dare one say, on the basis of experiences with the new principle of individuality? – that the *temporal dimension* and above all the *social dimension* were added. It will be difficult to judge the influence of Leibniz on this development; in any case, both that which, as a world, constituted individuality and, conversely, what, as individuality, constituted a world, gradually began to be imbued with historical and socially practical references; and it was this triad of referential dimensions which brought out the element of personal individuality in all its worldly uniqueness, its uniqueness as being-of-the-world. As a consequence, love, following education and sociability, now acquired a function of its own, for the factual development in time of the uniqueness of a given view of the world required that people had an influence on other people and incorporated this influence within it.

One aspect in particular of the semantics of love and individuality was new, but is not easily pinpointed – namely, the *functional* use of individual uniqueness. In the context of love this acts as an orientation that wards off entropy and tries to prevent love from going out. In order to make this point more clearly, let us return to the considerations of attribution theory presented in chapter 3. In allowing oneself to become involved in intimate relationships (and especially in sexually based intimacy), one seeks certainties that will transcend the momentary and ultimately finds them in the manner in which the partner knows that he is identical with himself: in his being-as-subject. Being-as-subject transcends the momentary because it is also the foundation of change in one's own being. In this fashion, only the other's personality is able, owing to its inherent dynamic stability, to endow love with permanence, and this is especially the case if his personality is taken to constitute a subject – world relationship, i.e. to contain all possible changes to it a priori. The momentary nature of all fulfilled intimacy had become consciously aware of its own fatality – one was able to read of it in the works of John Donne or Bussy Rabutin, Claude Crébillion and, finally, Stendhal. And this notion of a subject – shaped on an inevitably present ego who accompanied all possible changes in life – provided a response that both referred to this problem and was adequate to solving it.

Of course, this notion did not exclude, but rather incorporated change. Even lovers whose love was unstable were nevertheless subjects – and no one would know this better than the Romantics. In other words, what counted, as in all practice that orients itself to the subject of transcendental philosophy,[18] was to bring the subject down to the level of everyday operations and to test its viability. Its behaviour had to be observed in order to establish what stable attitudes could be attributed to it.

Such demands were bound to affect and change the semantics of intimacy. The more individual the personal element was conceived of as being, the more improbable it became that one would encounter partners *possessing the characteristics expected*. The initiation in and justification of the choice of a partner were thus no longer able to rely on such characteristics, but were instead transposed onto the symbols of the medium of communication, i.e. onto both the reflexivity of love and the history of the development of the social system for intimate ties.

The evolutionary conditions for such a further development of the symbolic medium of love and for the temporarily completed process of its formation under Romanticism did not originate in France, but rather in the Germany of the last third of the eighteenth century. The old European conceptual tradition that had survived here in an only slightly modified form, was oriented above all towards the basic difference of sensual and non-sensual love, and was now exposed to English and French imports: sentimentality (Richardson); Rousseau's unresolved oscillation between love and friendship; and the novel, degenerating from galantry to frivolity, albeit still precise in its observations. Mysticism and the Enlightenment thrived side by side. The rejection of sexuality on account of its supposedly animal nature was torn asunder in the throes of the Storm and Stress movement. On pietistic soil, sensibility became heightened to the point of pure self-torment; yet at the same time there was a wish to accord sexuality its rightful place and to save marriages (as Rousseau would have it) by making friendships out of them. Toward the turn of the century it also behove on one to take either an affirmative or a negative stance toward Kantian philosophy. The overall impression one gets is that the differences between the authors at this time are greater than the differences between the historical periods. No primary difference succeeded in establishing itself – neither that of sensual/non-sensual, nor that of *plaisir/ amour* or love/friendship. All retained a certain validity, the initial result being only that the self-esteem of the female (reading) public was enhanced. The dividing lines became smudged, and the contrasts lost their sharp contours. More than ever before, personal elements began to enter into literature, and literature was in turn interpreted with reference to the personal element[19] (and the contrast to the time of *amour passion*'s original emergence in the seventeenth century is particularly evident here). The semantics of intimacy seems for the time being to consist of a structured chaos, a fermenting and self-stimulating mass that inspired everyone to reach their own conclusions and thus opened the way for individualization beyond its mere self-presence in feeling. Some writers considered it necessary for semantic reasons, both in literature and in their own lives, to have two women in order to exhaust love's possibilities. Other writers employed details recognizably culled from their own lives.[20] This provoked variations in many different ways from which tangible results did not emerge until the genesis of the Romantic concept of love.

   The significance of this innovation is not adequately understood if examined only in terms of the changes in attitude toward particular topics, in that its objective was to establish a new concept of love that in turn allowed traditional elements to appear as if they were new in themselves. There is still no consensus as to what constituted the Romantic: was it an intended (no longer realizable) synthesis, or the insistence on the unity of subject and world, or even the deviation from normality that made all this innovation possible? In the context of the semantics of love what is above all conspicuous is that the old difference in the typical morphology of the semantics, the difference between idealization and paradoxicalization, now emerged as a new unity. Love itself was ideal and paradoxical, to the extent that it claimed to unify a duality. The point was to preserve and enhance the self in the act of self-devotion, and to consummate love, fully and yet reflectedly, ecstatically and yet ironically.

In all of this an innovative, typically Romantic[21] paradoxy asserted itself: the phenomenon of vision, experience, and enjoyment *being enhanced by means of distantiation.* Distance made it possible to retain the unity of self-reflexion and involvement that would otherwise be lost in the process of immediate pleasure. Thus, the accent was shifted from fulfilment to hope, to desire, and into the distance, and consequently, one not only had to seek progress in the process of love, but to fear it as well.

Evidently, attributes or virtues specific to certain social strata were no longer all that could be affirmed and rewarded by love. It was now a question of being an individual in one's own world. The asymmetry of the sexes remained as an asymmetrical attitude towards this problem. The man loved loving, the woman loved the man; therefore, her love was, on the one hand, deeper and more natural, but on the other also less free and reflected. As a result, the unity postulated by Romanticism remained bound to the man's domain of experience, although – and precisely because – the woman was the primary lover and enabled him to love. The *sociality* of loving thus came to be understood in terms of the *enhanced chance of a self-confident formation of the self* – and this led to a definitive rejection of any concept of self-love.[22]

One initial consequence of this was the complete integration of sexuality into love and the concomitant permission to do everything that had been denied its rightful place by the mutually-exclusive choice of either frivolous love affairs or a barren marriage. With regard to sexuality, there was now more at stake than the questionable endeavour to accord greater recognition to the animal in human beings;[23] and with regard to marriage, more was involved than some understanding consensus reached on fulfilling the duties entailed in one's role. Marriage was love and love was marriage – at least according to Fichte's concept of 'natural law'.[24] Although this could end up reducing most marriages to mere attempts at marriage, at least it was clear to the participants what was at stake. The faulty development of a semantics of love in the direction of the carefree and frivolous was abandoned, and ranking friendship – as something more stable and thus more valuable – higher than love also became unnecessary.

All this was part of the general departure from the old European semantics to be observed around 1800. In other respects also, human beings ceased to be defined in terms of what made them different from animals. Their greatest faculty, for example, was no longer assumed to be the ability to recognize universal truths, but instead the capacity to form a self-referentially constituted relationship to the world.[25] This faculty individualized people as subjects different from the world – and no longer as members of the exceptional human species as distinguished from the species Animal. This overall change in the orientation of human semantics also meant that the topic of love could be formulated in a new way and possessed a new set of connotations, for when love quite simply involves the human being as an individual, the under-standing of *social reflexivity* (and not only the individual reflexiveness of feelings) has to be posited at a deeper level. Social reflexivity – at least at the level of interpersonal interpenetration – becomes the constitutive prerequisite for the 'formation' of individual self-reflexion and vice versa.

The historical and theoretical basis necessary for an understanding of this development were outlined above (p. 107f.). As the medium love expanded and was universalized, so too imitations of predefined characteristics had to be forfeited, and love had to be based on its own facticity. For one thing, formulations became more explicit in indicating that by orienting himself to the other person, the lover was also invariably referring to himself: he wished to find his own happiness in the other's happiness.[26] Initially, this took the form of general concepts that need to be instilled with individual meaning, such as happiness, and *voluptas* and *taedium*. But self-referentiality of the subjects does not yet amount to reflexivity of the process. However, around the middle of the eighteenth century the emphasis on sensibility provided a bridge to reflexivity – if only because it served to emphasize the dynamic quality of the subjective and, in this respect as well, also did not distinguish between the sexes: *both* were expected to be sensitive. The self-enhancement of one's own sensibility, however, ultimately cast doubt on whether and how one existed intimately for the other person. Besides, it was evidently difficult to do without characteristics that provided a reason for love, such as wealth, youth, beauty and virtue, and thus it became necessary to fall back on the particular rights accorded to individuality.[27] As long as personal characteristics had been the basic criteria, it had been possible to love one another purely on the basis of hearsay. Once these prerequisites were dismantled, the process had only itself to rely on. Loving based on hearsay was replaced by the love of loving, which sought out its object and cultivated social reflexivity within mutual love. In other words, the reflexivity of loving comprised more than just the consciousness of the ego cofunctioning in love, and also more than a mere consciousness of the fact that one loved and was loved. Nor did the influence of intelligence on love, celebrated in France as *délicatesse*, get to the roots of the matter. It was possible to dispense with all this[28] once one had achieved reflexivity in love. This meant, among other things, that a corresponding feeling had to be emotionally affirmed and sought after and that one loved oneself as lover and beloved and also loved the other as lover and beloved, i.e. related one's feeling precisely to this coincidence of feelings. Love was aimed at an I and a you, *to the extent that* both were part of the love relationship – i.e. that each made it possible for the other to have such a relationship – and not because both were good, or beautiful, or noble or rich.

Reflexivity of loving is, in abstract terms, a capacity open to all talents and all situations and by no means an esoteric affair reserved for only a few great lovers or masters of the art of seduction. It does not necessarily require the heavy labour of passion, and can – but does not have to – lead to an intensification of feeling. What it did intensify, at least for the Romantics, was the enjoyable nature of feeling and the capacity to suffer because of feeling. 'Love for the sake of love'[29] became an existential maxim, and its most impressive proponent was Jean Paul.[30]

Nevertheless, under Romanticism things did not go so far as the admittedly conceivable 'democratization' of love in the sense of a capacity equally available to everyone. The form in which the semantics was celebrated, namely the unity of idealization and paradoxicalization, blocks what would otherwise be possible. Loving with 'Romantic irony' was not something intended for labourers or servant girls, for without being earmarked as specific to certain social strata, the universalism of Romantic love (like the bourgeois universalism of Europe in general) was nevertheless a highly selective idea in terms of the attitudes it presupposed.

The gain in reflexively grounded autonomy in the unconditioned love of loving corresponded to a new kind of differentiating consciousness. The love of loving could not be mere *amor amicitiae*, could not simply be loving the love of the other, just as it could not be reduced to mere loving. During Romanticism even the tension between capricious and reasonable elements which the Classical model had managed to somehow live with disappeared. Once reflexivity had been practised in love, the latter threatened to switch over into revulsion; the inner relationing of things could no longer be shaken off. The act of feeling transpired to not be quite the same as the felt feeling; spontaneity was lost, and both levels of feeling began to differ in their temporal position, all immediate feelings being felt to be superficial. The lover of love admired himself, was surprised, and peeved about himself as a lover – about the way, for example, in which he had adopted gestures in harmony with the partner, had not mastered techniques, had approached the other physically – and been sullied in the process. The problem could no longer be solved by means of Romantic irony; and it certainly no longer had anything to do with thoughtful reflexion about one's own interest in love. The problem became that of how the ego could remain identical with itself, as it had to feel feelings and love love; and this identity could then become the difference of both partners and of each in the other – and thus there were no restrictions placed on what one subsequently felt.

One comes across a similar problem of Romantic ambiguity if time is taken as the focal point instead of social reflexivity. In this case we can be guided by Stendhal, specifically chapter XXXII, 'De l'intimité', in *De l'amour* (1822).[31] Rousseau's influence is clearly visible. Intimacy is the concept taken to describe the

blending of the happiness of the two lovers, whereby the happiness
of both lies in precisely the same actions. This is only possible if
time is brought to a standstill and each person takes his or her cue
from that moment. Any attempt to draw upon knowledge and
memory would paralyse inner experience,[32] and any premeditation,
any actions which might have been considered beforehand, have
to be avoided, for this would render one insensitive to the
moment.[33] The *art d'aimer* was reduced to this law (and thereby
cancelled itself out), and consequently in love there was neither a
will that could determine action, nor any transparency (*candeur*).[34]
'On est ce qu'on peut, mais on sent ce qu'on est.'[35] What this now
meant was – leaving aside all the moral implications – *sensibilité*.
The conceptual reversal becomes clear if one remembers that
this was precisely the standpoint whence tradition had criticized
passion because it made the human being as vulnerable to the
momentary as an animal. At the same time, the reference to time
was situated at a deeper level than would be the case if
inconstancy and the typical time-span of a love story had been
thematized. Immersing oneself in the infinite moment was now
the condition for experiencing oneself in the self-referential
reference to love. All that one attempted to be, to remain, to
withstand, petrified into an unwieldy wooden hand with which
one could not love; or subsequently into vanity, replacing *amour
passion* with *amour de vanité*. Here as well, failure awaited one,
owing to the timeless existence – and stretched as far as the
impossibility of remembering, since one could now only remember
reproducible texts. And in the end the nineteenth-century novel
led to a reoccupation of the position from which love could be
reflected on: *amour passion* was succeeded by *amour de vanité*
– superior in that it not only had to negate all other forms of
plaisir, but itself as well.

The outcome of all this was a peculiar combination of circular
closedness and an openness towards anything that might enrich
love. Precisely the idea that all that matters to love was love
admittedly meant that love constituted a world of its own – but
one that was by this very fact also a world unto itself. More was
involved here than reciprocal adaptation, and also more than
making each other happy, which would soon inevitably cease in
the face of needs becoming exhausted and the relationship
becoming habit; love amounted to the constitution of a common

special world in which love was always able to inform itself anew by basing its reproduction on that which meant something to the other person. This was the only way that love could be marriage and the only way in which love could lend itself permanence.

Regardless of whether this self-referential closedness was subsequently pursued from a social or rather more from a temporal point of view, i.e. as a matter of individualizing a view of the world or as a matter of achieving a sensitive harmony uncoupled from time, the act of accepting such self-reference of love was probably the most important step forward taken in the development of the medium of love during Romanticism. This made it possible *to embed* the paradoxies, which in the form of contradictory descriptions or prescriptions had been components of the code of *amour passion, in love itself* – for instance in the sense of a spiritually permeated sensuality, of ironic eroticism, or of role switches based on love as the form of enhancement, etc. The problem stylized in this way was ultimately that of remaining identical with one's self while also becoming part of the other person.[36] And friendship was just the reverse: self-duplication by absorbing the other person into oneself (see, for example, the old notion of two souls in one breast). Couched in this semantic form, the concept of 'Romantic' love attempted to transcend *amour passion* in two respects: by incorporating an infinitely enhanceable individuality and through (the thus self-guaranteed) prospect of permanence, i.e. the reconciliation with marriage. Love became the basis of marriage, and marriage became the task of repeatedly earning love.[37] Equally, especially during the Romantic period, the element of exaggeration involved, the questions this raised, and the dangers to its existence, were also a part of the experience of love and, one might almost say, enjoyed.

One of the most important consequences of this was that the *difference* of *sincere* and *insincere* love collapsed, destroying the structural preconditions for information processing in the classical code of *amour passion*. Benjamin Constant's *Adolphe*[38] is the novel that attempts to grasp love in this situation. It was no longer possible to convey the difference between loving and no longer loving within communication[39] because all communication had become completely and thoroughly socially reflected. This in turn made information impossible, since the necessary differential scheme could not be assumed to exist and/or had to be handled differently for the sake of love. In other words, love itself became a main reason for the collapse of its codification.

In a much more general sense, it was typical for the spirit of Romanticism that it attempted to survive without objective criteria. As a result, the long-standing, common polemic against false devotion, fraudulent love, and hypocrisy[40] was abandoned. Instead an autonomous role was assigned to social practice which more or less as a matter of course initially oriented itself toward externalities and made use of deception and feigned attitudes in order to make a beginning. It thus allowed itself to be guided by social models, especially literary models – but only so as to make itself viable, to find characteristics which made its own life loveworthy. The literature that ushered in this change in attitude assumed the double function of effecting this change and of exposing it.[41]

Furthermore, the self-referential constitution of loving absorbed the *imagination* of the lovers. That a lover will see a smile without seeing the missing teeth is something which has always been observed and utilized to characterize his passion. Now, however, it was no longer a question of mere selection and imaginary supplementation of his perceptions, but of enhancing his feelings for the world. From this vantage point everything could acquire new qualities that were of value precisely because they were only valid for the lovers.[42]

Around 1800, traditional themes appear new when set against this background. They owe their innovative semblance to the stronger reflexive isolation of loving. For example, it had always been common knowledge that love would eventually wind up being a disappointment for the lovers;[43] yet Kater Murr stumbled upon this as if it were something new.[44] The technique of paradoxicalization was retained, and new topics were added to the commonly used paradoxes. Thus Stendhal named loneliness and worldliness as prerequisites for love.[45] Many innovations appear to be grafted artificially onto the old trunk of *amour passion*. And yet it was the novel and not non-fiction, sentimentality rather than galantry, narrative technique rather than the technique of codifying *maximes d'amour*, which apparently continued to have an impact.

This selective treatment of history was used – in keeping with the reflexive closedness of the affairs of love – to install chance as the trigger that set love off instead of the traditional sparking off by reasoned deliberation and galant skilfulness.[46] The insertion of this into the code led to an important innovation: the paradoxicalization of chance as a necessity, as fate, or also of chance as freedom of choice.[47] This inclusion, regardless of any other functions it might have possessed, took account of wishes to expand the spheres of contact and prepared the way for an extension of the code to encompass all classes of society. Whereas it had only been natural for courtly and subsequently galant love to be reserved for ladies whom 'one' already knew, meaning that the choice could be based on preliminary information,[48] the symbolic marker 'chance' was now used to socially differentiate at the very beginning of a love relationship, i.e. it no longer needed legitimation and was constructed in terms of a lack of prerequisites. The combination of chance and fate accordingly meant that a non-personalized beginning did not affect the significance of the love relationship negatively; on the contrary, being independent of any external moulding, this enhanced the significance the relationship bore, making it absolute in and of itself, so to speak.

Even Hegel allowed himself to be misled on this question, in that he understood 'chance' literally and not as a symbol of separation. In paragraph 162 of the *Guidelines to a Philosophy of Right* the following statement is made with regard to subjective and/or objective points of departure for matrimony:

At one extreme, the first step is that the marriage is arranged by the contrivance of benevolent parents; the appointed end of the parties is a union of mutual love, and their inclination to marry arises from the fact that each grows acquainted with the other from the first as a destined partner. At the other extreme, it is the inclination of the parties which comes first, appearing in them as *these* two infinitely particularized individuals. The more ethical way to matrimony may be taken to be the former extreme or any way at all whereby the decision to marry comes first and the inclination to do so follows, so that in the actual wedding both decision and inclination coalesce. In the latter extreme, it is the uniqueness of the *infinitely particularized* which makes good its claims in accordance with the subjective principle of the modern world. — But those works of modern art, dramatic and other, in which the love of the sexes is the main interest, are pervaded by a chill despite the heat of passion they portray, for they associate the passion with *accident* throughout and represent the entire dramatic interest as if it rested solely on the characters as *these individuals*; what rests on them may be of infinite importance to *them*, but is of none whatever *in itself.*

At the end of these passages light is shed once again on the principle of marriage as it used to be: the assumption that the act of marriage would, at least normally, be followed by affection and love. This could be expected as long as the demands placed on self-centred individuality and interpersonal interpenetration were not so very great. However, the modern world had long since dispensed with such a limitation. At the same time, with its differential symbols of passion and of chance, and the codificatory technique of paradoxicalization, the modern world had no principle at hand which offered the prospect of stability in marriage or other intimate relationships. Romanticism's response to this situation, in which the semantics of love came into conflict with demands that the personal world be endowed with permanent meaning, was to take flight into exaggeration.

14

Love and Marriage

The Ideology of Reproduction

Both English sentimentalism and eighteenth-century sexology, which claimed to be close to nature, had moved the problem of marriage into the foreground of debate on love. The increasing differentiation of the economy on the one hand as the sector of production, and family life on the other, also led to the family being relieved of having to fulfil any role over and above its immediate concerns. By the eighteenth century families from the upper social strata had already lost their significance as 'supporters of the state'. Socio-structural reasons for controls on marriage had thus ceased to exist, and what was there to prevent society from making the switch from arranged marriages to marriages of the heart?[1]

This innovation must be more clearly outlined from two different mutually reinforcing vantage points. On the one hand, the differentiation of other functional systems made it possible to do without family ties (created by marriage) as the pillar of political, religious or economic functions. These systems were now sufficiently autonomous to be able to assert themselves and ensure their own reproduction. People could as a consequence now accept that the different groups of relatives of which the married couple were members by virtue of their birth and nothing else were connected quite coincidentally by means of the latter's marriage, and that the connection between the relatives only had a bearing on the individual marriage in question and no significance beyond that. The original families were connected symbolically only by the married couple's children, only for this tie to become ever so thin once the children in turn married.

Because this process of connection and distantiation was detached from others of the social system's macrofunctions, people could, indeed were compelled to, conceive of families as something that had to be founded anew with every new generation. This notion admittedly existed in earler times as well (especially in cases in which members of the family were geographically separated), but the process of refoundation was now left to its own devices and bestowed a far greater importance on marriage in the family system than it had in the economy of the Old European household. Accordingly, the choice of a bride or groom had to be able to legitimate itself (regardless of what the individual had in mind in making the choice). It was this structural change that people, without being consciously aware of the fact, had prepared themselves for by developing the symbolic medium of love. The semantics, partly oriented towards extra-marital passions (France), partly towards domesticity (England) and partly towards education (Germany), was ready at hand and could now be set into operation.

The problem of leaving the door open for marriages based on coincidences that were no longer subject to regulation had, in other words, become topical in the course of changes in the *social structure* and informed further developments of the symbolic medium of love. At the time, however, the only semantic correlate available was *amour passion*, which, while being open to enrichment with new themes, could not itself resolve the issue of stability.[2] It was only possible to outbid it in terms of extravagance and to declare that leading a normal life was totally unintentional.[3] This exaltation was, however, to remain a special phenomenon which by no means covers everything that has since, in a sense no longer only related to novels, been termed 'Romantic love'.

By the end of the eighteenth century the unity of a marriage of love and conjugal love was generally professed to be the principle of the natural perfection of humankind.[4] One of the most important side benefits of this was that now not only the two parties' motives for marriage, but also the motives for marriage they attributed to each other, could converge. The difference between the sexes diminished – not only with reference to the respective motives of each, but also with respect to the motives for marriage which one imputed to the opposite sex.[5] Shielded by the unusual nature of the complex of 'Romantic love', the partners' respective expectations came to approximate one another; and the more surprising a love affair appeared to the outside, and the more clearly it distanced itself from normal behaviour, the more certain the lovers could be of themselves in ascribing to each other the same motives.[6] Difference and unanimity were brought together in a new relation of reciprocal enhancement.

However, this brought one face to face with the problem of finding an explanation for all the unhappy (or at least not particularly happy) marriages. These could no longer be regarded as the result of having been married off by one's parents out of considerations for class or property. 'Romantic' love therefore had to assume the task of explaining the reason for the existence side by side of both happiness and unhappiness in marriage.

In the course of the nineteenth century, the barriers to a marriage based on 'Romantic' love were taken down and thus had an effect on what was now seen and desired as 'Romantic'. Love became the sole legitimate reason for the choice of a partner, and all those moments of passion that were threatening, that endangered existence and put life and death in the balance had to be filtered out. What remained was an institutionalized understanding for enraptured passion and the assumption that this was a sort of test of one's willingness to marry as well as a promise of happiness of sorts. The families now had to be founded anew by each generation. What were now called 'relations' in a somewhat pallid sense of the word, were regarded rather more as potentially disruptive, and certainly not as something which facilitated getting married and making a marriage work. The parents had, at best, indirect means at their disposal to help or hinder their children in making contacts,[7] and the (objective) uncertainty and the risks involved in choosing a partner were accordingly great. The semantics of 'Romantic' love took on the function of turning this uncertainty into subjective certainty, serving as a sort of magical substitute for foresight. It at any rate provided presentational forms with which uncertainty could be treated as certainty in the course of interaction with the effect that uncertainty was socially affirmed and could thus indeed become certainty. Last but not least, the separating off of the two lovers had the function of allowing this transformational process to unfold free of objectifying social controls. Here again we come across specific problematic socio-structural situations influencing what is drawn from the rich stocks of the semantics of love and then reproduced.

One gets a clearer picture of this change if one considers that a declaration of love, if it were to be absolutely convincing,[8] always called for a second declaration. In the seventeenth century this had been the '*déclaration de sa naissance*';[9] it had to be said or proven that the lover was a prince or a suitor of the same rank as the lady.[10] In the nineteenth century this was replaced by the declaration of one's intention to marry.[11] This additional declaration no longer referred to the past, but to the future; and this was because the family no longer persisted through the generations, but had to be founded anew each time.

If one takes this necessity of a reorientation towards the future into account, then it becomes clear that Romanticism as a wide-ranging theory was not in itself sufficient. It was all very well to celebrate the unusual – on the occasion of marriage's liberation from social and familial constraints – with tempestuous orgies. This, however, hardly made provisions for the everyday love life of those who entered into marriage and later found themselves in a predicament for which they had only themselves to blame.

Romantic love could not therefore remain the sole answer to this new problem. Indeed, in the years after 1800 other thematic developments can be noted which fuse the semantics of love and sexuality and marriage in non-romantic terms, i.e. tune them down into the trivial, so to speak. Ample proof for this can be found in Senancour's book on love.[12] The foundation of love in sexuality was accepted with the proviso that this basis was simultaneously surpassed. Sexuality was in itself to be viewed only as '*un soulagement à obtenir: rien de plus*',[13] and was the condition for both the survival and enhancement of love.[14] The code-immanent function of this symbiotic mechanism was, in other words, taken very literally. While imagining that they were pursuing happiness, individuals actually served to reproduce humankind, and society had to provide forms for this – love and marriage – that allowed a combined maximum of order and freedom. As a consequence, a rather more peaceful, and certainly not turbulent, passionate atmosphere had to be achieved in love and marriage. The old *amour passion* was thus strongly relativized, if not actually rejected;[15] the sociological criticism of a marriage based solely on such passion was thereby anticipated.[16] Elitist values are still to be found in the concepts used to make demands of the other,[17] but one also comes across the notion that love was a solace for the mediocre, for members of the population (i.e. for everyone!) who were unable to achieve anything else in life.[18]

If one also consults Destutt de Tracy[19] and Schopenhauer,[20] then one finds that a theory already existed in the first decades of the nineteenth century which no longer took the semantics of love as a given quantity or as a form of cognition, but tried rather to conceive of it as a tripartite control mechanism. Primary ideas that influenced the formation of individual emotions were pinpointed at the level of literature, of novels, and of the *idéologie* (which we here term semantics). These in turn were held to direct the generative behaviour of people in a sort of 'meditation on the Genius of the species'.[21] Decisions on reproduction, and thus on the 'composition of the next generation',[22] were made in a completely individualized, unconstrained selective process in which the actual presence of controls remained hidden. Freedom and institution thus coincided.[23] The notions that lovers made for themselves modelled on novels had no purpose in themselves, but only in terms of this coincidence. Regardless of whether these arose in a paradoxical, uncontrolled and not readily constructable fashion, what was important was that they individualized the choice of a partner in order to serve an accumulative breeding of the human species; and one must first be aware of this function if one wishes to get anywhere close to understanding the deeper meaning of all the delight and pain, fear and hardship, and exuberance.[24]

The concept of *idéologie* cancelled out the eighteenth-century concept of nature. Scientifically researched material codified in civilization took the place of some force that had asserted itself solely by virtue of its own laws. This corresponded to the sort of biological sentimentalism that Proudhon decades later formulated in such vague, but meaty terms. The unity of love and marriage is presumed to be the unity of material and form, and the reproduction of humankind became the functional aim of this unity, the achievement of which was aided by certain ideals: 'l'influence de l'idéal était nécessaire aux générations de l'humanité, and 'l'amour est donc . . . la matière du mariage.'[25] The primary difference was thus either that of form and matter or of ideal and reality. As one could not decide in favour of the one side and against the other in this difference it provided the conceptual basis for the unity of sexually based love and marriage while suspending all earlier differentiations of form. Romanticism survived the naturalist and evolutionist tendencies of the second half of the nineteenth century, but only at a high cost: it was stripped of all deep-seated tension and took the form of a seemingly serious illusionism, soon to become exposed for what it was.[26]

Was Romanticism then only a last-ditch attempt to prevent the trivialization, the general accessibility of love? Or did the fixation on 'the love of one's life' have to be paid for with a curious sort of indecisiveness,[27] or indeed with the loss of the noble form? At any rate, the differentiation of single families resulted in a shift in the various plausible bases that sanctify the forever possible innovations.[28] Only now did the long-recurrent motive of lovers seeking marriage (and of novels ending with marriage being concluded) become topical. The old thesis of the incompatibility of love and marriage had to be covered up; the end of the novel was not the end of life. An attempt was made to limit the semantics of 'Romantic' love by omitting all elements that signal the existence of threats to love. Everybody, rather than just the heroes of novels such as Don Quixote, Emma Bovary or Julien Sorel, was given the chance to intensify the relationship via copied needs. Thus, a sort of Romanticism for the person on the street arose, one that in some cases could already be satisfied by the consumption of books and films – 'one of the few bright spots in a life normally bounded by the kitchen, the office and the grave'.[29] It was easily understood, realizable as if in a dream, intellectually undemanding and sterile. Only a few were able to actually live according to this form of Romanticism, but many could dream of it.[30] Furthermore, by being diametrically opposed to the normal career conditions prevalent in a society determined by markets and organizations, it included love and marriage as a particular form of social climbing that did not presuppose 'anything' and could, as a consequence, be considered fully individualized.

But will simple trivialization suffice? If love has to again be institutionalized as an ideal in order to give social cover to improbable behaviour and to psychologically prepare for it, will not the comparison of ideal and person typically become a disadvantage for the person in question? If a code is specialized in making abnormal behaviour appear normal, will it not fail if that behaviour is renormalized under the pressure of real psychological and social conditions? This old incompatibility has been rediscovered as a problem in marriage: as a dashing of precisely those expectations on which the marriage was originally based. Perhaps men are particularly vulnerable to exposure to such disappointment, if what Madame de Staël supposed is indeed true: that they compensate for their lack of heartfelt ties by their imaginations.[31] Sociologists have at least speculated that this shock of coming face to face with reality often endangers marriages which had begun as romances.[32] 'Romantic' love thus places divorces in a new, dramatic light. 'The world that loves a lover does not love a divorcé . . . He has got what he wanted and found it was not good for him.'[33] Religious, legal and family – political barriers recede, directing social judgement towards the divorcees themselves. Any open rejection can no longer be justified, but this does not necessarily place the person in a better light, for he knows that everyone else knows that he got himself into this situation in the first place. Perhaps the ideological misdirection of 'Romantic' love is to blame. This assumption launches a search for a completely different foundation for enduring intimate relations. The old (e.g. Puritan) notion of 'life's companion' is, without anyone actually remembering it, nowadays reborn in the guise of companionship. Marriage is not expected to provide one with a completely unrealistic ideal world and definitely not a perpetual affirmation of passionate feelings, but rather with a basis for communication and common action with regard to everything which is of importance to the partners involved.

Whereas the light literature of the first half of the twentieth century reconstructs, reinforces and stereotypes the trend toward differentiation of a Romantic complex that is reduced to a few particular characteristics,[34] the more strongly reflected reworking of the code would seem to have already induced this reorganization. What is more, empirical data shows that, unlike the picture conveyed by light literature and the interest in it, Romantic enthusiasm is not very widespread in notions of love; and this fact naturally serves to cool out the semantics.[35] What has this change brought about? An explanation occasionally given is that the increasing tolerance with regard to pre-marital sexual relations[36] and the far-reaching levelling of differences in sex-roles is not compatible with the notions of 'Romantic' love:[37] Romanticism presupposes ascetism, i.e. the postponement of satisfaction. Be that as it may, this would only explain the decline in the plausibility of Romantic notions of love and not the direction in which, as a generalized symbolic medium of love, they have been transformed.

The new semantics of intimacy to be developed can base itself on a factor which has never before influenced symbolic properties in this way, namely the *difference of impersonal and personal relationships*. This is not the old distinction between one's own group and those outside it, from which the tradition of a difference between *philos* and *philia* had grown.[38] We no longer have to do with a pre-given, natural grouping of persons, within which individual persons or small groups can only shift, if at all, by mobility (secession). The problem also no longer lies in the difference of religious (related to God) and secular (necessarily jealous) love, both of which can remain relatively indifferent with regard to the fates and personal characteristics of the other.[39] Thus, all the forms of relief afforded by such indifference become irrelevant. It is indeed no longer a question of the difference of marriage and loneliness which had kindled the imagination and sparked off the irony and disappointment of the Romantics. Rather, the difference that now determines the form the code takes lies at the level of social relations, in which the individual can or cannot immerse his whole self. The individual can – and this is new – provide cover for most of the demands made by his life only through impersonal relationships, i.e. through relationships in which he cannot communicate about himself, or, at the most, only within the narrow limits of the particular social system. This condition includes the actual creation of the self, namely one's personal development in the context of school and professional career. The experience of difference, the axis along which the self constitutes itself, is coloured in a specific manner by these socio-structural conditions. The need for another Self – and this means another Other Self and another Self of one's own – is deeply influenced by this and plays a part in constituting one's own identity.

In the nineteenth century one had been able to assume, in view of the situation which the industrial revolution created for the bourgeois strata, that this problem affected only the man. He alone worked outside the home. He alone had to cope with the unwholesomeness of the world. Only he was directly exposed to the indifference, carelessness and nastiness of his fellow men, and the woman compensated for this with her love. 'Le soir, il arrive brisé. Le travail, l'ennui des choses et la méchanceté des hommes ont frappé sur lui. Il a souffert, il a baissé, il revient moins homme. Mais il trouve en sa maison un infini de bonté, une sérénité si grande, qu'il doute presque des cruelles réalités qu'il a subies tout le jour . . . Voilà la mission de la femme, (plus que la génération même), c'est de refaire le coeur de l'homme.'[40] Given these socio-theoretical premises, the anthropological difference of man and woman had to be maintained at first, indeed driven to the extreme, before then being abandoned completely.

Once this basic experience of the difference of impersonal and personal relationships has become common knowledge, once it holds true for everyone regardless of social strata and sex, it must fix the desire for personal relationships, for fuller interpersonal interpenetration, at a deeper level and make it appear all the more unattainable. References to an economy of scarcity (helping each other) and a morality of industriousness are not completely dispensed with. These factors, the main supports of the traditional ethos of friendship, remain important; they are, however, degraded to the status of minimal requirements that must not be absent. Because such requirements are located in the field of impersonal relationships and can be fulfilled there, they can no longer form the starting point for what one expects from the other person in terms of a personal relationship. The ideals of love and friendship cannot emerge from such requirements. Indeed, such ideals can no longer consist of inflated demands with regard to how one gets by with scarce resources, industriousness, a willingness to sacrifice and a willingness to exert oneself; but then what else are they supposed to consist of?

It has been proposed that, in a society which offered everyone a highly complex environment with constantly changing relationships, marriage or quasi-marital relationships will be all the more intensified, for they can provide an anchorage in the shape of at least one lasting relationship for the whole person.[41] Empirical research also shows that families in a complex and variable environment tend to generate diffuse intimate internal ties rather more than families in which the individual roles are also clearly incorporated into the environment.[42] One can, however, hardly conclude that the respective systems are stable just by referring to the strong, so to speak, compensatory interest in intimate relationships. Precisely hopes and expectations that endeavour to find something that has not been fulfilled can set standards which are very difficult or impossible to meet. This is particularly the case when no socially standardized semantics is available as a yardstick towards which one can orient both one's assessment of future prospects and the regulation of one's own behaviour.

15

What Now?

Problems and Alternatives

The current semantics of love is more difficult to define in terms of one general formula than were any of its predecessors. A balance exists between rejecting and continuing traditional ideas in a disguised form. The form of the code appears to have undergone a transformation from the ideal via the paradox to a problem, namely, that of being able to find both a partner for an intimate relationship and tie him to it. Skepticism vis-à-vis high spirits of any kind is combined with a demanding, highly individualized set of expectations. The alternative to breaking off the relationship and instead going it alone is taken seriously as a course of action for life and meets with understanding. Ann Swidler, in one of the few adequate attempts at interpretation that exist, claims to have traced a shift within the paradoxical demands of loving towards a higher degree of compatibility with individual self-realization.[1] According to Swidler, this is no longer seen in youthful exuberance as a problem of the true love of a lifetime, but as a practical problem encountered as part of adulthood, and one which can be tackled by establishing ties, relinquishing them, and doing without them in the course of a long life.

In order to examine the changes in the nature of the problem which this reflects – albeit very roughly – we must again place things in the context of socio-structural transformation. It is common sociological knowledge that the communal living conditions of past social orders left little leeway for intimate relationships, and that social controls – but also social reassurances – were closely related to behaviour and still provided the individual person with enough consensual chances. Partners who entered into closer relationships usually knew each other beforehand and in a different context; entering into closer relationships therefore probably represented neither a significant expansion of one's prior knowledge, nor an acceptance of the deep structures in the partner's inner experience. There was little room for expectations to be enhanced with regard to personal harmony; it may be that 'affairs of the heart' were not as such even present, for society at that time offered no opportunity whatsoever for self-problematization. The most important factor in harmonizing personal relationships was probably that of harmony in external relationships; these only needed to be linked by friendship or by a common way of life.

The autonomization of intimate relationships, which Slater aptly refers to as 'social regression',[2] creates a totally new situation. External supports are dismantled, and the internal tensions become more acute. The capacity for stability now depends on purely personal resources – while at the same time being part of the involvement with the other person! Turning once again to an historical comparison, we find that around 1700 the idea of a stable love relationship was considered a sheer impossibility by the French, while during the same period the English moralists noted that an increase of love and hate in marriages accompanied an increase in sensibility.[3] More recent research has also repeatedly confirmed the propensity for conflict of intimate relationships.[4] This may be attributable to the fact that personal communication is not only the sole level at which agreement can be preserved in mutual love, but also the only one available for the resolution of differences of opinion with regard to concrete actions, role attitudes, appraisals of environment, causal attributions, questions of taste and value judgements. This may also be the case, however, because opinions or manners of behaviour can all too easily be attributed back to this level, precisely because people believe that such a linkage is afforded by love.

The first explanation which sociology came up with in the 1920s and 1930s was simple: all this stemmed from incorrect programming, for Romantic love did not agree with marriages.[5] Today this explanation has all but disappeared, and instead one is faced with the question of whether 'social regression', the freedom to shape intimate relationships in accordance with one's own personal views rather than in terms laid down by society, is not indeed the source of the problems. If this is the case, then we are dealing with a finding of a general and typical nature: namely, that modern society no longer experiences its achievements as *desiderata*, but rather equally as part of reality. This means that sociology must make a sharper distinction between socio-structural analysis on the one hand and the semantic analysis on the other, and that causal hypotheses should be employed with more caution.

The semantics of love ushered in the differentiation of intimate relationships; this was at first directed against marriage as a social institution, but later with a view to marriage as an institution founded by the lovers themselves. This tie to marriage appears to be in the process of loosening. The influence of parents has long been limited to the more informal precautionary method of encouraging or preventing contacts being made.[6] This form of control itself now also seems increasingly to be giving way to self-imposed considerations. Above all, however, the temporal frame started to assume the function of a social control. As one gets older, one comes under pressure – a generalized social pressure! – to find or at least come to accept an adequate matrimonial partner. These shifts still apply to the symbol with which society provides for permissible and protected exclusivity, but making this symbol available for quasi-autonomous use necessarily has certain consequences. This is particularly true in one respect: a marriage autonomized in this way does not afford adequate protection against the primary danger posed by intimate relationships, namely, their instability.

In view of this situation we shall disregard the question of the form and attractiveness of marriage for the moment and turn our attention instead to the overall problem of socially autonomized intimate relationships, i.e. marriages, and also extra-marital relationships, whenever they attempt to realize special demands placed on intimacy.

Even though a great deal has been said about intimacy, intimate relationships and so forth, we have still not designed a theoretical concept to deal with the subject adequately. One comes closest to capturing what is meant by characterizing it as a high degree of interpersonal interpenetration,[7] meaning that in relation to each other, people lower their relevance thresholds with the result that what one regards as relevant almost always is also held relevant by the other. Communicative relationships accordingly become more dense. Bearing in mind the typology of the adoption of patterns of selection treated in chapter 2, one can characterize intimacy by saying that in it the (selective) inner experience of the partner, and not just his actions, becomes relevant for the actions of the other person. French Classicism used various topoi to describe this: it claimed that nothing was trifling in love, emphasized that fulfilling one's duties was incompatible with love, and that it was not enough to do all that was demanded of one, but rather one had to anticipate the other's wishes. German Idealism would have put it differently: making the other's relation to the world one's own meant enjoying it with him. The high degree of verbalization of love relationships confirms this theory. Lovers can talk incessantly with each other because everything they experience is worth sharing and meets with resonance.

As in the case of all generalized symbolic media of communication, the question arises of whether it is possible to differentiate corresponding social systems and what consequences this has? Can intimate relationships be left open to autonomous self-regulation? Can they exist in themselves, without social supports, linked with the environment by processes that do not correspond to the nature or to the particular mode of information processing in intimate relationships?

This automatically leads us to a second question: is a semantics such as *amour passion*, which helped to advance and assert the process of differentiation, suitable when it comes to treating the factual contents that emerged as a result? It is one thing to make the impossible possible and then plausible; but enduring it is another. The nineteenth century was already swaying uneasily between exaggeration and trivialization, and today, more than ever before, the codification of intimacy has to keep access to the corresponding attitudes open to everyone. By utilizing a semantics of 'affect' Parsons speaks of 'generalized accessibility to an "attitudinal" entity'.[8] Is a semantics of passion, of excess, of extravagance, of no sense of responsibility towards one's own feeling, or even just a semantics of high spirits and of improbable happiness any longer of use in this context?

What we can say is that the semantic content of 'Romantic' and 'Romanticism' has been clandestinely replaced – not only if this is taken to signify actual Romanticism, but also if it is understood simply as the Romantic portrayal of love. For example, if one considers the items which Americans use to devise scales to measure 'Romantic' love, what they mean is roughly the feeling of being there for each other – no more and no less than that.[9] There is no longer any trace of the tradition of *amour passion*. The only difference that still counts here, apparently, involves access to sexual relationships – be this with or without emotional ties.[10] The symbiotic mechanism of sexual relationships is thus not only incorporated into the code; it is 'the thing itself', toward which one can have various attitudes. The difference between these is then defined as 'Romantic love'.

At first glance, such modest demands on meaning – and, after all, we are supposedly dealing here with the meaning of life! – contrast strikingly with the socio-structural importance and the inevitability of an autonomous treatment of differentiated intimate relationships. However, perhaps this is precisely the explanation; perhaps it is the development that we have characterized as differentiation, autonomization, social regression, which makes it too risky to burden the already precarious process of expectation-agreements with a balast of culturally hyperbolized models, demands, and linguistic forms. Moreover, in the course of this process the complexity of the internal adaptive capacity, and thus the complexity of the relevant environment, also increases. If one considers that the ego as well as the alter are concerned with the problem of relationships between person and environment, i.e. with a problem that cannot simply be pinpointed by describing the desired set of personal characteristics, it is difficult to imagine solutions availing themselves at the level of lasting semantics. Isolated words such as 'cameraderie' surely do not suffice to indicate the presence of such solutions, particularly since they stem from a sphere which, for the most part, is depersonalized nowadays. One even has to wonder whether and how the topic can be treated in literature. The tension between sexuality and morals, between necessarily secret and public matters that enabled something to be published in print which had to be practised privately out of the public eye is now absent. As a consequence, the corresponding interest in learning and vicarious experience also does not exist.[11] There is no relatively easy-to-manage, direct or indirect function for sexuality as a secret indicator of something desired. Not that one could do without sexuality as a symbiotic mechanism! But the thematization of sexuality or the treatment of subjects which represent sexuality in the semantics are both no longer connected to that closely related problem, i.e. no longer suggest quite so clearly that the need for intimate communication could be satisfied in this way. When the world is also at issue, sexuality is no longer an adequate symbol for interpenetration. This gives way, not least of all, to uncertainty with regard to the question of the significance to be attached to the difference between the sexes, if one looks at the problem of intimacy as it presents itself today. The differences between the sexes – which were emphasized in all love codes in the past, and around which asymmetries were constructed and enhanced – are toned down. Considering that this difference used to be an even more important criterion for marriage than money, the question today is what to do with the remains of a difference that cannot be legitimated?

One outgrowth of this liberation of sexual relationships from social control is – at least in the novel – that the conditioning of love has to be reversed. The idea of a long, drawn-out pining for fulfilment seems ridiculous. And yet, the ties and impressions left on a person by a sexual relationship lead only to unhappiness. The tragedy is no longer that the lovers fail to find each other, but rather in the fact that sexual relationships produce love and that one can neither live in keeping with it nor free oneself of it.[12]

One also finds reactions to this new state of affairs in non-fictional works that address the subject of sexuality directly in one form or another. They run in a different direction, however.[13] Nearly all of this body of literature is no longer intended to warn or inhibit people, but rather to provide counselling, positive and encouraging advice. The Victorian age's last grand attempt to negate sexuality as far as possible is now only treated ironically[14] and viewed as a mistake that almost defies comprehension. The medicinal semantics is replaced by a clinical, therapeutic concern for full orgasmic satisfaction,[15] which creates its own paradoxies;[16] and by the barely conscious, but all the more manifest semantics of sport. Physical activism symbolizes youth – both in sexual behaviour and in sport. It is a matter of performing and improving performance, not because one has to, but because one wants to do so voluntarily. The capacity for improvement in turn requires effort and attentiveness and – as in the case of all physical achievement – training. Achievement is contingent upon spatio-temporal differentiation from what goes on in everyday life. The relationship to the partner has to be 'fair', he has to be given a chance, too. And, as in sport, resorting to a form of physical behaviour that is socially defined as meaningful makes it possible to evade the uncertainties of meaning in all other domains of life.

The equality of the sexes is emphasized nowadays more than ever before, and the considerable differences in the way men and women experience sex therefore do not really come to the fore. This emphasis on equality results, paradoxically, in sexual matters and the semantics of love which reflect it being interpreted after the liking of men. The man's experience of sexuality and his behaviour have the advantage of being the more striking, indeed of being the more spectacular event and of having a clearly visible beginning and end. It is a more suitable focal point for orgasm-oriented forms of therapy. Ideas on how sexually oriented behaviour can be differentiated also seem to take what the man wants and not what the woman desires as their point of departure. When a woman loves, it is said that she loves forever. In the meantime, the man has other things to attend to.

In light of all this, the private sphere, in contrast to social demands, inclines toward differentiation and relaxation (also a 'male' symbol, by the way). What literature or film then pass off in the way of exalted moments to ensure their own survival is consequently no longer bought. Nevertheless, there is still a need for intimacy, for interpersonal interpenetration. Thus there is also a need for prejudices that structure experience, for a cultivated semantics, for form and above all for the capacity to learn. But the points of orientation for the codification of love as a symbolic medium have shifted; and in fact so radically that one can hardly tell whether and which topics of the semantics of love can be adopted and further employed.

The radical nature of this change, compared with the period from 1780 to 1830, for example, is not reflected in the radicalization of topics, in the exaggeration of idealization, of criticism, etc., but rather results from socio-structural developments and in the final instance, amounts to modern society's radicalization of the difference between personal and impersonal relationships. It is not much of an exaggeration to say that this difference can be experienced in *every* social relationship: impersonal relationships are 'only' impersonal relationships. Personal relationships are overburdened by the expectation that one will be in tune with the person, and this often dooms such relationships to failure – which in turn only serves to intensify the quest for them and makes the inadequacy of exclusively impersonal relationships all the more apparent.

In this way, and as never before, the personal/impersonal distinction becomes the *constitutive difference*, i.e. the difference that in the sense of Bateson's definition (a difference that makes a difference) *instils* information with its *informative value*. Without this difference it would not be possible to glean from the other's behaviour information relevant to his intimate sphere; and it would be equally difficult to determine the meaning of one's own actions without orienting oneself towards this difference whenever love (or a semantic equivalent) was supposed to be involved. In other words, at this fundamental level difficulties of *starting off* arise in experiencing as well as in acting, because in situations that are primarily structured by impersonal expectations one has to be able to see an interest in the personal and express this interest without availaing oneself of forms of approach which bear the hallmark of present society (galantry).[17]

This could mean that, contrary to earlier claims, a deeper understanding of love is hardly a suitable guide nowadays to entering into or warming to an intimate relationship. Notions based on exchange that have been blocked out of the code of real love may be more suited to this task,[18] although it is impossible to specify how selflessness and an orientation to the other person could become embedded as a dominant motif in a broader and deeper understanding of exchange. But is such a codification any less plausible than one based on the chance emergence of passion? Moreover, links to Romanticism would not be far removed (albeit to a Romanticism which is only seldom remembered), for that movement had, after all, declared that external gestures can be followed by corresponding feelings.

Other approaches often question how it is even possible to initiate personal communication in public situations and given the brevity of contact which is to be expected in such cases. The ability to talk about oneself appears to be the prerequisite for beginning an intimate relationship; it stimulates the addressee to talk about himself as well. The inclination to do this may depend to a large extent on psychological factors; but its realization depends on social situations. Moreover, the code of love defines an exclusive relationship, and as a consequence one only recognizes an attempt at love if elements suggesting that others are being excluded are also communicated in the process. Precisely this, however, is virtually impossible in an impersonal, public setting; for whoever switches over to the communication of personal or even intimate matters at the normal pace of conversation shows that he will do this habitually, so to speak, and with anyone.[19] In such circumstances a sensual, sexual accentuation of one's interest may facilitate making contact; in any case, even in public situations, it invariably signals a certain exclusivity with regard to the willingness to make contact.

It is also necessary to clarify the shape semantic formulations that claim validity and permanence would take in a contemporary setting. The constitutive traditional differences (sensual/non-sensual love and *plaisir/amour* that covered this over)[20] were strongly influenced in the semantics of love by general societal values – be it in the form of idealization, or in that of paradoxicalization. However, these general values thus bestowed greater informative value on the constitutive difference with which this could then build up themes and points of orientation in the area of personal affection. The constitutive difference was equally an informative difference. This has changed. Hardly any directives for the codification of the intimate domain can be inferred from the personal/impersonal difference – but perhaps the current unclear situation is misleading. On the one hand, it is *universally* relevant and not restricted to the classical triad of young/beautiful/rich. In principle it is valid for *all* conceivable situations, to the extent that one can view them from the vantage point of interpersonal interpenetration. However, this is precisely why the difference does not yet indicate either the form in which social systems for the intimate domain based on it may emerge, or which of the mutually accepted rules will apply. An answer to *this cannot also* be found to lie in the application of the constitutive difference, i.e. cannot also be found to be totally individual and personal, for the difference in and of itself does not ensure the

availability of an option of intimacy in concrete situations, but
instead makes this more difficult.

The same change can be observed in a second case, which can
be formulated as a *trivialization of the self*. Love is no longer
reserved for a few great lovers, nor is it oriented any longer
toward the example they set. Romanticism and the Romantics
themselves had tried their hand at making the 'ideal' work for the
last time in literature and life; they had lived and suffered with it
in the reciprocal relationships of conception and reality and of
man and woman. But one cannot possibly expect everyone to do
so, not even within a particular class of society. Universalization
requires that the self be accessible to anyone as the basis for
intimacy. This is what was meant by the concept of the subject in
transcendental philosophy, and early Romanticism still oriented
itself towards such a concept. 'The highest task of education is to
be at one and the same time the master of one's transcendental
Self and to be the Self of one's Self,' as Novalis puts it.[21] However,
the transcendental idea becomes deformed as something idealistic
when transposed onto a thoroughly empirical love and marriage.
It fails to allow for precisely what it claims to entail, namely, the
formation of individuality. A recognition of the single-mindedness
of true individuality – or at least of every real individual, which
includes failures! – has to assert itself against the culture of
individuality. Both what a person expects in terms of recognition
for his Self within personal relationships, and what he wishes to
realize in terms of being able to speak freely about himself, do
not involve something ideal, but rather something factual. In
other words, they centre not on the portrayal of humanity from a
particular point of view, but rather on what has somehow come
together to form a life – a life that wishes to be understood. The
problem is how such different things can still form a unity, and
not how this should as a 'whole' provide the 'meaning of life'; and
today the ego's Self is no longer called the transcendental Self,
but rather identity.[22] The concept does not have a logical, but
rather a symbolic relevancy, in that it proves that in a society
characterized by predominantly impersonal relationships it has
grown difficult to find the point at which one can experience
oneself as a unity and function as a unity. The ego's Self is not the
objectivity of subjectivity in the transcendental-theoretical sense.
The ego's Self is the result of self-selective processes; and this is

precisely why it is also dependent upon others for its being
selected by others. The problem now is not enhancement, but
selection from among one's own adaptive capacities.

Accordingly, what one is looking for in love, in intimate
relationships, is first and foremost *the validation of self-portrayal.*[23]
It is not so much a question of the lover's overestimating or even
idealizing the beloved. The beloved, who feels continuously called
upon to be better and continuously experiences the discrepancy
between this and reality, tends to find this rather unpleasant, at
least in the long run. If self-portrayal as the 'formation' of one's
own individuality is freed from social control, i.e. is made
somehow contingent, it in particular will need a social foundation.
The threshold of consciousness – the point at which one registers
one's own 'self-presentation in everyday life'[24] – is considerably
lowered under modern living conditions. In such cases, one is
particularly dependent on the tact of others who are indifferent
enough not to pick up on the discrepancies between being and
semblance – or on someone who believes in the unity of being
and semblance or at least makes this the subject of his own self-
portrayal, which one must in turn believe in.

This affirmation of self-portrayal, even if arbitrarily selected,
has to be learned and practised while paving the way for intimate
relationships. But can this task be standardized in the form of a
behavioural code? This, in any case, would have the effect of
resurrecting the form taken by paradoxical constitution. Love
would again have to be provided for as a unity of illusion and
reality, while at the same time being offered as a credible example
of how to live one's life. Regardless of how observers may choose
to see it, it is difficult to accept that lovers lack credibility
towards themselves and each other, precisely because they love
one another.

If the question of the validation focuses solely on self-portrayal,
then the semantics of love has to be adapted to suit this. The
change affects above all the *primary symbolism of the
differentiation of intimate relationships,* and it shifts the position
taken by elements of the 'against what' and the 'for what' that are
also intended as part of the semantics. This is where the concept
of *passion* fails, for it had the purpose of warding off attempts by
family and society to exercise controls, by emphasizing the
irrational, even pathological lack of responsibility for one's own

feelings and actions. Ardour and exaltation are however now no longer necessary and are replaced by a principle which is difficult to pinpoint, and which attempts to express that the *lover himself is the source of his love*, this also being what spontaneity must now mean. Love should not wait for an inquiry before making itself known; it must pre-empt every wish and question so as not to seem like a duty or a conciliatory gesture.[25] Love must now allow itself to be provoked. Its actions should not be reactive, but 'proactive'. This is the only manner in which it can react to the beloved's inner experience as well as to his actions and view of the world, and can move freely about in an as yet undefined situation. This is the only way in which the lover can preserve his own freedom and self-determination, by anticipating the wishes of the person who is the centre of his attention. And then the paradox of voluntary submission, of wanting to stay in chains, is also lifted, and one sees what is most important in everyday life: being able to act as the Self of one's own ego, as the source of one's own love.

In keeping with this pattern, as opposed to the reflexive thought of a long history of literature,[26] the importance of *sincerity* in communication among lovers is again being emphasized more strongly.[27] On the one hand, more is demanded than sincerity alone with regard to the difference of 'true love' and mere seduction; on the other, a simple and easily-prescribed principle is involved, which brushes aside 300 years of insight into the indissoluble connection of sincerity and insincerity entailed in human existence and the development of love.[28] Quite apart from the question of whether he whom one loves would even allow one to tell him everything one had to say: should one be sincere, even in cases where the moods are in a state of constant change? Should the other person be hooked up to one's own temperature like a thermometer?[29] Above all, however: how is one supposed to be sincere toward someone who is not sincere towards himself? And, after all, is not every existence an unfounded projection, a draft that requires supports and buffer zones based on insincerity? Can one communicate one's own sincerity at all, without becoming insincere by so very doing?

The influence of therapists on morals (and of morals on the therapists) is difficult to estimate, but it is surely to be feared: unstable health, i.e. the constitution of a person in need of a cure, takes the place of love and the only notion of love then developed is that of a reciprocal long-term therapy on the basis of an insincere understanding that has been reached with regard to sincerity.

But then, one is forced to ask, what can love possibly be if it is supposed to give every individual a chance to identify with himself and to be the Self of his ego? It may seem as if the steady decrease in the ideals expected of the other (which also means doing without all surrogate ideologies such as 'growth of personality', etc.)[30] would make it easier to solve the problem. The truth of the matter thus deprives the semantics of love of something that had been an indispensable help for its formulation, namely, the process of exaggerating things to the point where they became either ideal or paradoxical. At the level of cultivated semantics this used to be the form in which the manifold was formulated and systematized as a unity, thus making it capable of being handed down from generation to generation. A surrogate principle is nowhere in sight. It may therefore be that relaxing the demands made with respect to everyday life and trivial matters enhances the improbability of these demands being fulfilled, since no form can then be found for them.

Nevertheless, the traditional semantics of instability and of love-induced suffering can at least still be used – as a point from which a problem can be formulated. The code of *amour passion*, as shown above, differentiated itself off from marriage and captured the inner impossibility of love as both excess and finiteness. Modern theories also apparently follow this lead when they ascertain symptoms of impossibility attached to love. Ties, for example, are seen by psychotherapist Dieter Wyss as being self-destructive.[31] But the outcome of all this for a society which attempts to bring love and marriage together is judged not to be the untimely end of both, but rather *the need for the partners to learn*. In light of the dynamics of dissolution which inheres in all the forms ties take, loving as a problem of *preserving* the improbable becomes something conscious – and is thus rendered viable for marriage. The act of preserving means preserving improbable chances of communication, for which a general, socio-structurally given need is assumed to exist. The singularity of the other person, whom one loves and has in mind when experiencing the world and acting, is absorbed into one's own sense of life as the result of a *processing of disappointments*. This is particularly true of those respects in which he is different from oneself; also different than one would wish him to be; and finally, different to the way he would be if his characteristic features were ideally stylized.

In light of all this one could assume that the codification of intimacy will develop in the direction of a programme of understanding. In principle, the concept of understanding postulates two things:

1 the incorporation of the *environment* and *environmental relationships* of an observed system into the observation, so that simultaneously one can become acquainted with the observed person's source of inner experience and the aim of his actions

2 the incorporation of *information* and *information processing*, i.e. the incorporation of the contingencies and comparative schemes, with reference to which messages in the observed system are then experienced and treated as selections.

And all this involves postulating

3 the incorporation of the necessities for self-portrayal, and the internal facilities used for such a purpose, into what goes to make up the object of understanding.

Understanding in this sense is also a quasi-impossibility, an ideal entity that can only be approached by means of approximations. And this is particularly true of the demand that one be prepared to act in accordance with the standards set by an understanding inner experience. The reconstruction of the code in terms of understanding would not cause a limitation of the framework of demand or a compromise with the realities at hand. If taken to the extreme, understanding is just as improbable as is rebirth in the other person, '*soumission*', or permanent excess. Such a turn taken within the code can only mean that a semantics which demands the improbable is being adapted to changed conditions of plausibility.

This suggests that there may be some reason for believing that idealization and paradoxicalization as code forms could be replaced by problem orientation. Totalizing regulations lead to problems that can be pinpointed exactly and, above all, expected, and which are neither simply ignored by referring to the ideal, nor adequately formulated as a paradox. Thus the imperative that one allow oneself to become involved in the other's view of the world gives rise to the question of whether one should also adopt, recognize and confirm unfounded fears, self-damaging views and life-endangering habits. Psychological acuity in everyday life and modern sensibility put this question firmly at the centre of the love ethic. And precisely if one sympathizes – very closely and on the basis of intimate knowledge – with how the other seeks a symbiosis with 'his' environment which in turn has a negative feedback on him – it is here, above all, that love calls out for affirmation and contradiction at one and the same time. Passion comes to an end; the ideal leads to disappointment; the problem is never solved. An advantage of problem orientation is that it assigns the lovers the task of demonstrating their love in the way they tackle the problem – painfully devoid of hope and yet lovingly. This theme of self-destructive attitudes is new, and is absent from the traditional semantics of love, which only had the purpose of treating characteristics and attitudes of people toward each other, and it may very well be that this and not the traditional paradoxes is the point at which the impossibility of love – can be negated.

Against this background one can interpret the tendency to reject the idea of getting married in favour of simply living together. This can be seen as the expression of a kind of over-determined scepticism which stems from knowing the problems and taking them seriously. Not getting married lends expression to a certain reservation – and in such a way that the rejection of the binding symbol, marriage, at the same time allows one to avoid symbolizing the reservation which had led to rejection. This rejection of form in favour of free love was already being voiced in novels written in the second half of the eighteenth century. And the occasional figure of a generous and under-standing uncle who allowed his nephew to bring along 'his affair' has long been established. Nowadays, in any case, such terminology would no longer be suited to a correct description of the facts. 'Living together' has gained social recognition. What is so surprising about this is not the fact as such, but instead that recognition is granted without any adoption whatsoever of generalized symbolic ties and without any kind of obligations being expected. Is the interest in personal relationships in itself considered strong enough? Or is choosing an 'alternative' already sufficient legitimation?

Finally, in view of the primary difference of personal and impersonal relationships, the problem of codification also acquires a semantic form which disconnects itself from tradition's attempts to define it. Codification is a kind of semantic duplication of views that further the acquisition and processing of information. Based on the idealization of the subject of love one was only able to think in terms of perfection and privation, but not in those of a bivalent codification in the strict sense.[32] The code's transformation to accord with the principle of *amour passion* provides better points of adaption. Owing to the unquestioning nature of *plaisir*, the capacities for sincere and insincere love then went their separate ways, in relation to access to the very last favour. Romanticism subjectivized the problem in the reflexive bivalency of surrendering and preserving oneself at the same time. In order to make such dualities possible, the unity of the code in both cases was couched in the form of a paradoxy by means of statements such as 'confinement' or 'deliberate passion'. As one can see, exceptional semantic performances strewn with many problems arise once an attempt is made to put them into practice in everyday life.

Once society has laid down the structural guidelines for this contradictory interest in impersonal and personal relationships, the problem of codifying intimacy becomes much easier to solve. This means that the semantics of love can be simplified, even trivialized; but it does not mean, of course, that loving as such becomes easier. The code now calls for a universal bivalency of all events guided by the distinction between the personal and the impersonal. Love is necessary for this as the differentiation of a referent with regard to whom the world can then be assigned a value other than that of being normal; and in the eyes of whom the lover himself can also be someone not normal. Naturally, the reality of worldly things is not duplicated, but only the world itself. The duality remains a semantic artefact. It constitutes a double typology of adaptive capacities in all forms of experience and action from the vantage point of anonymous validity, on the one hand, and from the viewpoint of the person one loves, on the other.

   In retrospect, the esoterics of passionate love appear to have been a kind of transitional semantics that attempted to devise a binary code for intimate relationships without having an adequate anchorage in the structures of the social system. Thus, in a not so strongly impersonal society where dominant stratification still persisted, it was possible to learn with the guidance of literature to allow oneself to become totally involved in the person of one's choice and to live in him on his terms; at first both occasionally and outside of marriage, and then even within the framework of institutional ties. The semantics had to try and create the motifs for this on its own, so to speak; accordingly, it swung back and forth between beauty and virtue, on the one hand, and 'animal' sensuality on the other. Today's society may perhaps be more accommodating as far as motivating the construction of a purely personal world is concerned, but one is also probably only just beginning to discover how improbable this is.

16

Love as a System of Interpenetration

Having devoted so much space to describing the morphological changes in the semantics of love, we shall now summarize them from the point of view of systems theory. Intimate relationships are social systems which are expected, particularly by the participants, to do complete justice to the views and needs of those involved. The function and meaning ascribed to such social systems therefore direct our attention to the systems of individual persons. Intimate relationships have to do justice to what the person expects of them, or else, as a social system, they run into difficulties. This interconnection of personal expectation and threat to social cohesion is defused by the insistence on pair relationships: this is the function of the code's prescription that one can only love one person at one and the same time.

Referred thus to the individual's personal system, we must inquire what relevance intimacy has for relations of the individual person to system and environment. In this context a distinction is important that has a great significance in more complex societies with extensively differentiated systemic relations. One must distinguish between the relations of a system to its *environment* and the relations of the system to *individual systems in its environment*. The system's environment is a unity (regardless of how this is subdivided) by virtue of the system, whereas the subsystems within the system's environment themselves generate their own respective unity. Everything which the system cannot dispose over in the form of self-referential reproduction belongs to the environment, which, of course, therefore includes all other systems as well. Other systems are, however, also (and in contradistinction to the environment as a whole) marked off by their own forms of self-referential reproduction. For the system, 'its environment' is the abstract Other; other systems, in contrast, are Others determined by themselves.

This difference is itself the result of evolution. It is heightened in different systems to differing extents by the fact that a distance develops between systems and their environments, that systems find other systems in their environments, and by the fact that this occurs with reference to an increasing number of increasingly distinct other systems, with the effect that individual systems are no longer representative of the environment. One can assume that it was initially religion which managed to bridge this difference and hold it together. It realized a system in the environment of other systems, a system which could interpret the world for the other systems. Its symbol – God – meant 'one and all', which is what it claimed to achieve. This function of world representation by one system in the environment of other systems is affected by the Reformation and by transformations in the societal system that were even more far-reaching during the sixteenth and seventeenth centuries. The differentiation of a code for intimate relations can be seen as a concomitant and complementary occurrence. This does not mean that love takes the place of religion (although on occasions there were outbreaks which claimed to do precisely this). In functionally differentiated societies functional areas can only develop by substituting themselves for themselves, i.e. religion can only be replaced by religion. But if instead of substitution the position remains empty, i.e. if no one system *in* the environment represents *the whole* environment, then special problems arise for all the functional areas.

Unique solutions to this difficulty are sought in the area of intimate relationships. The copying of religious forms fades into the background. In the case of pair relationships, after all, it is not very easy to leave the task of representing the world up to the other person, although concepts in the code such as (absolute) submission and conquest had at first seemed to suggest this was possible. To aim at such a unity of the world and the pair relationship leads, as we have seen, to paradoxy. All that is available to the nineteenth century, after the rejection of a copying of religious forms, is copying as an activity in itself. The absolute becomes a gesture. The unattainable becomes symbolized by the dandy, the clown and the street urchin.[1] The only possible response to this is to break with tradition. The lovers' conduct is no longer patterned on novels, but rather on psychotherapy.

However, the *difference* between one's own environment and other systems in one's environment can be seen if grasped in sufficiently abstract terms to be linked back to tradition and to contain new perspectives. The problem of this *difference* becomes a problem of the social system that has developed by means of intimate relationships. The system no longer depends on qualities, virtues or the harmony of characters; what is important is the other person in my environment who bestows meaning upon my world, but can only do so if I accept him and his environment as my own. 'Reciprocity of perspective' is also far too simple a formula to describe this and focuses too much on the reciprocal thematization of the persons involved. Rather, we have to do here with the capacity of a social system for acquiring and processing information, in which each piece of information is supposed to affirm the unity of the common world, and thus in which the difference can blossom forth in each piece of information. 'My wallet has disappeared' – the first time this happens it is excusable, but is it, the second or third time round? And will there not come a time when one of the two will suspect that the other person views the information differently?

We replaced the notion of reciprocity of perspective with the (much richer and much more demanding) concept of inter-personal interpenetration. This has various consequences for the topic of love, each of which leads in a different direction. Most importantly, the imagery of a fusion of two hearts is cancelled out and replaced.[2] Interpenetration does not fuse different systems into a unity. It is no *unio mystica*. It functions only at the operational level of a reproduction of elements, in this case the units of occurrence embodied by inner experience and action. Every operation, every action and every observation with which one system reproduces sequences of events thus also occurs in the other. Each operation has to be aware of the fact that, as an action of the one system, it is at the same time the inner experience of the other, and this is not only an external identification, but rather the very condition of the reproduction of such action. One can only act in love in such a manner that one can live with what the other person experiences inside. Actions must be inserted into the world of the other person's inner experience, and reproduced out of it; and they must not lose their freedom, their self-chosenness and the expressive value they lend to lasting inclinations in the process. They must precisely not appear as submission, docility, acquiescence or as an attempt to avoid conflict. No love can be satisfied with an 'oh, all right'. It demands that only he who loves can act in a loving manner.

Acting out of love, in other words, does not mean conforming, and does not only want to please or to fulfil wishes. The terminology of *soumission* and *complaisance* is no longer adequate in this context, if indeed it ever was. What is important is to find meaning in the world of someone else. As this world can never be problematical, so, too, the meaning affirming it can also never be unproblematical. This meaning may oppose the moods or spirits of the other person. It may transform the world of the beloved by its presence. It has to run the risk of winding up not knowing what is good for the other person and *nevertheless* holding on to love.

As the basis for interpretation and action, love orients itself towards the world of another system; in other words, in its consummation it changes what it observes. Love cannot distance itself, but makes itself part of its 'object'. Its object does not stay put, for it absorbs the operation and as a consequence changes. The being experienced by the other becomes a component of operative reproduction. Self-reproduction and external reproduction remain divided according to systemic context, and yet are nevertheless consummated *uno actu*.

That is, if and as long as the interpenetrative relationship guides inner experience and action. Each partner can, of course, attempt to disengage himself or herself from this; but even such disengagement occurs within the synchronization of the intimate relationship. This was demonstrated taking the example of the termination of a love affair, and what appeared at first sight to be a strange conclusion, namely, that the person who is still in love has to declare the love to be terminated. The Marquise de M. was able to; Ellenore was not.[3]

All communication within intimate relationships is subject to the incommunicabilities which it itself constitutes. We found this to be the insight discovered and covered up in the eighteenth century.[4] This can also be clarified with the aid of the concept of interpenetration. Under conditions of interpenetration each action consists of two parts: on the one hand, what it intends, and, on the other, what it signifies for attribution processes. This also forms the basis of the famous double-bind theory.[5] Prospects of lastingness can only be anchored at the level arrived at by attribution; communication remains negatable. Thus, this difference can never be compounded in one act of love, or rather this is always possible, but only from the eternal perspective of the moment. Every utterance separates the speaker from what he has said, thus destroying innocence in the process. Part of love must involve respecting this fact. The only other choice is to attempt to force insincerity, if not schizophrenia into existence.

Interpenetration should also be understood to mean lovers conceding each other the right to their own world and refraining from integrating everything into a totality. The *universality* of the significative reference of love does not need to grasp *all* topical inner experience and action; indeed, it cannot do so. Just as is the case with the significative reference of religion or law, nothing is by nature irrelevant, and yet there is no compulsion to take every step in line with the code. Only if it is dispensed with can universality in the strict meaning of the word be achieved. Only somebody who still thinks nowadays in terms of novels and Romanticism will be surprised to find out that lovers do not accord much significance to the topos of 'shared activities', 'shared values and goals'.[6] If this could be substantiated, then one would have a basis for claiming that the real emotions and thoughts on love are more mature than traditional semantics prescribe.

It is not nearly as far-fetched as it might seem to try to escape from the demands love makes that cannot be fulfilled into the haven of monotony, i.e. to attempt to curb the inflow of information.[7] But this also means dispensing with any optimization of the function of love, dispensing with the capacity for complete affirmation of one's own world by means of the other. Prescriptions of this or some other sort can have varying results. If one leaves this aside, then what remains is the thesis of a differentiated social system with improbable structures and improbable functions. To reiterate: each piece of information which is taken up in this system and processed tests the compatability of the environments (whereby each participant belongs to the environment of the other and is thus also tested). The system collapses (even if the partners remain 'together') when this ceases to be the common basis that reproduces the system by giving all information the function of reproducing the system. This is the counterpart in systems theory to a code which requires that in the course of interaction one tunes oneself in, through one's actions, to the inner experience of the other person. The unity of the code postulates the unity of the social system of intimate relationships, and the unity of this system is the unity of difference, which forms the basis of its information processing. One cannot 'found' anything on 'difference'. There is thus, as has always been maintained, no basis for love.

If one postulates the existence of functionally specific, differentiated self-referential social systems as intimate relationships between two people and if one understands intimacy as interpenetration, then one can probe retrospectively whether and in what ways the semantic tradition of *amour passion* and Romantic love provided points of orientation for this. With regard to the total stock of the traditional semantics of love, one can dispense with both the exaggerated paradoxicalizations and the significative elements of passion and excessiveness which were meant, above all, to legitimate differentiation. What remains indispensable, however, is the neo-humanist, Romantic concept of a worldly individual who constitutes his or her own world. The notion of self-reference, of love for love's sake, is equally indispensable, for this prescribes that, in the area of intimacy, systems themselves have to produce those conditions which are necessary if they are to come about and be reproduced. This is a continuation of the old notion that love lays down its own laws, not abstractly, but concretely in each case, and only with validity for that case.[8] What will have to be conceded more radically than ever before is that love itself cancels out all the characteristics which could have served as a basis and a motive for it. Every attempt to 'see through' the other person ends up in empty space, in the unity of true and false, of sincere and insincere, a vacuum for which there are no criteria of judgement. Therefore, it is not possible to say everything. Transparency only exists in the *relationship* of system and system, and by virtue, so to speak, of the difference of system and environment, which constitutes the system in the first place. Love and love alone can be such transparency:

> A face in front of
> one
> neither now any more sub-ject
> only reference
> intangible
> and fixed.
>
> (Friedrich Rudolf Hohl)

Notes

PREFACE TO THE ENGLISH EDITION

1 Stuttgart, as of 1972.
2 Cf. also Reinhart Koselleck (ed.), *Historische Semantik und Begriffsgeschichte,* (Stuttgart, 1978); and *Vergangene Zukunft: Zur Semantik geschichtlicher Zeiten,* (Frankfurt, 1979), or Wolf-Hagen Krauth, *Wirtschaftsstruktur und Semantik: Wissenschaftssoziologische Studien zum wirtschaftlichen Denken in Deutschland zwischen dem 13, und 17, Jahrhundert,* (Berlin, 1984); for other case studies, see Niklas Luhmann, *Gesellschaftsstruktur und Semantik,* 2 vols., (Frankfurt, 1980—1).
3 A recent work which is particularly important for the problems touched on here: Jürgen Habermas, *Der philosophische Diskurs der Modern: Zwölf Vorlesungen,* (Frankfurt, 1985).
4 For a closer look at a projected general sociological theory in this connection, see Niklas Luhmann, *Soziale Systeme: Grundriß einer allgemeinen Theorie,* (Frankfurt, 1984).
5 See particularly Humberto R. Maturana and Fransisco J. Varela, *Autopoiesis and Cognition: The Realization of the Living,* (Dordrecht 1980); Heinz von Foerster, *Observing Systems* (Note the ambiguity in the title!), (Seaside Calif., 1981).
6 *Laws of Form,* 2nd ed., (London 1971), p. 3.
7 From the standpoint of systems theory, this is an application of the concept of autopoiesis. For sketches that develop this further cf. Niklas Luhmann, *Politische Theorie im Wohlfahrtsstaat,* (Munich, 1981); also, 'Die Einheit des Rechssystems', in *Rechstheorie,* 14 (1983), pp. 129—54; *A Sociological Theory of Law,* (London, 1985), p. 281ff.; 'Die Wirtschaft der Gesellschaft als autopoietisches System', in *Zeitschrift für Soziologie,* 13 (1984), pp. 308—27.
8 For a critical discussion of Parsons see Niklas Luhmann, 'Generalized Media and the Problem of Contingency', in Jan J. Loubser et al. (eds), *Explorations in General Theory in Social*

Science: Essays in Honor of Talcott Parsons, (New York, 1976), vol. II, pp. 507—32.

9 As shown in the present study, this can also come about because precisely these problems are reflected in the semantics of the medium, i.e. for example, one falls in love with one's own illusions about the other person.

10 See also Niklas Luhmann, *Trust and Power,* (Chichester, 1979), especially p. 48ff.

INTRODUCTION

1 Gesellschaftsstruktur und Semantik, 2 vols., (Frankfurt, 1980—1).

1 SOCIETY AND INDIVIDUAL

1 Translators' note: we have followed the German original and used 'him' as the pronoun for 'individual' or 'person' except where the author used the German female case *die,* signifying explicitly that a woman was referred to. We would like to take this opportunity to extend our sincere thanks to Professor Luhmann for his careful and critical reading of our draft translation. Without his helpful comments the text would no doubt not have been as accurate to the original as we hope it now is.

2 See, for example, Emile Durkheim's famous concluding remarks in *De la division du trevail social. Etude sur l'organisation des sociétés supérieres,* (Paris, 1893), English translation *On the Division of Labor in Society* (New York, 1933); and also his *Leçons de sociologie: Physique des moeurs et du droit,* (Paris, 1950), English translation *Professional Ethics and Civil Morals,* (London, 1957); Georg Simmel, *Grundfragen der Soziologie (Individuum und Gesellschaft),* (Berlin/Leipzig, 1917), p. 71ff; Louis Dumont, *Homo Hierarchicus: The Caste System and Its Implications,* (London, 1970). For the much discussed semantic developments that ran parallel to this see also Norman Nelson, 'Individualism as a Criterion of the Rnaissance', *Journal of English and Germanic Philology,* 32 (1933), pp. 316—34; Angel Sanchez de la Torre, *Los comienzos del subjectivismo juridico en la cultura Europea,* (Mardid, 1958); Colin Morris, *The Discovery of the Individual 1050—1200,* (London, 1972).

3 The extent to which social ties and controls exist that influence the individual is a quite separate issue. In this context there is a wide

range of freedom in some societies from regulation, without one being able to interpret this as a recognition or a demand for individuality. See, in particular, John F. Embree, 'Thailand — A Loosely Structured Social System', *American Anthropologist,* 52 (1950), pp. 181—93; and, taking this theme up, Hans-Dieter Evers (ed.), *Loosely Structured Social Systems: Thailand in Comparative Perspective,* (New Haven, 1969).

4 See, for example, François de Callieres, *La Logique des amans ou l'amour logicien,* (Paris, 1668), p. 118: 'L'individu est proprement un sujet separé de tout autre, et qui ne se peut diviser sans estre destruit.'

5 This has, amongst other things, the following significance for a concept of individuality. The old direction of specification: being → human being → member of a class → inhabitant of a town or country → member of a profession → member of a family → individual, loses its meaning. Rather, it is individuality, one of the most conrete characteristics of man, that now becomes the most general. What had in past times to be viewed as highly contingent must accordingly now be conceived of as a necessity and characterized by its reference to the world. Yet, this new concept, this definition of the individual as *uniquely constituting the world,* suspends the notion of the individual as *nature* that was valid until approximately 1800.

2 LOVE AS A GENERALIZED SYMBOLIC MEDIUM OF COMMUNICATION

1 See, for greater detail, Niklas Luhmann, 'Einführende Bemerkungen zu einer Theorie symbolisch generalisierter Kommunikationsmedien', in Luhmann, *Soziologische Aufklärung,* vol. 2. (Opladen, 1975), pp. 170—92; Luhmann, *Macht,* (Stuttgart, 1975); Luhmann, 'Die Unwahrscheinlichkeit der Kommunikation', in Luhmann, *Soziologische Aufklärung,* vol. 3, (Opladen, 1981), pp. 25—34.

2 All these descriptions are of course limited in applicability, for they refer to the enhancement of an adaptive capacity in a very specific sense. This by no means excludes the event of that capacity becoming possible for other reasons and/or indeed its evolution breaking down for other reasons.

3 Michel de Montaigne, *Essais,* vol. I, 28, quoted from the 1950 Paris edition, p. 224.

4 Talcott Parsons in his 'Religion in Postindustrial America: The Problem of Secularization', *Social Research,* 41 (1974), pp. 193—225,

states that affects and/or love 'in my present sense is a *medium* of interchange and not the primary bond of solidarity itself'. Other sociologists also treat the semantics of love as a 'cultural imperative' and/or as an ideological prescription. See Willard Waller and Reuben Hill, *The Family: A Dynamic Interpretation,* 2nd edition, (New York, 1951), p. 113; William J. Goode, *The Family* (Englewood Cliffs, NJ, 1964).

5 'Il y a des gens qui n'auraient jamais été amoureux s'ils n'avaient entendu parler de l'amour,' one can read in La Rochefoucauld's 'Réflexions ou sentences et maximes morales', no. 136, quoted from his *OEuvres complètes,* (Paris, 1964), p. 421. Even in the eighteenth century precisely this element of a prior, equally playful learning of love is retained, despite the personal and individual ethos of love. This experience of play within the world-transforming discovery of the partner is in clear evidence in Klopstock's work, e.g. 'Der Verwandelte' ('Dich zu finden, ach Dich, lernt ich die Liebe'). quoted from *Ausgewählte Werke,* (Munich, 1962), pp. 66—8; or in his letter to J. A. Schlegel of August 1952: ' . . . daß meine Wahl, nachdem ich die Liebe so lange gelernt habe, auf ein Mädchen fallen müsse, die mich sehr glücklich machen könne . . .,' quoted from *Briefe von und an Klopstock,* ed. J. M. Lappenberg, (Brunswick, 1867), p. 108f. Clearly no contradiction was felt to exist between prior mental practice and the enthusiasm of involvement.

6 A formulation of Georg Simmel's, from his 'Über die Liebe (Fragment)', in *Fragmente und Aufsätze,* (Munich, 1923), pp. 47—123, (p. 62).

7 Dieter Wyss develops this concept in *Lieben als Lernprozeß,* (Göttingen, 1975), p. 42f., p. 46, and then demands that it be broken with by means of learning processes. Pascal Bruckner and Alain Finkielkraut are also sceptical of the chances of today's lovers in their *Le Nouveau Désordre amoureux,* (Paris, 1977), p. 140ff.

8 For the conceptual framework used here see Luhmann, 'Erleben und Handeln' and 'Schematismen der Interaktion' in Luhmann, *Soziologische Aufklärung,* vol. 3, (Opladen, 1981), pp. 67—80 and 81—100.

9 To facilitate comparison with other media complexes, see the frequently used table given below, which projects the double attribution capacities of inner experience and/or action onto the position of alter and ego, whereby ego is always the one who has to accept or reject such communicative selections.

	Ego experiences	*Ego acts*
Alter experiences	$A_e \longrightarrow E_e$ truth value relations	$A_e \longrightarrow E_q$ love
Alter acts	$A_a \longrightarrow E_e$ property/money art	$A_a \longrightarrow E_a$ power/law

10 To be distinguished from the self-references within the observing, loved person, a distinction to which we shall return shortly.

11 'Liebe ist das gasprächigste aller Gefihle und besteht zum groben Teilganz and Gesprächigkeit', Robert Musil notes in his *Der Mann ohne Eigenschaften*, (Hamburg, 1952, reprinted 1968), p. 1130, (English translation; *Man Without Qualities*, London, 1979).

12 Of course, these always remained analogies or metaphors. Only the Middle Ages and the second half of the nineteenth century were naive enough and trusted sufficiently in science to presume that actual psychosomatic pathological properties were involved. See, for a critical view of this Gaston Danville, 'L'Amour est-il un état pathologique?', in *Revue philosophique*, 18 (1893), pp. 261—83; and Danville, *La Psychologie de l'amour*, (Paris, 1894), p. 107ff. Even nowadays empirical research still exists that concentrates on affirming or disproving the connections between Romantic love and emotional immaturity, for example, see Dwight G. Dean 'Romanticism and Emotional Maturity: A Preliminary Study', in *Marriage and Family Living*, 23 (1961), pp. 44—5; and his, 'Romanticism and Emotional Maturity: A Further Exploration', in *Social Forces*, 42 (1964), pp. 298—303; William M. Kephart, 'The "Dysfunctional" Theory of Romantic Love: A Research Report', in *Journal of Comparative Family Studies*, I (1970), pp. 26—36.

13 See Robert Mauzi, *L'idée du bonheur dans la littérature et la pensée française au XVIIIe siècle*, (Paris, 1960, 4th edition, 1969), p. 466 for a summary of eighteenth-century notions: 'L'amour est un mystère, le plus irrationnel des mouvements de l'âme, devant lequel l'esprit demeure désarmé; il est une mystification, où l'imagination ne cesse d'escamoter et de métamorphoser la nature; il est une aliénation, qui sépare l'homme de lui-même et le voue à toutes les tortures; enfin l'amour ne suffit jamais à lui-même.' The same theme from a modern viewpoint is treated in Francis E. Merrill, *Courtship and Marriage: A Study in Social Relationships*, (New York, 1949), p. 23ff.; Waller and Hill, *The Family*, p. 113ff.;

Vilhelm Aubert, 'A Note on Love', in his *The Hidden Society,* (Totowa NJ, 1965), pp. 201—35.

14 See the interpretation of the role of patients and their institutionalization in Talcott Parsons, *The Social System,* (Glencoe III., 1951), particularly p. 428ff.

15 See for a general overview Luhmann, 'Symbiotische Mechanismen', in *Soziologische Aufklärung,* vol. 3, (Opladen, 1981), pp. 228—44. Specifically on the eroticism of this see also Parsons, *Societies: Evolutionary and Comparative Perspectives,* (Englewood Cliffs NJ, 1966). p. 31f.

16 Even for communication that contradicts the spoken message. One need only think of the eye-language frequently treated in descriptions of love.

17 On the system of religion and on the symbolic media of 'belief', see Luhmann, *Funktion der Religion,* (Frankfurt, 1977), particularly p. 134ff., and on the lack of a symbolic media specifically for education see Luhmann and Karl Eberhard Schorr, *Reflexionsprobleme im Erziehungssytem,* (Stuttgart, 1979), p. 54ff.

18 Simmel's treatment of the 'erotic' in the fragment 'Über die Liebe', tackles this problem, but without finding a clear conceptual solution to it.

19 See also the discussion of loyalty and thankfulness in Georg Simmel, *Soziologie: Untersuchungen über die Formen der Vergesellschaftung,* 2nd edition, (Munich/Leipzig, 1922), p. 438ff. (p. 444ff.), English translation *On Individuality and Social Forms,* (Chicago, 1973).

20 See on this point Rupprecht Gerds, 'Tabu statt Liebe', in Helmut Kentler et al., *Für eine Revision der Sexualpädagogik,* 3rd edition, (Munich, 1969), pp. 89—113, (p. 108f.).

21 Henry Fielding's *An Apology for the Life of Mrs. Shamela Andrews,* (London, 1741, reprinted Folcroft Pa., 1969) exposes this.

22 Jean Guittan, *Essai sur l'amour humain,* (Paris, 1948), p. 9, speaks with reference to the nineteenth century of a 'sexologie positive'. For an exhaustive study see Michel Foucault, *History of Sexuality,* vol. 1, (London, 1979). Material from the USA is to be found in Sidney Ditzion, *Marriage, Morals and Sex in America: A History of Ideas,* 2nd edition, (New York, 1969).

23 A functional knowledge of this sort does not arise at first in the context of sociological research and theory. That the deferral of enjoyment enables an intensification of love and that love actually consists of hoping for love are both topics that have been debated since the seventeenth century, and knowing this knowledge has not led to a loss of motivation. Love is characterized as something that

deviates from the lovers' notions of it. Despite this awareness of the illusory traits of love, the power of love was nevertheless judged to outweigh it. The lovers also love their illusions, and with reference to sexuality the secret guarantee of this would seem to be that it functions.

24 See, for more detail, pages 79ff, 94ff.

25 We shall see below that the irrationality of this evaluation of the problem and the fact that it cannot be accepted both become less pronounced (but only somewhat).

26 What cannot be overlooked is that universality both has limits and yet creates an inequality of opportunity. This results, after differentiation of a medium, above all from the limits of the semantic expression of sexuality, i.e. from the relative self regulation of the basic mechanism. Clearly, some have it easier than others in this respect, regardless of the semantic codification of their behaviour.

27 'J'avais lu quelques romans, et je me crus amoureux,' reports the hero in Charles Duclos's *Les Confessions du Comte de . . .*, (1741), quoted from the 1970 Lausanne edition, p. 38. The polished elegance of this formulation is noteworthy, in that it only indicates the presence of a common occurrence.

28 Similar problems exist in other common areas that tend towards improbable communication. See, for details on religion, Luhmann, *Funktion der Religion,* (Frankfurt, 1977); for art, Luhmann, 'Ist Kunst codierbar?', in Luhmann, *Soziologische Aufklärung,* vol. 3, (Opladen, 1981), pp. 245—66.

29 On relations at home see Howard Gadlin, 'Private Lives and Public Order: A Critical View of the History of Intimate Relations in the United States', in George Levinger and Harold L. Rausch (eds), *Close Relationships: Perspectives on the Meaning of Intimacy,* (Amherst, 1977), pp. 33—72; David H. Flaherty, *Privacy in Colonial New England,* (Charlottesville Va., 1972), particularly p. 70ff.

30 See in particular Guy E. Swanson, 'The Routinization of Love: Structure and Process in Primary Relations', in Samuel Z. Klausner, *The Quest for Self-Control: Classical Philosophies and Scientific Research,* (New York, 1965), pp. 160—209. See also William J. Goode, 'The Theoretical Importance of Love', in *American Sociological Review,* 24 (1959), pp. 339—64.

31 From this point of view it is not unimportant that uncle-nephew relationships belong to the examples marked off at an early stage by ritualization and which are at the same time, protected. See S. N. Eisenstadt, 'Ritualized Personal Relations', *Man,* 96 (1956), pp. 90—5.

32 See Jean Maisonneuve, *Psycho-sociologie des affinités,* (Paris, 1966), p.322ff, in particular p. 343.

3 THE EVOLUTION OF COMMUNICATIVE CAPACITY

1 In this context see Luhmann, *Gesellschaftsstruktur und Semantik,*
2 vols., (Frankfurt, 1980—1).

2 This quite well-known divergency is to be found not only in
behaviour geared toward observation, but also in partner
relationships in which both people alternately act or observe. See,
for example, the results in table 4.2 (category 7) in Harold H.
Kelley, *Personal Relationships: Their Structures and Processes,*
(New York, 1979), p. 101.

3 See the overview in Lauren G. Wispe, 'Sympathy and Empathy', in
International Encyclopedia of the Social Sciences, vol. 15, (New
York, 1968), pp. 441—7.

4 For remarks on this function of the 'grand world' see Stendhal, *De
l'amour,* (1822, reprinted Paris, 1959), p. 33f. *On Love,* translated by
G. Sale and S. Sale, (London, 1981). See also Christian Garve,
Ueber Gesellschaft und Einsamkeit, vol I, (Breslau, 1797), p. 308ff.

5 *The Sufferings of Young Werther,* (London, 1966), letter of
16 June.

6 'Soins' was the technical term for this in the seventeenth century.
What was an equally developed art was to avoid the occasions that
provided such opportunities. See François Hedelin, Abbé
d'Aubignac, *Les Consiels d'Ariste à Célimène sur les moyens de
conserver sa réputation,* (Paris, 1666).

7 See Kelley, *Personal Relationships,* p. 93ff.

8 The literature of the second half of the seventeenth century inferred
from this that illusion was the main ingredient of love, whereas that
of the first half of the eighteenth century opted for insecurity. This
point in the system would appear to be have been replaced nowadays
by the management of attribution conflicts, to which we shall
return.

9 Kelley, *Personal Relationships.* p. 81, p. 84f., calls this (deviating
from normal usage) a 'double contingency'.

10 See further Harriet B. Braiker and Harold H. Kelley, 'Conflict in
the Development of Close Relationships', in Robert L. Burgess and
Ted L. Huston (eds), *Social Exchange in Developing Relationships,*
(New York, 1979), pp. 135—68.

11 One underestimates this problem if one only points to the positive
functions of conflict (as has been usual in sociology in recent years).
See, for example, John Scanzoni, *Sexual Bargaining: Power Politics
in the American Marriage,* (Englewood Cliffs NJ, 1972), p. 61ff.

(Note also the orientation towards economic and political metaphors and the absence of any deeper analysis of intimacy in 'sociological' descriptions of this type.)

4 THE EVOLUTION OF THE SEMANTICS OF LOVE

1 This is treated extensively in Ruth Kelso, *Doctrine for the Lady of the Renaissance,* (Urbana III., 1956, reprinted 1978), p. 136ff.

2 One can of course always say that it was the problems which were the latent driving force for a revision of the code. But does this get us any further?

3 This interpretation follows the approach taken by Maurice Valenca, *In Praise of Love: An Introduction to the Love-Poetry of the Renaissance,* (New York, 1958).

4 The deep structure of this complex is, for its part, open to changes — predominantly in the last two decades of the seventeenth century. The *suspected motives* are initially radicalized with religious means (above all by the Jansenites), posited as universal and then left in the lurch, so to speak. The *technique of disclosure* adjusted itself to this. Instead of a disclosure of sinfulness and egotism, now (since La Bruyère) it involved disclosing man's mediocrity and the banality of his motives. *Frivolity,* which was able to draw its own security from the insight that all could be disclosed and therefore that frivolous behaviour was sincere, now lost its courageous character and became the last haven from banality, i.e. one could flee banality by pretending it. All this proved to be unnecessary at that point when one was able openly to declare one's loyality to a cultural codification of behaviour (under the influence of the religion in culture). What must also be noted here is that it was not the disclosure of sins, but rather that of the mediocrity of human motives which decisively spotlighted the stratified construction of the social system. Once the bourgeoisie tried to reduce both social strata to the common denominator of banality, the aristocracy could only flee into frivolity.

5 'Une systematisation exclusive et consciente de son instinct sexuel', says Danville in *La Psychologie de l'amour,* (Paris, 1894), p. 63. Th. Ribot in *La Psychologie des sentiments,* (Paris, 1896), p. 244ff. takes a similar view. The decisive turning point in this evolutionary process he holds to be 'l'apparition du choix individuel' (p. 251).

6 In the statement 'Delicacy, we perceive, is like "eggs", "fresh eggs", and "strictly fresh eggs" ' Robert P. Utter and Gwendolyn Needham

in *Pamela's Daughters,* (New York, 1936, reprinted 1972), p. 47 summarize this experience.

7 If one views Stendhal's development from *De l'amour* (1822) to the great novels of later years one can see that this version only gradually became established.

8 See Luhmann, *Gesellschaftstruktur und Semantik,* vol. I, p. 31f.

9 This description comes from Stendhal, *De l'amour* (Fragments divers, no. 105), quoted from Henri Martineau's edition, (Paris, 1959), p. 276. The thought dates back to Edward Young, *Conjectures on Original Composition,* quoted from *The Complete Works,* vol. 2, (London, 1854), pp. 547—86.

10 As in other functional areas, autonomy is only seemingly desired, sought and fought for, or so the semantics assumes when trying to defend love against the intrusion of reason, religion, the family and interests. Seen in socio-structural terms, however, autonomy arises because the type of differentiation adopted by society becomes rearranged into a sort of compulsive sequence. The semantics has to then take this account by utilizing new processes of signification. See, for a parallel problem in the functional area of education, Luhmann and Karl Eberhard Schorr, *Reflexionsprobleme im Erziehungssytem,* (Stuttgart, 1979), p. 46ff.

5 FREEDOM TO LOVE

1 Jean Corbinelli's *Sentimens d'amour, tirez des meilleurs poetes modernes,* 2 vols., (Paris, 1671), a collection of excerpts ordered according to headings, provides a good working summary; see also the somewhat pedantic compilations of *questions d'amour* with responses of Charles Jaulnay, *Questions d'amour ou conversations galantes. Dediées aux belles,* (Paris, 1671). Precisely such second-hand collections demonstrate the interest in codification.

2 See, for instance, Flaminio Nobili, *Trattato dell'Amore Humano,* (1567) with notes in the margins by Torquato Tasso (reprinted, Rome, 1895). On the Middle Ages, (which did not follow Ovid in this respect, a poet otherwise held in high regard — rather the morality of love was emphasized) see also Egidio Gorra, 'La teorica dell'amore e un antico poema francese inedito' in his *Fra Drammi e Poemi,* (Milan, 1900), pp. 199—300, (p. 223ff.).

3 See for late Medieval stylizations, for example, William George Dodd, *Courtly Love in Chaucer and Gower,* (1913, reprinted Gloucester Mass., 1959), particularly p. 78f.

4 For surveys of the individually very heterogeneous sources see

Luigi Tonelli, *L'amore nella poesia e nel pensiero del Rinascimento,*
(Florence, 1933); John Charles Nelson, *Renaissance Theory of*
Love: The Context of Giordano Bruno's Eroici Furori, (New York,
1958). For an example see 'Amor mi sprona in un tempo et affrena',
etc, in Petrarch's Sonnet CLXXVIII, quoted from *Le rime di*
Francesco Petrarca, ed. Giuseppe Salvo Cozzo, (Florence, 1904),
p. 181f.; if one reads Jean de la Fontaine's elegies (OEuvres, vol. 8,
(Paris, 1892), pp. 355—76), one finds nothing substantially new.

5 At any rate, the inversion of the hierarchy of perfection typical for
the seventeenth century, where the apex is no longer salvation but
the sensual fulfilment of love, is to be seen in this last favour. See
also Gorra, 'La teorica dell'amore', p. 219ff.; Nelson, *Renaissance*
Theory of Love, p. 52.

6 Peter Dronke determines that this — and not the usual topoi of
courtly love — is what is actually new about the Medieval
contribution to the semantics of love. See his *Medieval Latin and*
the Rise of the European Love-Lyric, 2 vols., 2nd edition, (Oxford,
1968).

7 A characteristic detail in this context is to be found in Madame de
La Fayette's *Princesse de Clèves.* Love commences with a dance —
admired by all present — that culminates in perfect harmony
although the two partners do not know each other.

8 See on this subject Aristotle's *Nichomachean Ethics,* (Oxford, 1980)
Book Eight which triggered off wide-ranging discussions. The type
of attraction is dosed according to social position, even and precisely
when friendship or love presupposes reciprocal equality or creates
it. One person's attraction is worth more than that of another, so to
speak. And this therefore excludes love alone sufficing for love to
be gained.

9 On this aspect of *amour lointain* see Erich Köhler, *Esprit und*
arkadische Freiheit, (Frankfurt, 1966), p. 86ff. and above all the
differentiating, sociological analysis presented by Herbert Moller,
'The Social Causation of the Courtly Love Complex', in
Comparative Studies in Society and History, I (1959), pp. 137—63.

10 And the French register quite clearly the disadvantages of this
institution: once the controls have been lifted or avoided, one no
longer needs to count on the inner resistance of the lady. But
precisely this was what had been of interest in France. An example
of this comparison, often made, is Saint-Evremond, *Sur les*
comédies, quoted from *OEuvres en prose,* vol. III, (Paris, 1966),
pp. 42—60. There a Spanish lady remarks on French galantry 'Que
d'esprit mal emploié . . . A quoi bon tous ces beaux discours, quand
ils sont ensemble.' See further Pierre Daniel Huet, *Traité de l'origine*
des romans, (Paris, 1670, reprinted Stuttgart, 1966), p. 91f.

11 See the instructions given in Fransesco Sansovino, *Ragionamento d'amore,* (1545), quoted from the edition in Guiseppe Zonta (ed.), *Trattati d'amore del cinquecento,* (Bari, 1912), pp. 151–84, (p. 170ff.).

12 One of the *questions d'amour* in Jaulnay, *Questions d'amour,* p. 42 is aimed at this distinction: 'de seduire une prude precieuse ou de fixer une coquette' (*prude* here means as much as *prudente*).

13 Ibid., p. 68.

14 On p. 29f. above we already specified that this was a general aspect of the development of generalized symbolic, self-referential systematized communicative media.

15 This is described clearly by an instruction to a married lady with reference to freedom and its use and the stimulations for suitors connected with this in François Hedelin, Abbé d'Aubignac, *Les Conseils d'Ariste à Célimène sur les moyens de conserver sa réputation,* (Paris, 1666),

16 We shall return to this point in the treatment of the prehistory of Romantic love. Here the innovation also originates from a situation in which semantics is overdetermined by the convergence of heterogeneous stimulants. See below p. 123f.

17 Louise K. Horowitz, *Love and Languages: A Study of the Classical French Moralist Writers,* (Columbus Ohio, 1977) limits this even more sharply: to the years 1660–80. This does indeed pinpoint the essential, if somewhat blurred defining boundaries. For the simultaneous transformation of interest in the novel, see also Max Freiherr von Waldberg, *Der empfindsame Roman in Frankreich,* vol. 1, (Strasburg, 1906), p. 1ff.

18 See, particularly for the *précieuses* movements in the years 1650–60, Daniel Mornet, *Histoire de la littérature française classique 1660–1700: Ses caractères véritables, ses aspects inconnus,* (Paris, 1940), p. 25ff. A good description of this, set against the background of the changing ethical attitudes at court, is provided by Edouard de Barthelemy, *Les Amis de la Marquise de Sablé,* (Paris, 1865), introduction, pp. 1–72.

19 See 'Interaktion in Oberschichten', in Luhmann, *Gesellschaftsstruktur und Semantik,* vol. I, pp. 72–161, particularly 87f., 96ff.

20 In the late formulation of this shift, at the end of the eighteenth century, we can read: 'Il semble que l'amour ne cherche pas les perfections réelles; on dirait qu'il les craint. Il n'amie que celles qu'il crée, qu'il suppose.' Chamfort, *Maximes et pensées,* quoted from *OEuvres complètes,* vol. I, (Paris, 1824, reprinted Geneva, 1968), pp. 337–449 (416).

21 See, for instance, the exhaustive treatment of reconnaissance strategies in d'Alquié, *La Science et l'école des amans: Ou Nouvelle*

découverte des Moyens infallibles de Triomfer en Amour, 2nd edition, (Amsterdam, 1679) p. 49ff., p. 64ff. This accords with the insight that it is not enough to love to gain love, but that one has to move tactically, bring presents, etc. See René Bary, *L'Esprit de cour ou les conversations galantes,* (Paris, 1662), p. 233ff.

22 'Courage, Messieurs les amants!' comments a listener to the story: Gelaste (Molière?). See *Les Amours de Psyché et de Cupidon,* (Paris, 1669), quoted from the edition in *OEuvres de Jean de la Fontaine,* vol. 8 (Paris, 1982), p. 224ff.

23 *Morale galante ou L'Art de bien aimer,* vol. I, (Paris, 1669), p. 101ff.

24 Ibid., p. 119.

25 Thus the title of Chapter XVII in Stendhal's *De l'amour,* (1822), quoted from the edition by Henri Martineau (Paris, 1959), p. 41.

26 See further Jacques Ferrand, *Traité de l'essence et guérison de l'amour,* (Toulouse, 1610); see also Aldo D. Scaglione, *Nature and Love in the Late Middle Ages,* (Berkeley, 1963), p. 60ff.

27 The lack of any attempt at individual characterization of the lovers in the novels of the seventeenth century has often been noted. See, e.g., Egon Cohn, *Gesellschaftsideale und Gesellschaftsroman des 17. Jahrhunderts,* (Berlin, 1921), p. 107ff.

28 See Jaques Ehrmann, *Un paradis désespéré: L'amour et l'illusion dans 'L'Astrée',* (Paris, 1963). On the weak characterization of figures in the novels of the time, see also Sevo Kevorkian, *Le Thème de l'amour dans l'œuvre romanesque de Gomberville,* (Paris, 1972), p. 23ff.

29 See Mornet, *Histoire de la littérature française classique,* p. 318ff; Bernard Bray, *L'Art de la lettre amoureuse: Des manuels aux romans (1550—1700),* (The Hague/Paris, 1967). This book of sample letters shows in particular that elegant formulations and abundant compliments were of principle importance — for letters of all sorts, including love letters. The lover can only be inspired by patterns external to love, e.g. the latter takes the form of a recommendation, or thanks or writes owing to some other occasion. See, e.g., Jean Puget de La Serre, *Le Secrétaire de la cour ou la maniere d'écrire selon le temps,* (reprinted Lyon, 1646); Boursault, *Lettres de respect, d'obligation et d'amour,* (Paris, 1669), which includes the remarkable 'Lettres à/de Babet'. Also worthy of note is Raymond Lebèque, 'La sensibilité dans les lettres d'amour au XVIIe siècle', in *Cahiers de l'Association internationale des ètudes françaises,* 11 (1959), pp. 77—85, who proposes that the genuineness of emotional expression — and therefore also its public perception — increased in the last third of the seventeenth century in direct proportion to the fact that women now started writing love letters.

30 See C. Rouben, 'Un jeu de société au Grand Siècle: Les "questions"

et les maximes d'amour', *XVIIe Siècle,* 97 (1972), pp. 85—104. See also René Bray, *La Préciosité et les précieux,* (Paris, 1960), p. 148ff. On further developments in England, see Wilhelm P. J. Gauger, *Geschlechter, Liebe und Ehe in der Auffassung von Londoner Zeitschriften um 1700,* doctoral thesis, (Berlin, 1965), p. 49ff., which deals with questions addressed to a newspaper and answered by the editors with a view to a public that in general (so one assumes) is interested in this. The pattern of question and answer is thus already detached from the context of differentiation according to birth.

31 Often built into novels. See, e.g. Du Peret, *La Cour d'amour ou les bergers galans,* 2 vols., (Paris, 1667), particularly vol. I, p. 31ff.; Anonymous, *L'Escole d'amour ou les heros docteurs,* 2nd edition, (Grenoble, 1666), in particular the teaching passages, p. 90ff.; on the Medieval tradition see also Pio Rajna, *Le corti d'amore,* (Milan, 1890); Paul Remy, 'Les "cours d'amour": légende et rèalité', *Revue de l'Université de Bruxelles,* 7 (1954—5), pp. 179—97; Theodor Straub, 'Die Gründung des Pariser Minnehofes von 1400', *Zeitschrift für romanische Philologie,* 77 (1961), pp. 1—14; Jacques Lafitte-Houssat, *Troubadours et cours d'amour,* 4th edition, (Paris, 1971).

32 Jean Regnault de Segrais's *Les Nouvelles Françoises ou les Divertissements de la Princesse Aurelie,* (Paris, 1657, quoted from the 1981 Geneva reprint) is a very typical example of this.

33 The important reservations that could be raised here arise from the material itself, and will be returned to later.

34 For insights into this discussion see Paolo Russo, 'La polemica sulla "Princesse de Clèves" ', *Belfagor,* 16 (1961), pp. 555—602, 17 (1962), pp. 271—89, 385—404.

35 A good impression of this is to be gained from Bary, *L'Esprit de cour;* and his *Journal de conversation,* (Paris, 1673). See further, from the quill of a participating observer, Michel de Pure, *La Pretieuse ou le mystère des ruelles,* 4 vols., (Paris, 1656—8, quoted from the edition by Emile Magne, Paris, 1938—9); or also in the form of a novella: François Hedelin, Abbé d'Aubignac, *Histoire galante et enjouée,* (Paris, 1673). See also Georges Mongrédien, *Madeleine de Scudéry et son salon,* (Paris, 1946).

36 Count Bussy Rabutin's maxims for the case of suspicions being cast on the beloved attest to the strength of this point of view:

> Vous me montrez en vain que vous êtes innocente.
> Si le public n'en voit autent,
> Je ne puis pas être content.

Quoted from 'Maximes d'amour', in Bussy Rabutin, *Histoire amoureuse des Gaules,* (Paris, 1856, reprint Nendeln/Liechenstein.

37 See *Recueil de pièces galantes en prose et en vers de Madame la Comtesse de La Suze et de Monsieur Pellisson,* 4 vols., (reprint, Paris 1684, vol. I), p. 267: 'L'Amour triomphe avec plus d'éclat dans un coeur qui a esté formé d'un sang noble, et la noblesse donne mille advantages aux Amants.' On the indispensability of wealth see also François de Callieres, *La Logique des amans ou l'amour logicien,* (Paris, 1668), p. 6ff., p. 2ff. The use of wealth to promote love belongs, however, to the conflicting nature of the code. On the one hand, one can read in Bary, *Journal de Conversation,* p. 178, quite clearly that 'point d'argent point de Dorimene, que point d'argent point de Suisse'. On the other hand: 'Il faut être dupe ou Allemand pour gagner les femmes par la dépense', LCDM. = le Chevalier de Mailly, *Les Disgraces des amants,* (Paris, 1690), p. 64.

38 Evidence of this is to be found in Max Freiherr von Waldberg, *Die galante Lyrik: Beiträge zu ihrer Geschichte und Charakteristik,* (Strasburg, 1885), p. 44ff.; Henry T. Finck, *Romantic Love & Personal Beauty. Their Development, Causal Relations, historic & national peculiarities* (London, 1887); Vilhelm Aubert, 'A Note on Love', in his *The Hidden Society,* (Totowa NJ, 1965), p. 201ff.

39 See Hugo Friedrich, 'Pascais paradox', *Zeitschrift für romanische Philologie,* 56 (1936), pp. 322—70.

40 See Gregory Bateson, Don D. Jackson, Jay Haley and John Weakland, 'Toward a Theory of Schizophrenia', *Behavioural Science,* I (1956), pp. 251—64.

41 See Gregory Bateson, 'The Cybernetics of "Self": Toward a Theory of Alcoholism', *Psychiatry,* 34 (1971), pp. 1—18, reprinted in his *Steps to an Ecology of Mind,* (New York, 1971).

42 This gets lost in such formulations as 'The Double Bind: Schizophrenia and Gödel', a chapter heading in Anthony Wilden, *System and Structure: Essays in Communication and Exchange,* (London, 1972), p. 110.

43 The transition from dual to triadic constellations and its creation of a capacity for circular self-reference seems to me to be the decisive development stage. See, for details, Luhmann, *Politische Theorie im Wohlfahrtsstaat,* (Munich, 1981).

6 THE RHETORIC OF EXCESS AND THE
EXPERIENCE OF INSTABILITY

1 See p. 39f. above.

2 This complex of paradoxy and casuistry is also by Ilse Nolting-Hauff, *Die Stellung der Liebeskasuistik im höfischen Roman,* (Heidelberg, 1959), p. 15.

3 The same question is raised with regard to the Middle Ages in Peter Dronke, *Medieval Latin and the Rise of the European Love-Lyric,* vol. 1, (Oxford, 1965), pp. xvii, 2, 50f., 57, etc.

4 Paris, 1669, quoted from the edition in *OEuvres de Jean de la Fontaine,* vol. 8, (Paris, 1892), pp. 1—234.

5 Bussy Rabutin, *Histoire amoureuse de France,* (no place or date), p. 242. See also Rabutin, *Histoire amoureuse des Gaules,* p. 389. And in *exactly* the same manner, for the opposing party of *précieuses:* 'L'amour n'est pas seulement une simple passion comme partout ailleurs, mais une passion de nécessité et de bienséance: il faut que tous les hommes soient amoureux' can be read (in Madame de Scudéri's *Cyrus,* in the edition by de Planhol, *Les Utopistes de l'amour* (Paris, 1921) p. 64. However, the methods used are different: the libertines attempted to achieve permanence by means of change, the *précieuses* by refusing to grant the final favour.

6 *Recueil La Suze-Pellisson,* vol. 1, p. 242.

7 Jaulnay, *Questions d'amour,* p. 83.

8 From this vantage point Rabutin, for example, *Histoire amoureuse des Gaules,* p. 390f.) opposes the topos of 'suddenly being hit by Cupid's arrow', for one does not love if one does not wish to love.

9 See on this Marie-Dominique Chenu, 'Les passions vertueuses: L'anthropologie de Saint Thomas', *Revue philosophique de Louvain,* 72 (1974), pp. 11—8.

10 De Callieres, *La Logique des amans,* p. 84. On the concept of love in *L'Astrée* which is also valid here, see Ehrmann, *Un paradis désespéré.* See also, however, the influential attempt to redefine this, as long ago as 1649, in art. 27 of Descartes's *Les Passions de l'âme.* Here the soul itself becomes the actual location of attributions of passions and the spirit becomes the factor determining their creation, retention and enhancement.

11 De Callieres, *La Logique des amans,* p. 85.

12 Ibid, p. 86.

13 See Charles Vion d'Alibray, *L'Amour divisé: Discours académique,* (Paris, 1653), p. 12f.

14 See for the transformation of 'passion' in general Eugen Lerch ' "Passion" und "Gefühl" ', *Archivum Romanicum,* 22 (1938), pp. 320—49.

15 There are Augustinian precursors of this. See, e.g. Abbé de Gerard, *Le caractere de l'honeste-homme morale,* (Paris, 1682), p. 21ff. (p. 45).

16 There is a detailed elaboration on this in Le Boulanger, *Morale galante,* vol. 1, p. 29ff. The text is dedicated to the Dauphin and emphasizes in particular the heroic force necessary to control such

an almost insurmountable passion. Thus, a class of warriors can continue the heroism ascribed to it in love affairs and pass the results off as galantry and enjoyment.

17 This is already true in the Middle Ages. See, for evidence, John F. Benton, 'Clio and Venus: An Historical View of Medieval Love', in F. X. Newman ed., *The Meaning of Courtly Love*, (Albany NY, 1968), pp. 19—42 (p. 31).

18 This is at any rate the case in a story by Madame de Villedieu in her *Annales galantes*, vol. 2, (Paris, 1670, reprinted Geneva, 1979), particularly p. 26ff.

19 'Il est impossible d'aimer sans de violence,' states Jaulnay, *Questions d'amour*, p. 19. 'L'amour aussi bien que la guerre demande beaucoup de soins,' is to be read in *Recueil La Suze-Pellison*, vol. 1, p. 237. On the metaphor of 'besieging', see also vol. 3, p. 177ff. On the dissemination of the metaphor of combat, see further d'Alquié, *La Science et l'école des amans*, throughout; Louis Ferrier de las Martinière, *Précepts galans*, (Paris, 1678), p. 86 and elsewhere: and the same author's *Ovide amoureux ou l'ecôle des amans*, (The Hague, 1698), p. 24f. and elsewhere; Ortigue de Vaumoriere, *L'art de plaire dans le conversation*, (1688; 4th edition, Paris, 1701), p. 395. The man thereby prizes the lady's resistance as the condition of the enhancement of his efforts, and the lady equally holds the tenacity and duration of the man's efforts in high esteem, and both know that both know this. This knowledge of knowledge provides both with the necessary security and the opportunity to treat themselves as opponents of equal birth. 'L'amour est une espéce de guerre où il faut pousser ses conquête le plus avant et avec le moins de relâche que l'on peut. Un Amant qui remerciroit sa Maîtresse paroîtroit comme satisfait d'elle, et cette espéce de repos ne plaît jamais tant que les empressements et les inquiétudes,' (de Vaumoriere, op. cit.).

20 'Aussi tost qu'on a donné son coeur a une belle on ne doit songer qu'a luy plaire, on ne doit avoir d'autre volonté que la sienne; et de quelque humeur qu'on soit, il faut se faire violence pour se regler sur ses sentimens. Il faut estudier toutes ses pensées, regarder toutes ses actions pour y applaudir et s'oublier soy-mesme pour ne souvenir que d'elle et pour rendre hommage à sa beauté' (*Recueil La Suze-Pellison*, vol. 1, p. 222f.). In this context, submission does not in itself suffice, and *douceur* must also play a role; what is of importance is the form, not the method (ibid., p. 249). Submission should not just be an advertising gag and cease once love has fallen on willing ears; it must endure as long as the love does (ibid., p. 255).

21 The relation of this to courtly love remains a topic much debated since mysticism seems of itself to produce a dogma of unconditional submission. See, e.g. Moshe Lazar, *Amour courtois et Fin'Amors dans la littérature du XIIesiècle,* (Paris, 1964), passim, particularly p. 68f.

22 See Heinz Pflaum, *Die Idee der Liebe: Leone Ebreo,* (Tübingen, 1926). For the transition to sociable, courtly love conversation, see particularly p. 36ff. Further, Friedrich Irmen, *Liebe und Freundschaft in der Französischen Literatur des 17, Jahrhunderts,* doctoral thesis, (Heidelberg, 1937), particularly p. 35ff.

23 See René de Planhol, *Les Utopistes de l'amour,* p. 51ff.; Antoine Adam, 'La théorie mystique de l'amour dans l'Astrée', *Revue d'histoire de la philosophie,* (1936), pp. 193—206; Kevorkian, *La Thème de l'amour,* p. 163ff.

24 Ibid. fol. 29 R.

25 Le Boulanger, *Morale Galante,* vol. 1, p. 97 states: "Amour à le bien definir, est une generale alienation de la personne qui ayme: c'est un transport sans contract et sans esperance de retour, par lequel on se donne tout entier et sans aucene reserve, à la personne aymée.'

26 A corresponding remark from *L'Astrée* ('il est vrai, sauf dans le cas où elle commanderait de n'être pas aimée') is to be found in Gustave Reynier, *La Femme au XVIIesiècle: ses ennemis et ses défenseurs,* (Paris, 1929), p. 17.

27 On the other hand, this also means 'Incompatibilité de l'union des coeurs avec la division des interests' (Jaulnay, *Questions d'amour,* p. 60) and from this it follows that love cannot change the difference in interests, or overcome it. The differentiation qua excessiveness also renders love powerless vis-à-vis everything other than oneself.

28 Laurent Bordelon, *Remarques ou réflexions critiques, morales et historiques,* (Paris, 1690), p. 162f.

29 See the stereotyped imputation of perfect beauty, as an objective fact (although in the land of illusion) in *L'Astrée,* and then the conscious inclusion of this illusion in the code of love in the second half of the century, for example in Jaulnay, *Questions d'amour,* pp. 8, 23ff. See in particular its derivation from narcissism, ibid., p. 23: 'La preoccupation dans une presonne qui a bien de l'esprit est une finesse de l'amour propre qui ne nous fait voir l'objet aimé que par l'endroit où il nous peut plaire, *afin d'authoriser son choix'* (my italics, NL.).

30 See Anonymous (Bussy Rabutin), *Amours des dames illustre de nostre siecle,* 3rd edition, (Cologne, 1682), p. 5; *Recueil La Suze-Pellisson,* vol. 3, p. 140.

31 Thus in *Recueil La Suze-Pellison,* vol. 1, p. 140.
32 Rabutin, *Histoire amoureuse des Gaules,* p. 369.
33 Jaulnay, *Questions d'amour,* p. 35.
34 Madame de Villedieu, *Nouveau Recueil de quelques pièces galantes,* (Paris, 1669), p. 120.
35 Benech de Cantenac, *Poesies nouvelles et autres œuvres galantes,* (Paris, 1661), p. 69.
36 Le Boulanger, *Morale galante,* vol. 2, p. 78.
37 Accordingly, the close inter-connection of happiness and suffering, hope and worry in love is one of the standard themes of literature. It is precisely their diametrical opposition to one another that make happiness and suffering so strongly dependent on each other, so that it is impossible to break this circular self-reference from outside with other properties. However, as a result of this closed semantic structure, the whole code can be rejected because of its content of suffering and the unreasonable expectations it involves — thus for example in de Mailly, *Les Disgraces des amants,* or in the new enthusiasm for friendship that commenced around 1700 (see below, p. 79ff.).
38 François Hedelin, Abbé d'Aubignac, *Histoire galante et enjouée,* (Paris, 1673), p. 126ff., (quotations from p. 129, p. 157f., p. 140).
39 Anonymous, 'L'Escole d'amour', p. 92. See the use of the same formulation in a critical, disapproving context at the end of the classical epoch: Bordelon, *Remarques ou réflexions,* p. 297.
40 But the necessity of embedding this in periphrasis is still justified here with reference to the ideality of the idea!
41 A formula most assuredly meant ironically, but one that is nevertheless used naively here. A little further on one can read (p. 100) that love often rests on stupidity, and refers to

> . . . une femme, un beau visage
> Qui bien souvent n'a rien en soy
> D'aymable que ie ne sçay quoi.

This is, of course, rejected in the school of love.
42 New edition by F. Deloffre and J. Rougeot, (Paris, 1962); see also 'La Solitaire', in de Villedieu, *Nouveau Recueil,* pp. 108—126.
43 Horowitz, *Love and Languages,* p. 131f. remarks that 'Guillerages' careful choice of metaphor, his overly lyric tones, bordering on the banal, testify not only to Mariane's naivete, but also to a sense of her control by a potent code. Mariane is surely determined to love, determined by love, but it is as, if determinism is here viewed as seduction by powerful myths'. See also the arguments against genuineness and in favour of a stylistically conscious (code-

conscious) composition in Leo Spitzer, 'Les "Lettres portugaises" ',
Romanische Forschungen, 65 (1954), pp. 94—135. Older literary
history, in contrast, admired the genuineness of the letters, See, e.g.
Max Freiherr von Waldberg, *Der empfindsame Roman in
Frankreich,* vol. 1, (Strasburg, 1906), p. 45ff.

44 Irmen, *Liebe and Freundschaft,* concentrates on this point.

45 Or, one must add, to preserve the self from slander by the lady —
an alternative often used following the *querelles des femmes* in the
sixteenth century.

46 Antoine Baudeau de Somaize, *Le Dictionnaire des précieuses.*
(1660/61), quoted from the 1856 Paris edition, (reprinted
Hildesheim, 1972), p. 131ff. What should be noted here is that irony
and ridiculousness could be utilized particularly vis-à-vis the
précieuses, because this group tried to retain elements of ideality
within their unswervingness, whereas in the ideational field of
marriage, paradoxicalization would promise greater success.

47 Thus, for example, one can read in a letter printed in de Cantenac,
Poesies nouvelles, p. 124ff.: 'Je souspire quelquefois, mais mes
souspirs ne me coûtent iamais des larmes, mes chaisnes sont commes
des chaisnes de parade, et non pas comme celles qui pesent aux
criminels' (p. 125), and this was intended as an answer to the
question 'de quel façon ie vous aime'. Or the rejoinder contained in
a letter by Le Pays, *Amitiez, amours, et amourettes,* expanded
edition, (Paris, 1672), p. 120, 'Voila bien du style de Roman tout
d'une haleine, direz-vous. Hé bien voicy du langage commun pour
vous contenter,' etc.

48 Michel Le Pure, *La Prétieuse ou le mystère des ruelles,* vol. 3,
(Paris, 1657), quoted from the edition by Emile Magne, (Paris,
1939), p. 78.

49 'Qu'en amour assez, c'est trop peu; quand on ayme pas trop, on
ayme pas assez,' is one of the maxims of *Histoire amoureuse de
France,* Rabutin, p. 329, *Histoire amoureuse des Gaules,* p. 385); or
in Jaulnay, *Questions d'amour,* p. 79: 'Il est de la nature de l'amour
qu'il soit dans l'excez et si on n'aime pas infiniment, on n'aime pas
bien.'

50 Bary, *L'Esprit de cour,* p. 246. See also the criticism of a rival in
Abbé de la Torche, *La Toilette galante de l'amour,* (Paris, 1670),
p. 77ff.: his calm, or even composure is considered to render him
almost incapable of coping with the demands of love and thus did
not deserve the love of his beloved.

51 This can be shown quite nicely by referring to the fifth letter of a
Portuguese nun who, after the end of her love affair, seeks a return
into 'ma famille qui m'est fort chère depuis que je ne vous aime

plus'. This point was made by Spitzer, 'Les "Lettres Portugaises" ', p. 106.

52 Ronald M. Berndt, *Excess and Restraint: Social Control Among New Guinea Mountain People,* (Chicago, 1962).

53
> Quand vous aimes passablement,
> On vous accuse de folie;
> Quand vous aimez infinement,
> Iris, on en parle autrement:
> Le seul exces vous justifie.
> (Rabutin, *Histoire amoureuse des Gaules,* p. 384f.)

54 One of the many variations on this theme is to be found in Le Boulanger, *Morale galante,* vol. 2, p. 79: 'Le droit d'estre aimé sert souvent d'obstacle pour l'estre, et l'Amour n'est plus Amour, sitost qu'il est devoir.'

55 *Lettres nouvelles de M. Boursault,* (Paris, 1698), p. 428f., quoted from von Waldberg, *Der empfindsame Roman,* p. 106. Here, the relative 'backwardness' of developments in the British Isles becomes apparent (a 'retardedness' that, however, served later to prepare a better point of departure for a recombination of love and marriage). The attempt was made here to weaken the canon of marital duties by means of love, but initially this creates no real stimulants for a reformulation of the semantics of love. See, for the starting point of English developments, James T. Johnson, *A Society Ordained by God: English Puritan Marriage Doctrine in the First Half of the Seventeenth Century,* (Nashville, 1970), particularly p. 104ff. The stark difference between marital duty and love granted voluntarily, as was emphasized in France, had a highly stimulating effect.

56 'A l'esgard des Amants, il n y'a point de bagatelles en Amour' (Jaulnay, *Questions d'amour,* p. 45f.). 'Enfin, pour vous le faire court, Rien n'est bagatelle en amour' (Rabutin, *Histoire amoureuse des Gaules,* p. 378). Similarly, BDR. (de Rèze), *Les OEuvres cavalières ou pièces galantes et curieuzes,* (Cologne, 1671), p. 19 (a further collection of *questions d'amour* and answers).

57 This is put negatively in a contribution to the *Receuil de Sercy,* 'Ces malheurs font un cercle duquel toutes les parties se tiennent l'une l'autre, et n'ont point du tout d'issue' ('Discours de l'ennemy d'amour, et des femmes', in *Receuil de pièces en prose, les plus agréables de ce temps, composées par divers Autheurs,* (Paris, 1658), pp. 332—55 (p. 338f.).

58 By taking this approach Amour defends herself in a debate with Amitié against the reproach that she is tyrannical, in *Receuil La*

Suze-Pellisson, vol. 3, p. 127ff. See also de Callieres, *La Logique des amans,* p. 125f.

'Il n'y a point de raison qui authorise les manquemens en amour, c'est un signe infaillible ou qu'on a jamais aimé, ou qu'on commence à cesser d'aimer,' stresses Jaulnay, *Questions d'amour,* p. 93. And it follows from this that he who *cannot pardon someone* can love all the more *strongly* (p. 96). See also p. 110ff., on granting pardon for mistakes that have confessed to. This is no contradiction, but rather an indication of the specification of the code of love. Such mistakes are unpardonable as allow inferences on love to be made; love cannot pardon its own mistakes, but only those of others. This is why Rabutin can say:

> Je excuse volontiere et bien plutôt j'oublie
> Un crime dont on fait l'aveu
> Qu'une bagatelle qu' on nie.
> (*Histoire amoureuse des Gaules,* p. 377)

60 See, e.g. Mario Equicola, *Libro di natura d'amore,* new edition, (no place, 1526), fol. 145ff; Nobili, *Trattato dell'Amore,* fol. 31 R. See also d'Alibray, *L'Amour divisé,* p. 8f., or de Chalesme, *L'Homme de qualité ou les moyens de vivre en homme de bien et en homme du monde,* (Paris, 1671), who puts love and hate alongside each other simply as dangerous proclivities.

61 *Livre de chançons,* printed in Corbinelli, *Sentimens d'amour,* vol. 1, p. 121. What is more, there is documentary proof for this point of view in the famous *Lettres portugaises* (cf. n. 42).

62 See on this Werner Schneiders, *Naturrecht und Liebesethik: Zur Geschichte der praktischen Philosophie im Hinblick auf Christian Thomasius,* (Hildesheim, 1971), p. 194ff. for references.

63 Thus Quinault in answering one of the *questions d'amour* put by the Comtesse de Brégy, printed in the Comtesse de B. (Brégy), *OEuvres galantes,* (Paris, 1666), p. 103f.

64 This is stated in La Rochefoucauld's Maxime 72: 'Si on juge de l'amour par la plupart de ses effets, il ressemble plus à la haine qu'a l'amitié', quoted from *OEuvres complètes,* (Paris, 1964), p. 412.

65 'C'est en vain qu'on establiroit de dessein certaines regles en amour, il ne prend loy que de soy-même. Les regles là seroient mesmes d'une dangereuse suite, parce que le coeur qui ne peut souffrir de constrainte nous forcerait à les rompre' (Jaulnay, *Questions d'amour,* p. 67).

66 See the derivation of this from a basic concept in Rabutin, *Histoire amoureuse des Gaules,* p. 348: 'Aimez! et vous serez aimé.' Or with

reference to learning: 'L'amour sçaura bien vous former; Aimez, et vous sçaurez aimer' (p. 352; see also p. 376). The fact that this argument was used, and the manner in which it was argued in the context of seduction are to be seen in Le Pays, *Amitiez, amours, et amourettes,* p. 110f. Romanticism was to declare this, in keeping with Madame de Staël's words, to be typical male behaviour and something that placed women uncomfortably under zugzwang. See her *De l'influence des passions sur le bonheur des individus et des nations,* (1796), quoted from *OEuvres complètes,* vol. 3, (Paris, 1820), p. 135.

67 The works of Ferrier de la Martinière cited above concentrate on this.

68 'L'amour ne permettant pas que l'on face [sic!] de reflexions sur ce qui nous en peut encore arriver' (Jaulnay, *Questions d'amour,* p. 33).

69 See above, p. xx on the problem of the ability to learn.

70 *La Logique des amans.* On the problem of proofs and the doubts these could, in the final instance, not remove, see also Jaulnay, *Questions d'amour,* p. 48ff., p. 104ff. The optimistic version is given here as: whoever really loves inevitably gives proof of this. Love cannot be hidden. Like a fire it makes its presence felt, either by the flickering light or at least by the smoke. (This last comparison is made in *Receuil La Suze-Pellisson,* vol. 1, p. 229.) For a modern-day version of the same problem (and as an indication that the casuistry of love has not completely died out) see Judith Nilstein Katz, 'How Do You Love Me? Let Me Count The Ways (The Phenomenology of Being Loved)', *Sociological Enquiry,* 46 (1975), pp. 11—22.

71 The man's *soins* and *empressements* are always being offered as signs of love — but one differentiates between *marques* and *épreuves,* for the former are, in the final instance, no proof. Accordingly, one of the *questions d'amour* reads: 'Si les dernières faveurs sont la nourriture; ou le poison du veritable amour' (in de Rèze, *OEuvres cavalières,* p. 16).

72 There is a novel on this theme by Madame de Villedieu, *Les Désordres de l'amour,* (1675, quoted from the edition by Micheline Cuénin, Geneva, 1970).

73 This is the gist of the anonymous contribution 'La Justification de l'amour in *Receuil de Sercy,* vol. 3, pp. 289—334 (p. 307). Recently this text has been attributed to La Rochefoucauld; see the edition under that name by J. D. Hubert, (Paris, 1971). Precisely in the point cited here the difference to the *Maximes* is evident. However, as the imputed authorship will no doubt continue to be debated we

will consider the text anonymous and quote from the original
edition. See also Louise K. Horowitz, *Love and Language: A Study
of the Classical French Moralist Writers,* (Columbus Ohio, 1977),
p. 33ff.
74 Jean de la Bruyère, *Les caractères ou les moeurs de ce siècle,*
quoted from *OEuvres complètes,* (Paris, 1951), p. 137.
75 Jaulnay, *Questions d'amour,* p. 31. See also de Callieres, *La Logique
des amans,* p. 90; *Receuil La Suze-Pellisson,* vol. 1, p. 241; Rabutin,
Histoire amoureuse des Gaules, p. 361f.
76 One need only think in this context of the extent to which texts of
supposedly real, lived love affairs slipped back into literature — an
example would be the 'Lettres à/de Babet,' see above, chapter 5,
n. 29.
77 Rabutin, *Histoire amoureuse de France,* p. 238.
78 See Erving Goffman, 'On Cooling the Mark Out', *Psychiatry,* 15
(1952), pp. 451—63, and also Jaulnay, *Questions d'amour,* p. 80ff.
and in particular p. 109, who lists soft treatment, attempts to shake
off the other as a last honour, paid to the past love, and an 'honeste
procedé purement politique'. What also forms the main part of the
discussion is the question of whether it is necessary to return the
letters, to preserve the secrets, etc. See also Jaulnay, ibid., p. 121ff.
on the thorny problem of whether one should say that one is no
longer in love, and if so how. An ebbing in one's efforts is advised,
accompanied by letting the other person guess.
79 See the following passage in de Planhol, *Les Utopistes de l'amour,*
p. 69, from the novel Clélie: 'Je veux qu'on aime par générosité
lorsqu' on ne peut plus aimer par inclination, et je veux même, si
l'on ne peut plus aimer par inclination, et je veux même, si l'on ne
peut plus aimer du tout, qu'on se contraigne pourtant à agir comme
si l'on aimait encore: puisque c'est en cette seule occasion qu'il est
permis de tromper innocemment, et qu'il est même beau de le
faire.' Note the tone evidencing a law being laid down!
80 *Libertins et amoureuses: Documents inédits,* (Paris, 1929), p. vi.
81 'Par le mérite qui organise, pour ainsi dire, l'attente', Myrrha
Lot-Borodine remarks in *De l'amour profane à l'amour sacré:
Etude de psychologie sentimentale au Moyen Age,* (Paris, 1961),
p. 73.
82 'Recommencez vos soins jusqu'aux bagatelles,' Rabutin (*Histoire
amoureuse des Gaules,* p. 386) suggests in order to effect this and
he also advises that one repeatedly state that one loves: 'Le passé
chez l'amant ne se compte pour rien; il veut qu'à toute heure on lui
dise ce qu'il sçait déja fort bien' (p. 396).
83 See the 'Discours sur les passions de l'amour' (incorrectly) attributed

to Pascal in *L'OEuvre de Pascal,* (Paris, 1950), pp. 313—23, (p. 319, p. 321).

84 See d'Aubignac, *Consiels.* Or in a later, already psychologistic form: 'J'étais un peu trop moi-même, et je m'en aperçus trop tard: l'espoir s'était glissé dans l'âme du comte' (in the Contes Moraus von Marmontel, in 'Heureusement', quoted from the *OEuvres complètes,* vol. 2, (Paris 1819, reprinted Geneva 1968), pp. 83—95 (p. 85).

85 An awareness of these temporal-social limitations is at first lent the form of a series of prescriptions, and at a later date is to be found predominantly in novels. See, e.g., Claude Crébillon, *Lettres de la Marquise de M. au Comte de R.,* quoted from the 1970 Paris edition. Here the sense of time (derived from the code and literature on it) is inserted into the process of love in a bivalent manner. The awareness that love *cannot endure* effects a *deferral* of fulfilment and this creates the intensification of emotion necessary for love. To this extent, the reflexivity of time functions as an equivalent to virtue, the rhetoric of which is used and at the same time repealed. Thus, the Marquise allowed, particularly in opening letters, concessions to peek through in the form in which she conveyed that she would have to fear that such concessions, if made, could be exploited, and she therefore (!) saw herself forced not to make them: she therefore (!) was only able to continually remark that she was not in love.

86 See on this Christian Garaud, 'Qu'est-ce que le Rabutinage?', *XVIIe siècle,* 93 (1971), pp. 29—53 (p. 35ff on *'embarquer')*; C. Rouben, 'Histoire et géographie galantes au Grand Siècle: L'Histoire amoureuse des Gaules et la Carte du pays de Braquerie de Bussy-Rabutin', *XVIIe siècle,* 93 (1971), pp. 55—73 (p. 65).

87 For instance *Receuil La Suze-Pellisson,* vol. 1, p. 218f.

88 Ibid., vol. 3, p. 129f. By the way, this topic is particularly suited to thematization in the novel. See d'Aubignac, *Histoire galante,* p. 96ff. or also Claude Crébillon, *Les Egarements du coeur et de l'esprit',* quoted from the 1961 Paris edition, p. 50ff. English translation *Wayward Head and Heart,* (London, 1979).

89 Jaulnay, *Questions d'amour,* p. 4f; de Villedieu, *Nouveau Receuil,* p. 133.

90 See Jaulnay, *Questions d'amour,* p. 53ff.

91 L'esperance entretient l'amour, affoiblit les douleurs et redouble les plaisirs,' it is stated in *Receuil La Suze-Pellisson,* p. 237. This also testifies to the link here to the one-sidedness of the perceptional framework. The interconnection of hope and impatience, hope and disquiet, hope and fear is for ever being emphasized. Hope itself is once again temporalized: at the beginning of an affair it assumes

more the form of fear and gains in strength only in the course of the affair (Jaulnay, *Questions d'amour,* p. 29).

92　See, e.g. C. Rouben, *Bussy Rabutin épistolier,* (Paris, 1974), p. 88ff.

93　A good illustration of this is the second story in Madame de Villedieu's *Les Désordres de l'amour,* p. 67ff., summarized in Maxime V (p. 85f.):

> Le bonheur des amans est tout dans l'esperance;
> Ce qui de loin les ęblouit,
> Perd de pres son éclat et sa fausse apparence;
> et tel mettoit un plus haut prix
> A la félicité si long-tems desirée,
> Qui la trouve à son gré plus digne de mépris,
> Quand avec son éspoir il l'a bien comparée.

94　Here as well the onward march of psychological observation is noteworthy. Pierre de Villiers, *Reflexions sur les defauts d'autruy,* (Amsterdam, 1695), p. 132, states: 'La beauté et la laideur reviennent presque au même; et l'une et l'autre diminuë à force de les voir, et on aurait de la peine à dire pourquoi une belle femme paroist moins belle, et une laide moins laide, la seconde fois qu'on la voit.'

95　See above, p. 51.

96　See on this point and for further evidence on the eighteenth century Georges Poulet, *Etudes sur le temps humain,* vol. 2, (Paris, 1952), English translation, *Proustian Space,* (Baltimore, 1977); Clifton Cherpack, *An Essay on Crébillon fils,* (Durham NC, 1962), p. 28ff.; Laurent Versini, *Laclos et la tradition: Essai sur les sources et la technique des Liaisons Dangereuses,* (Paris, 1968), p. 436ff.

97　Compare, for example, the two epistolary novels by Claude Crébillon, *Lettres de la Marquise de M. au Comte de R.* and *Lettres de la Duchesse de . . . au Duc de . . .* in *OEuvres complètes,* (London, 1777), vol. 1 and vols. 10 and 11 respectively, quoted from the 1968 Geneva reprint. Both ladies struggle with their virtue at the superficial level of self-presentation. For both, the real problem is not actually virtue, but the knowledge that love cannot endure. Their decisions differ. They both become unhappy.

98　Here again it is difficult to say how much of this is really *new* for the seventeenth and eighteenth centuries. Probably it is this temporally related, reflective context, which shows semantic influences. But, the simple warning that, quite apart from moral questions, adultery is not worth it, because the partner will be unreliable, is most certainly not new. Evidence of this can be found in the *Livre des Trois Vertus* (1405) by Christine de Pizan, in Charity C. Willard, 'A Fifteenth-Century View of Women's Role in Medieval Society:

Christine de Pizan's Livre des Trois Vertus', in Rosemarie Thee Morewedge (ed.), *The Role of Women in the Middle Ages,* (London, 1975), pp. 90–120, in particular p. 111ff.

99 There is no lack of indications by experts, but literary historians have still not conducted the necessary thorough re-evaluation.

100 It must be noted that *L'Astrée* takes a stand against both, against inconstancy and against the differentiation of love and marriage; indeed, it consciously opposes the dominant view of the time. But the weaknesses in this view force it to be transposed into the land of shepherds. It is almost impossible, in particular, to imagine how passion in the sense of the self-renunciation of one's personality and absolute submission to marriage was supposed to be practised. The novel is accorded the role of creating the necessary illusionary formulae, even if the author stresses that oaths to eternity and submissiveness should not only be made, but should be meant sincerely. In the second half of the seventeenth century, criticism of the novel is directed at precisely this point. See the Abbé de Villars, *De la délicatesse,* (Paris, 1671), p. 8ff. The reader is supposed to not be interested in a love that would lead to marriage because this is not possible; he is held to wish that his weaknesses will be given authority, and is interested in *amour déréglé.*

101 See as representative of many, de Cantenac, *Poesies nouvelles,* p. 7ff.

102 One can of course also ask oneself: who is the addressee of this literature? Naturally, only married people! Seen in this manner, one can detect behind the rejection of *marriage* the necessity of providing orientational directives *for marriages* that can be concluded without love on the basis of family interests and which are then confronted with love. See in particular, d'Aubignac, *Conseils.*

103 In de Cantenac, *Poesies nouvelles,* p. 1.

104 *Histoire amoureuse des Gaules,* p. 382.

105 Anonymous, *L'Amour marié la bizarrerie de l'amour en estat de mariage,* (Cologne, 1681), p. 2.

106 Rabutin, *Histoire amoureuse des Gaules,* p. 381f.

107 Charles Cotin, *OEuvres galantes en prose et en vers,* vol. 2, (Paris, 1665), p. 519.

108 *Amitiez, amours, et amourettes,* p. 333ff.

7 FROM GALANTRY TO FRIENDSHIP

1 In terms of historical substitution it is noteworthy that Ferrier de la

Martinière stressed that it was not the Muse, but *expérience* and *usage* that guided his pen: *Précepts galans,* p. 10; *Ovide amoureux,* p. 3f. This legitimates preparation of the code for intentional usage.

2 This interesting (one could almost say 'bourgeois') argument is to be found in Jacques de Bosq, *L'Honeste Femme,* new edition, (Rouen, 1639), p. 322: 'Plusieurs peuvent avoir le mesme jugement, mais il est mal-aisé qu'ils ayent la mesme inclination.'

3 See, for the history of the concept, Else Thureau, *'Galant': Ein Beitrag zur französischen Wort und Kulturgeschichte,* (Frankfurt, 1936); for further information see Christoph Strosetzki, *Konversation: Ein Kapitel gesellschaftlicher und literarischer Pragmatik im Frankreich des 18, Jahrhunderts,* (Frankfurt, 1978), p. 100ff; Roger Duchêne, *Réalité vécue et art épistolaire: Madame de Sévigné et la lettre d'amour,* (Paris, 1970), p. 35ff.

4 A wealth of pointers to this double-sidedness are contained in Max Freiherr von Waldberg, *Die galante Lyrik: Beiträge zu ihrer Geschichte und Charackteristik,* (Strasbourg, 1885). Parsons would probably speak here of 'interpenetration'.

5 This is Jaulnay's definition, *Questions d'amour,* p. 98.

6 Jaulnay, *Questions d'amour,* p. 2, makes this clear from the outset: Love is *not only* 'desir d'estre aimé de ce qu'on l'amie', i.e. not love for love's sake as Jean Paul was later to say, but 'quelque chose de plus, parce que l'on cherche à plaire devant que d'esperer d'estré aimé, et le desir d'y reussir precede celuy d'estre heureux.' Similarly Bary, *L'Esprit de cour,* p. 233.

7 Rouben, 'Histoire et géographie galantes', p. 67ff also shows that mutually opposing moral perspectives can meet in intending a generalization of behavioural maxims.

8 On the *précieuses*'s marital problems, see Gustave Reynier, *La Femme au XVIIe siècle,* (Paris, 1933), p. 87ff.; some further short indicators are to be found in the *Dictionnaire des précieuses* by Antoine Baudeau de Somaize, 2nd edition, (1660/61), quoted from the 1856 Paris edition, (reprinted Hildesheim, 1972); or Eulalie's (the Comtesse de la Suze's) lament on the tyranny of marriage, and the conversation that follows in Michel de Pure, *La Prétieuse ou le mystère des ruelles,* vol. 2 (1656), quoted from Emile Magne's edition, (Paris, 1938), p. 276ff.

9 See for example du Four de la Crespelière, *Les Foux amoureux,* (Paris, 1669); by the same author, *Les Recreations poëtiques, amoureuses galantes,* (Paris, 1669).

10 Instructive on this point is Octave Nadal, *Le Sentiment de l'amour dans l'œuvre de Pierre Corneille,* (Paris, 1948).

11 *Receuil de pièces en prose,* (Paris, 1660).

12 Ibid., p. 306f., p. 321f. See also Kelso, *Doctrine for the Lady of the Renaissance,* p. 171f., p. 178f.
13 Ibid., p. 309.
14 For an example of the 'Sentences ou Maximes contre l'amour' typical for this by Le Chevalier de Mailly, in LCDM., *Les Disgraces des amants,* (Paris, 1690), pp. 61—73 (p. 68): 'Les femmes pleurent la mort de leurs Amans, moins par le regret de leur perte que pour faire croire que leur fidelité merite de nouveaux Amans.'
15 See Abbé Goussault, *Le Portrait d'une femme honnête, raisonnable et véritablement chrêtienne,* (Paris, 1694); & by the same author (but erroneously attributed to Fléchier), *OEuvres complètes,* vol. 2, (Paris, 1856), pp. 973—1050, in particular p. 1028ff — here at a stage clearly before the appropriation of values from the bourgeois strata. For the temporally parallel developments in England, see Joachim Heinrich, *Die Frauenfrage bei Steele und Addison: Eine Untersuchung zur englischen Literatur- und Kulturgeschichte im 17/18, Jahrundert,* (Leipzig, 1930), particularly p. 113ff.
16 See Catherine Bernard, *Les Malheurs de l'amour: Première nouvelle. Eléonor d'Yvrée,* (Paris, 1687); by the same author, *Le Comte d'Amboise: Nouvelle galante,* (The Hague, 1689).
17 *De la charité chrêtienne, et des amitiés humaines,* quoted from *OEuvres complètes,* vol. 15, new edition, (Versailles, 1812), pp. 1—50.
18 Explicitly, ibid., p. 12.
19 Ibid., p. 8.
20 Ibid., p. 6.
21 See the characteristic and influential Anne-Therèse Marquise de Lambert, *Traité de l'amitié,* quoted from *OEuvres,* (Paris, 1808) pp. 105—29. See also Louis-Silvestre de Sacy, *Traité de l'amitié,* (Paris, 1704). Similarly also the Marquis de Caraccioli, *Les Caractères de l'amitié* quoted from the 1767 Paris edition. A survey of the literature is to be found in Frederick Gerson, *Le Thème de l'amitié dans la littérature française au XVIIIe siècle,* (Paris, 1974).
22 'Il nous faut songer de plus que nos amis mous caractérisent; on nous cherche dans eux; c'est donner au public notre protrait, et l'aveu de ce que nous sommes,' writes the Marquise de Lambert, *Traité de l'amitié',* p. 114.
23 'La galanterie est bannie, et personne n'y a gagné (ibid., p. 159ff. And another author suggests: 'La Galanterie autrefois si cultivée, si florissante, fréquentée par tant d'hônnetes gens, est maintenant en friche, abandonée: quel desert!' Anonymous, *Amusements sérieux et comiques,* (Amsterdam, 1734) p. 98, and only two pages in this book are devoted to galantry despite its title!). Similarly the Abbé

Nicolas d'Ailly, *Sentimens et maximes sur ce qui se passe dans la societé civile,* (Paris, 1697), p. 34. On the whole the judgement passed on galantry is neither moral nor psychological; see, for example, the *Contes moraux* by Marmontel.

24 Marquise de Lambert, *Traité de l'amitié,* p. 114f.; Jacques Pernetti, *Les Conseils d'amitié,* 2nd edition, (Frankfurt, 1748), p. 77ff.; Marquis de Caraccioli, *La Jouissance de soi-meme,* new edition, (Utrecht/Amsterdam, 1759), p. 407; Marie Geneviève Thiroux d'Arconville, *De l'amitié,* (Paris, 1761), p. 1f., 7f., 80ff. and elsewhere.

25 See, for details, Gauger, *Geschlechter, Liebe and Ehe*; on love and friendship see in particular pp. 59ff., 147ff. & 291; see also Lawrence Stone, *The Family, Sex and Marriage in England 1500—1800,* (London, 1977), p. 219ff.

26 See, for details, Albert Salomon, 'Der Freundschaftskult des 18. Jahrhunderts in Deutschland: Versuch zur Soziologie einer Lebenform', *Zeitschrift für Soziologie,* 8 (1979), pp. 279—308: Wolfdietrich Rasch, *Freundschaftskult und Freundschaftsdichtung im deutschen Schrifttum des 18. Jahhunderts vom Ausgang des Barock bis zu Klopstock,* (Halle, 1936); Ladislao Mittner, 'Freundschaft und Liebe in der deutschen Literatur des 18. Jahrhunderts', in *Festschrift Hans Heinrich Borcherdt,* (Munich, 1962), pp. 97—13; Friedrich H. Tenbruck, 'Freundschaft: Ein Beitrag zu einer Soziologie der persönlichen Beziehungen', *Kölner Zeitschrift für Soziologie und Sozialpsychologie,* 16 (1964), pp. 341—456.

27 Thus, for example, Johann Gottfried Herder, 'Liebe und Selbstliebe', in *Sämtliche Werke,* (ed. Suphan), vol. 15 (Berlin, 1888), pp. 304—26, in particular p. 311ff: 'Liebe soll nur zur Freundschaft laden, Liebe soll selbst die innigste Freundschaft werden' (p. 313). Further pointers in Paul Kluckhohn, *Die Auffassung der Liebe in der Literatur des 18. Jahrhunderts und in der deutschen Romantik,* 3rd edition, (Tübingen, 1966), p. 150ff. The reverse induction is also frequently to be found — in poetry and in reality: initial close friendship first, and then marriage to the sister of the friend (see Mittner, 'Freundschaft und Liebe', p. 101ff.).

28 'Je veux donc que l'amour soit plutot la suite que le motif du mariage; je veux un amour produit par le raison' it is stated regarding the *union intime* of marriage in la Maitre de Claville, *Traité du vrai mérite de l'homme,* vol. 2, 6th edition, (Amsterdam, 1738), p. 127. Thus, what are clearly English influences are incorporated. See also Ian Watt, *The Rise of the Novel: Studies in Defoe, Richardson and Fielding,* (London, 1967), in particular the notes on p. 160.

29 See Bourdier de Villemert, *L'Ami des femmes, ou Philosphie du beau sexe,* new edition, (Paris 1774), on this variant.
30 Ibid., quotations on p. 22f, p. 21f. and p. 19.
31 In Fléchier, *OEuvres complètes,* sp. 1046.
32 See Gauger, *Geschlechter, Liebe und Ehe,* p. 281ff. A brilliant illustration of this is also to be found in the novel by Claude Crébillon, *Les égarements du coeur et de l'esprit,* (1736—8), quoted from the 1961 Paris edition. See further for a modern version of this William Samson, *A Contest of Ladies,* 2nd edition, (Garden City NY, 1959), p. 4f.
33 *De l'amour,* p. 153.
34 One can speak here of cultural fictions being put to the test. There are some that dissolve on being seen through, and others that prove their strength in precisely this situation. See James W. Woodard, 'The Role of Fictions in Cultural Organization', *Transactions of the New York Academy of Sciences,* II, 8 (1944), pp. 311—44.
35 See Luhmann, 'Interaktion in Oberschichten', in *Gesellschafts-struktur und Semantik,* vol. 1, p. 72ff.
36 Typically, for example, in Jaulnay, *Questions d'amour,* p. 9: 'Il faut presque d'avouer, que l'Amour n'est autre chose que l'Amour-propre.' Only reason, and then only faintly, is in a position to raise the reservation that one can at least think of uninterested love. Similarly undecided, Madame de Pringy, *Les Differens Caracteres de femmes du siècle avec la description de l'amour propre,* (Paris, 1694): self-love as droit naturel, aimed not just at conservation but also at happiness and satisfaction, yet which, if exaggerated, becomes the source of all problems.
37 See on this Luhmann, 'Frühneuzeitliche Anthropologie', in *Gesellschaftsstruktur und Semantik,* vol. 2, p. 162ff.
38 See, for the fact that this view can be passed down in time, especially Vilhelm Aubert, 'A Note on Love', in his *The Hidden Society,* (Totowa NJ, 1965), pp. 201—35.
39 See Luhmann, 'Gesellschaftliche Struktur und semantische Tradition', in *Gesellschaftsstruktur und Semantik,* vol. 1, p. 9ff.

8 THE PRIMARY DIFFERENCE

1 *Steps to an Ecology of Mind,* (San Fransisco, 1972), p. 315. See also p. 271f., p. 489f.
2 See on this Reinhart Koselleck, 'Zur historisch-politischen Semantik asymmetrischer Gegenbegriffe', in his *Vergangene Zukunft: Zur Semantik geschichtlicher Zeiten,* (Frankfurt, 1979), pp. 211—77.

3 See for detail Luhmann, 'Der politische Code: "konservativ" und "progressiv" in systemtheoretischer Sicht', in *Soziologische Aufklärung,* vol. 3, (Opladen, 1981), pp. 267—86.

4 *La Logique des amants ou l'amour logicien* (Paris, 1668).

5 We will retain the French terminology, because *plaisir* is untranslatable.

6 See specifically Garaud, 'Qu'est-ce que le Rabutinage?' p. 47; Rouben, 'Histoire et géographie galantes', p. 65.

7 See on this point the recent discussion on the unique manner in which consciousness needs no criteria with reference to itself, particularly taking up the thoughts of Sidney Shoemaker, *Self-Knowledge and Self-Identity,* (Ithaca NY, 1963); also his 'Self-Reference and Self-Awareness', *Journal of Philosophy,* 65 (1968), pp. 555—67.

8 Quoted from *L'OEuvre de Pascal,* (Paris, 1950), pp. 312—23, (p. 316).

9 Both the difficulty and the only approximate nature of the insights into the facticity of a self-reference devoid of any evaluative criteria prove that the difference of true and false, although declared insignificant, were in fact still used. The *précieuses* adopted quite a different stance: 'Il ne peut y avoir de vray plaisir dans les plaisirs criminels,' can be read in Madeleine de Scudéri, 'Des plaisirs', in *Conversations sur divers sujets,* vol. 1, (Lyon, 1680), pp. 36—64 (p. 56). But the thrust of the difference in opinion scratches only the surface of the argument, because even Madeleine de Scudéri still terms *plaisir* things that are in fact criminal.

10 *De l'amour,* p. 16.

11 The discussion on a 'knowledge' that cannot be corrected has obscured this difference under the terminology in which it has been conducted. See for a rectifying portrayal Richard Rorty, *Der Spiegel der Natur: Eine Kritik der Philosophie,* (Frankfurt, 1981), p. 112, for example. English original, *Philosophy and the Mirror of Nature,* (Oxford 1981).

12 Thus d'Alquié, *La Science et l'école des amans,* p. 87ff.

13 Thus the recommendations of the Comte de Versac in the novel by Crébillon, *Les Egarements du coeur et de l'esprit,* p. 172.

14 The difference is lent uncommonly strong emphasis in de Villiers, *Réflexions sur les défants d'autray,* p. 130: 'Un homme qui ne sent point d'amour place bien mieux qu'un autre ces soins qui engagent les femmes: plaire est un art qui demande du sang froid et de la raison pour y réussir, la passion qui oste l'un et l'autre n'est gueres capable d'apprendre et de suivre les preceptes de cet art.'

15 See, in contrast, the (probably English) innovation of an intentional

presentation of the unintentionality of the approach above p. xxf.

16 Thus judges Mornet, *Histoire de la littérature Française classique,* p. 97ff, providing what is still the best overall depiction of this theme.

17 Thus Le Pays, *Amitiez, amours, et amourettes,* p. 349.

18 p. 81f.

19 For this problem see Dieter Henrich, ' "Identität" — Begriffe; Probleme, Grenzen', in Odo Marquard and Karlheinz Stierle, (eds), *Identität,* (Munich, 1979), pp. 133—86 (p. 178).

20 A good insight into the technical means and the mentality as well as the risk of coquetry is to be found in an exemplary letter in de Cantenac, *Poésies nouvelles,* pp. 199 (misprinted as 159) to 206 (misprinted as 266).

21 In this context, precisely to use love to seduce a coquette comes to be seen as a masterpiece of the art of love. 'Si l'on peut espérer à la fin de se faire aimer d'une coquette,' is one of the questions that Bussy Rabutin tries to answer (quoted from Mornet, *Histoire de la littérature française classique,* p. 34). See above, chapter 5, n. 12. The manner in which one difference adapts itself to another in order to direct perception and ambition towards higher improbabilities is to be seen clearly here.

22 Cotin thematizes this in his epigramme 'Fausse complaisance':

> Il est vray, ie ne m'en puis taire.
> Tyrsis pour moy n'a point d'appas;
> Son exceβif desir de plaire,
> Est cause qu'il ne me plaist pas.
> (*OEuvres gallantes,* vol. 2, p. 528).

23 De la Bruyère, *Les Caractèses ou les moeurs de ce siècle,* p. 125 stated on this point: 'Il arrive quelquefois qu'une femme cache à un homme toute la passion qu'elle sent pour lui, pendant que de son côté il feint pour elle toute celle qu'il ne sent pas.' One can clearly perceive in this or in similar observations by other authors — now completely moralist in outlook — the manner in which the new refinement and the insight into social reflexivity cancel out the old difference of idealism and sarcasm, mystical and Gallic tradition in questions revolving around women.

24 Crébillon, *Lettres de la Marquise de M.,* p. 203.

25 The extensive literature on this subject can be summarized to read that absence changes the situation of the lovers in all cases: a short absence intensifies loves (not least because letters present an opportunity to state one's love more strongly than one could if present). A long absence, in contrast, leads to doubts, indifference

and the affair being broken off. See, e.g. Jaulnay, *Questions d'amour,* p. 86ff. See also Rabutin, *Histoire amoureuse des Gaules,* p. 374: 'L'absence est à l'amour ce qu'est au feu le vent. Il étaint le petit, il allume le grand.'

26 'Tout est siècle pour eux, ou bien tout est moment', it is stated in Rabutin, op cit, p. 238.

27 'C'est pour la complaissance qu'on commence tous les projets amoureux' (*Receuil La Suze-Pellisson,* vol. 1, p. 258).

28 We have already discussed the fact that an ebbing of efforts could be used tactically to communicate this more considerately (p. 71). Information necessitated at certain phases is always also potential communication. Refusing to *communicate this,* despite the great evidence for the need thereof, is the theme of *Adolphe* by Benjamin Constant.

29 In the opinion of the author of the *Discours sur les passions de l'amour,* p. 319, this makes love affairs last longer.

30 This is so because it is forever being stressed that even fulfilled love cannot dispense with its continual provision with new *plaisirs,* with exchanging niceties and signs of favour in a more conventional meaning of the term. *Amour* is in no way a higher stage of development that renders all complaisance superfluous. See, for example, *Receuil La Suze-Pellisson,* vol. 1, p. 255.

31 'Representez vous', René Bary admonishes everyone who shies away from love, 'que la jeunesse n'a point de retour; que l'age qui la suit n'a point de consolateurs' (*L'Esprit de cour,* p. 73). A remoralization is, on the other hand, to be expected if shortly afterwards one was to orient oneself towards long-term perspectives and a weighing up of advantages and disadvantages: 'Qui commence à aimer, doit se preparer à souffrir,' warned de Mailly, *Les Disgraces des amans,* p. 61.

32 See above, p. 73f.

33 See the contribution 'Le justification del'amour, in *Receuil de Sercy.*

34 Anonymous, *Les caracteres du faux et du veritable amour et le portrait de l'homme de lettre amoureux,* (Paris, 1715).

9 LOVE VERSUS REASON

1 See F. Joyeux, *Traité des combats que l'amour a eu contre la raison et la jalousie,* (Paris, 1667), pp. 1—23. We quote from the same text in Le Pays, *Amitiez, amours et amourettes,* (the extended edition, Paris, 1672), pp. 43—58. See also *Receuil La Suze-Pellisson,* vol. 3, pp. 127—58.

2 *Caritas ordinata, amor rationalis.* We do not have space to go into this rich and controversial tradition, which Thomasius tried to continue, in any detail. For an extensive study see Werner Schneiders, *Naturrecht und Liebesethik: Zur Geschichte der praktischen Philosophie im Hinblick auf Christian Thomasius,* (Hildesheim, 1971).

3 This is also a good example of the custom, widespread in the seventeenth century, of depicting specific facts as social relations by means of allegorization, in this way instilling them with reflexivity.

4 P. 56. See also the measurement of the strength ('force') of love in terms of its ability to bridge differences either upward or downward in the social hierarchy, in de la Torche, *La Toilette galante,* p. 179ff. For a *question d'amour* on this theme see also de Brégy, *OEuvres galantes,* p. 111f.

5 P. 57.

6 One therefore also comes across the statement that Love usurps terrain that in itself belongs to Reason — thus de Brégy, *OEuvres galantes,* p. 113.

7 This in turn belongs to the corpus of politico-geographical allegories common after 1653, i.e. the Cartes de Tendre etc. See as an example for many Louis Moreri, *Le Pays d'amour: nouvelle allegorique,* (Lyon, 1665).

8 P. 48.

10 EN ROUTE TO INDIVIDUALIZATION

1 Consensus of this sort naturally stimulates contradiction. See the collection of statements in Corbinelli, *Sentimens d'amour,* vol. 2, p. 164ff.

2 Whoever admonishes this must write a whole book about it: thus Charles Vion d'Alibray, *L'Amour divisé: Discours academique. Où il est prouvé qu'on peut aimer plusieurs personnes en mesme temps egalement et parfaitement,* (Paris, 1653). The assertion of exclusivity, in contrast, requires only one sentence. This unequal distribution of the onus of the argument illustrates more than do the arguments themselves what was, despite all proofs, nevertheless plausible.

3 *L'Amour divisé,* p. 18.

4 See Aristotle, *Nichomachean Ethics.,* (Oxford, 1980) Book Seven which is still founded on the basic form of friendship and conceived of such a relationship as *the* enhancement of ethics.

5 Madame de la Fayette, *La Princesse de Clèves,* (quoted from

OEuvres, ed. Robert Lejeune, vol. 2, Paris, 1928), p. 257f. (my italics, N. L.). The claim to individuality here is not based on an anticipation of future forms of existence, but on the preservation of past ideals although it was already evident that these could not be put into practice. See the excellent interpretation of this by Jules Brody, 'La Princesses de Clèves and the Myth of Courtly Love', *University of Toronto Quarterly,* 38 (1969), pp. 105—35.

6 *OEuvres galantes,* vol. 2, p. 566. See also the verses of Brébeuf printed in Corbinelli, *Sentimens d'amour,* vol. 2, p. 28: the beauty of the beloved justifies inconstancy, because it is also to be found in others.

7 Also in *L'Astrée,* however!

8 Thus, for instance, in the essay 'De la connoissance d'autruy et de soi-mesme' by Madeleine de Scudéri, *Conversations sur divers sujets,* vol. 1, (Lyon, 1680), pp. 65—135, in particular, p. 72f: A closer scrutiny of the friend would cause the friendship to dissolve, which would mean to lose one's enjoyment of the friend, the standard admonishment here being: 'Il ne faut jamais détruire son plaisir soy-mesme.'

9 *Questions d'amour,* p. 14. Similarly Rabutin, *Histoire amoureuse des Gaules,* p. 387.

10 Ibid., p. 15.

11 One could also interpret the background of this to mean that only religion can secure identity for eternity — 'il doit être tousiours le même dans l'Eternité, il n'est jamais dans le tempo' (François de Grenaille, *Le Mode ou le charactere de la religion etc,* Paris, 1642, p. 25).

12 See Joachim Heinrich, *Die Frauenfrage bei Steele und Addison: Eine Untersuchung zur englischen Literatur- und Kulturgeschichte im 17/18. Jahrhundert,* (Leipzig, 1930); Rae Blanchard, 'Richard Steele and the Status of Women', *Studies in Philology,* 26 (1929), pp. 325—55.

13 See on this point Ian Watt, *The Rise of the Novel: Studies in Defoe, Richardson and Fielding,* (London, 1957, reprinted 1967), p. 135ff.

14 See on this point Sidney Ditzion, *Marriage, Morals and Sex in America: A History of Ideas,* 2nd edition, (New York, 1966), particularly p. 13ff., p. 35ff.

15 Again, the Renaissance is instructive in the contrast it provides to this. See Ruth Kelso, *Doctrine for the Lady of the Renaissance,* (Urbana III., 1956, reprinted 1978).

16 See specifically with reference to the higher aristocracy Randolph Trumbach, *Aristocratic Kinship and Domestic Relations in Eighteenth-Century England,* (New York, 1978); also, with a wider

scope, Lawrence Stone, *The Family, Sex and Marriage in England 1500—1800,* (New York, 1977).

17 For adjustments to this in the French translations of Richardson see Servais Etienne, *Le Genre romanesque en France depuis l'apparition de la 'Nouvelle Heloïse' jusqu'aux approches de la Révolution,* (Brussels, 1922), p. 119ff.

18 See François de Caillieres, *La Logique des amans ou l'amour logicien,* (Paris, 1668) — with an overly pedantic imitation of the code for logic that is hardly typical of thought contemporary to him.

19 See Hermann Schmalenbach, 'Die Genealogie der Einsamkeit', *Logos,* 8 (1920), pp. 62—96; further, for the interpretation of the genesis of the friendship cult based on this see Wolfdietrich Rasch, *Freundschaftskult und Freundschaftdichtung im deutschen Schrifttum des 18. Jahrhunderts: Vom Ausgang des Barock bis zu Klopstock,* (Halle, 1936), p. 36ff. On the ambivalence of Nicoles's view of things see also Luhmann, 'Interaktion in Oberschichten', in *Gesellschaftsstruktur und Semantik,* vol. 1, pp. 72—161 (p. 109ff.).

20 In the *Confessions du Comte de . . .* by Charles Duclos (1741), quoted from the 1970 Lausanne edition, p. 82, one comes across the following: 'Une dévote emploie pour son amant tous les termes tendres et onctueux de l'Ecriture, et tous ceux deu dictionnaire de la dévotion la plus affectueuse et la plus vivre.' One should also note that the paths of charitable devotion demand that the same inconspicuous and unnoticed mobility be adopted as was necessary to tread the paths of love.

21 Clear evidence of this in Boudier de Villemert, *Le Nouvel Ami des femmes, ou la philosophie de sexe,* (Amsterdam/Paris, 1779), p. 122ff. The *chercher à plaire* becomes suspicious *per se.* What was formerly equally probable, i.e. the sincere binding of two hearts in the context of galantry, now becomes conceded only in terms of it being an exception: 'Il est vrai qu'au milieu de cette galanterie universelle il se forme des engagemens de préférence ou le coeur soit veritablement de la partie?' (p. 125). Romanticism was to go a step further here and to assume that a necessary condition for the formation of genuine love lay in the insincerity and superficiality of forms. See in particular Benjamin Constant, *Adolphe,* (1816), quoted from *OEuvres,* (Paris, 1957), pp. 37—117.

22 Thus, at any rate, the teachings of the Comte de Versac in Crébillon, *Les égarements,* p. 168ff. Note the game with semantic self-reference, created by paradoxes: insincerity means to be sincere to oneself; the imitation of others is the path to individuality (indeed, it is termed *singularité*). It is the negative projection of the world,

and not the ideal variant, that enhances adaptive capacity of this form.

23 Thus the Marquise de M. in the novel by Claude Crébillon, *Lettres de la Marquise de M. au Comte de R.,* 1732, quoted from the 1970 Paris edition. See, for instance, letter XIII, p. 71: 'Je sens des mouvements que je n'ose démêler: je fuis mes réflexions, je crains d'ouvrir les yeux sur moi-même, tout m'entraîne dans un abîme affreux; il m'effraie, et je m'y précipite.' The most important precursors of the seven 'genuine' letters to be found in Boursault, *Lettres nouvelles de M. B., avec sept lettres amoureuses d'une dame à un cavalier,* (Paris, 1697).

24 See Luhmann, 'Temporalisierung von Komplexität: Zur Semantik neuzeitlicher Zeitbegriffe', in *Gesellschaftsstruktur und Semantik,* vol. 1, pp. 235—300.

25 Emphasis is no longer lent to the fact that precisely this is a characteristic shared with the animal kingdom. For the reference of passion to the present for example Joseph Joubert, *Pensées et lettres,* ed. Raymond Dumay, (Paris, 1954), p. 65; Charles Duclos, *Considérations sur les moeurs de ce siècle,* (1751; Lausanne, 1970), p. 358.

26 Thus, with reference to Claude Crébillon, Clifton Cherpack, *An Essay on Crébillon Fils,* (Durham NC, 1962), p. 28.

27 See on this point Henri Peyre, *Literature and Sincerity,* (New Haven, 1963), in particular p. 13ff.

28 The fragility precisely of this strategy had, of course, been recognized at a much earlier date. The Princesse de Clèves's love begins, already almost in a cul-de-sac, with a dance. But it was the dramaticism of Classicism that generated language as a counterbalance which could be taken seriously — which, at a later point, was no longer possible.

29 *Maximes et pensées,* in *OEuvres complètes,* vol. 1, (Paris, 1824, reprint Geneva, 1968), pp. 337—449, (p. 421).

30 For an overview of the main tendencies in English and French literature that prepared the way for *liaisons dangereuses,* see Laurent Versini, *Laclos et la tradition,* (Paris, 1968), p. 121ff.

31 We shall return to this in chapter 13.

32 See above, p. 68f., p. 95f.

33 This refers to differentiation from truth that had since been granted a scientific validity. In comparison: 'altra cosa non puo pagar colui che ama, che eser amato,' in Sansovino, *Ragionamento d'amore,* p. 163; similarly Nobili, *Trattato dell'Amore,* fol. 17f.; or, 'L'Amour ne se paye que par l'Amour' in *Receuil La Suze-Pellisson,* p. 244, where (particularly clear in Sansovino) most emphasis is given to a

differentiation from equally influential economic considerations. For the inverse decision, whereby the attractedness of the other person is not accorded relevance, see Cicero, *Laelius 58.*

34 Quoted without reference to source in Maurice Donnay, 'Marivaux ou l'amour au XVIIIe siècle', *La Revue des Vivants,* 6 (1929), pp. 843—67, (p. 848).

11 THE INCORPORATION OF SEXUALITY

1 See, for example, de Planhol, *Les Utopistes de l'amour,* p. 115ff. Of the German authors of 'galant novels' above all Hunold follows this path. See Herbert Singer, *Der galante Roman,* 2nd edition, (Stuttgart, 1966). According to Singer, even in the literary form taken by the novel no substantial innovations emerge. These have to be imported at a later date from England.

2 See on this Robert Mauzi, *L'Idée du bonheur dans la littérature et la pensée française au XVIIIe siècle,* (Paris, 1960), in particular p. 180ff.

3 For much evidence of this see Valentini P. Brady, *Love in the Theatre of Marivaux,* (Geneva, 1970).

4 Thus the *Confessions du Comte de . . . :* 'Nous vivons, nous pensons, nous sentons ensemble'; thus it ends, à la mode anglaise, one could add.

5 See for numerous indications of this Paul van Tieghen, 'Les Droits de l'amour et l'union libre dans le roman française et allemand 1760—1790', *Neophilologus,* 12 (1927), pp. 96—103.

6 See Louis-Sebastien Mercier, *L'Homme sauvage, histoire traduite de . . .,* (Paris, 1767). It is also clear here that incest is considered good if there is no reference to time, no past and no future (e.g. p. 68).

7 Thus, for example, in the novels of the Officer of the Guards Loaisel de Tréogate.

8 An extensive discussion also occurs with regard to this, above all with respect to the use of contraceptive techniques which in turn facilitate (1) the free availability of sexual enjoyment and (2) the extension of intimacy in relationships with children. See as typical for this Marcel Lachiver, 'Fécondité légitime et contraception dans la région parisienne', in *Sur la population française aux XVIIIe et XIXe siècles: Hommage à Marcel Reinhard,* (Paris, 1973), pp. 383—401; Jean-Louis Flandrin, *Familles: parenté, maison, sexualité dans l'ancienne société,* (Paris, 1976), p. 204ff. English translation, *Families in Former Times,* (Cambridge, 1979).

9 In *Marriage and Morals,* (1929), quoted from the 1972 London, reprint, p. 36.

10 A much-discussed development. See, e.g., Stone, *The Family, Sex and Marriage,* p. 143ff., p. 253ff.; Robert Muchembled, *Culture populaire et culture des élites dans la France moderne (XVe—XVIIIe siècles).* (Paris, 1978), p. 230ff. On the problem of sleeping together, see Flandrin, *Familles,* p. 97ff. On the whole, talk is somewhat one-sidedly of 'repression' in this context. (See for example, Jos van Ussel, *Sexualunterdrückung: Geschichte der Sexualfeindschaft,* (German translation, Reinbek, 1970). This could give rise to the false impression that opportunities to satisfy sexual needs were limited, an assumption that is somewhat false. What is characteristic is rather that sexuality is differentiated from other areas of life. More intimacy then means more freedom. The church's regulation of permitted and forbidden positions in sexual intercourse is then relinquished, and love as the permissive principle takes the place of what is necessary for procreation.

11 Comtesse de B. (Brégy), *OEuvres galantes,* (Paris, 1666), p. 113.

12 See Pierre Charon, *De la sagesse,* quoted from *Toutes les OEuvres de Pierre Charron,* (Paris, 1635, reprinted Geneva 1970), vol. 1, p. 76ff.

13 Starting with — is this a coincidence? — a hero of the semantics of love: Peter Abelard. See in particular his *Ethics.* Quoted from the edition by D. E. Luscombe, (Oxford, 1971).

14 See in this point once again Nadal, *Le Sentiment de l'amour;* Horowitz, *Love and Languages.*

15 See for a detailed overview Paul Kluckhohn, *Die Auffassung der Liebe in der Literatur des 18. Jahrhunderts und in der deutschen Romantik,* 3rd edition, (Tübingen, 1966), in particular p. 42ff., p. 82ff.; also Edward Shorter, 'Illegitimacy, Sexual Revolution and Social Change in Modern Europe', *Journal of Interdisciplinary History,* 2 (1971), pp. 237—72; Georges May, *Diderot et 'La Religieuse'; Etude historique et littéraire,* (Paris, 1954), in particular p. 98ff.; Aram Vartanian, 'La Mettrie, Diderot, and the Sexologie in the Enlightenment', in *Essays on the Age of Enlightenment in Honor of Ira O. Wade,* (Geneva, 1977), pp. 347—67. See also for the socio-historical aspects Helmut Möller, *Die kleinbürgerliche Familie im 18. Jahrhundert: Verhalten und Gruppenkultur,* (Berlin, 1869), p. 279ff. Of course there are many precursors of this. An example of such an early development would be that gradually conjugal sexuality comes to no longer be justified exclusively in terms of procreation (see, e.g., André Biéler, *L'Homme et la femme dans la morale calviniste,* (Geneva, 1963); James T. Johnson, *A*

Society Ordained by God: English Puritan Marriage Doctrine in the First Half of the Seventeenth Century, (Nashville, 1970) or individual cases of the theme's treatment outside of more or less pornographic literature, e.g. in Montaigne's work.

16 See, e.g. François Lebrun, *La Vie conjugale sous l'ancien régime,* (Paris, 1975), p. 85ff.

17 This is at the same time one of the points of reference for a comparison of religious, sexual and political liberation movements that play nature off against the conditions of nature. See Edward A. Tiryakian, *Sexual Anomie in Prerevolutionary France,* MS, February 1981).

18 'Je suis fâché de n'avoir jamais pu concevoir l'amour indépendent des sens,' a somewhat worried Pernetti confesses, *Les Conseils d'amitié,* p. 78 and then slightly more explicitly, p. 79.: 'l'attrait mutuel des sexes fait la base de l'amour.' Or see Jean Blondel, *Des hommes tels qu'ils sont et doivent être: Ouvrage de sentiment,* (London/Paris, 1758), p. 140ff. 'Il n'est pas du véritable amour, de l'amour le plus pur, d'anéantir les sens. Il ne pourroit' (p. 142). Diderot's *Encyclopédie* defines *sub voce amour* love as 'une inclination dont les sens forment le noeud' (author, Vauvenarges), vol. 1, (Paris, 1751), p. 367.

19 For an overview of this aspect see René de Planhol, *Les Utopistes de l'amour,* (Paris, 1921).

20 To prove this with just one typical quotation: 'La volupté . . . sera donc l'art d'user des plaisirs avec délicatesse, et de les gouter avec sentiment,' is to be read in Anonymous (Thémiseuil de Saint-Hyacinthe), *Receuil de divers écrits,* (Paris, 1736), p. 130.

21 Claude Crébillon, *La Nuit et le moment, ou les matinées de Cythère,* quoted from *O Euvre complètes,* vol. 9, (London, 1777), p. 15; (reprinted Geneva 1968), vol. 2, p. 61. Precisely the passage from which the quote is taken shows a dissillusioned mixture of bitterness, matter-of-factness and cynacism, not completely free of the expectation that things should really be different.

22 This amounts to the initial preparation for an awareness of the code as it was later to be formulated by the *idéologues.* See below, p. 149ff.

23 The consequences this had can be seen to have even effected literary style. Crébillon's often maligned tortuous style meets the requirement fully by keeping the different perspective separate and yet also connecting them to one another.

24 Memoirs as a literary canon provide a good insight into this, by means of which one can also control to what extent life influenced novels and vice versa. A poignant example would be the Comte

Alexandre de Tilly, *Mémoires: Pour servir à l'histoire des moeurs de la fin du 18e siècle,* quoted from the 2nd edition, 3 vols., (Paris, 1828). On the connection of novels and (one could almost say) life world and of Tilly's role in this context see also Laurant Versini, *Laclos et la tradition: Essai sur les sources et la technique des Liaisons Dangereuses,* (Paris, 1968), p. 25ff. Police reports (published meanwhile) provide information on courtesans and their prices. See Camille Piton (ed.), *Paris sous Louis XV: Rapports des Inspecteurs de Police au Roi,* 5 vols., (Paris, 1909—14).

25 A good read on this is Robert P. Utter and Gwendolyn B. Needham's *Pamela's Daughters,* (New York, 1936, reprinted 1972). The usual treatment of this, that takes only the nineteenth century into account, notes only the historical and national particularity and tries at no point to explain it. See for the USA Milton Rugoff, *Prudery and Passion,* (London, 1972); further as a complementary picture, Steven Marcus, *The Other Victorians: A Study of Sexuality and Pornography in Mid-Nineteenth Century England,* 2nd edition, (New York, 1974).

26 See Kluckhohn, *Die Auffassung der Liebe,* p. 140ff. for an overview.

27 See *Neue Abhandlungen über den menschlichen Verstand,* Book 2, chapter 20, arts. 4 and 5, quoted from Leibniz, *Werke,* vol. 3. 1, (Darmstadt, 1959) p. 224ff.

28 See Christian Thomasius, *Von der Kunst, vernünftig und tugendhaft zu lieben . . . Oder: Einleitung zur Sitten Lehre,* (Halle, 1692).

29 See on this Georg Jäger, *Empfindsamkeit und Roman,* (Berlin, 1969), p. 44ff.

30 'En vérité, ce serait une sottise que d'avoir avec eux de la vertu; on n'a, pour s'en pouvoir défendre, tout au plus besoin que de gout' (Crébillon, *Lettre de la Marquise de M.,* p. 114). See also Jean de la Bruyère, *Les Caractères ou les moeurs de ce siècle,* quoted from *OEuvres complètes,* (Paris, 1951), p. 115: 'Pour les femmes du monde, un jardinier est un jardinier, et un maçon est un maçon; pour quelques autres plus retirées, un maçon est un homme, un jardinier est un homme. Tout est tentation à qui la craint.'

31 See Watt, *The Rise of the Novel,* p. 164f. This theme also exists in France — but there it is in contrast used to portray the man who modestly loves a woman of higher social station as an innocent victim. Thus in the anonymously published novel, *Les Amours d'Euméne et de Flora, ou Histoires véritables des intrigues amoureuses d'une grande Princesse de notre siècle,* (Cologne, 1704).

32 Quoted from Kluckhohn, *Die Auffassung der Liebe,* p. 260, n. 1.

33 We shall ignore the difficult problem of homosexuality as a secret stake held in the concept of friendship. On the literariness of this topic see Hans Dietrich, *Die Freundesliebe in der deutschen Literatur*, (Leipzig, 1931).

31 By the middle of the eighteenth century such a point of view became modelled on the expression of great passion contained in the image of the woman hopelessly offering herself.

35 I shall return to this, see below, p. 130ff.

36 See the indicators in chapter 7, n. 27. See also, however, de Villemert, *Nouvel Ami des femmes,* p. 130. See further *Die kleinbürgerliche Familie,* p. 305ff.

37 K. W. von Drais, *Drei Vorlesungen über Liebe, Geschlechter und Eheglück, dreien Damen gehalten,* (Gotha, 1783), p. 14.

38 Ibid., p. 22.

39 Jakob Mauvillon, *Mann und Weib nach ihren gegenseitigen Verhältnissen geschildert,* (Leipzig, 1791), p. 273. See also (this time from the point of view of the woman) Johann Gottlieb Fichte, *Grundlage des Naturrechts nach Prinzipien der Wissenschaftslehre,* (1796), quoted from *Ausgewählte Werke,* (Darmstadt, 1962), vol. 2, p. 308ff: 'The Deduction of Marriage'.

40 Op. cit., p. 273.

41 *Essais,* III, (Paris, 1950), p. 952.

42 'C'est la consentement et non pas la satisfaction des sens qui fait l'essence du mariage' (François de Grenaille, *L'Honneste mariage,* Paris, 1640, p. 57).

43 The following quotations from Jacques des Coustures, *La Morale universelle,* (Paris, 1687), p. 42ff are very typical: 'Le mariage est . . . tres necessaire à l'Etat, il faut se secrifier à son utlité, et tâcher par sa conduite d'en faire son propre bonheur . . . [p. 50]. Je ne voudrois pas non plus que cette union fut causée par une grande passion, puisqu'il n'y en a point d'eternelles . . . [p. 51]. Cela n'empêche pas qu'on ne doive sentir et marquer à sa femme une tendresse extreme . . . [p. 52]. Il me semble que cette familiarité, qui est entre le mary et la femme, altère le charme de cette union [p. 53]. In other words we have to do not with passion violente, but with anticipatory, personal and confidential treatment as the correlate to socially necessary institutional stability at the level of everyday affairs. This, in turn, could not be secured by fluctuating emotions, but only by marrying within the same social stratum.

44 Some accurate observations on this are to be found in Emil Lucka, *Die Drei Stufen der Erotik,* 12th—15th editions, (Berlin, 1920), p. 258ff. Sociology has, incidentally, been more interested in the reproaches rather than the thing itself. See as representative for

many, Vilfredo Pareto, *Le Mythe vertuiste et la Littérature immorale,* (Geneva, 1971).

12 THE DISCOVERY OF INCOMMUNICABILITY

1 *Annales galantes,* vol. 4, p. 180f.
2 Quoted from Servais Etienne, *Le Genre romanesque en France depuis l'apparition de la 'Nouvelle Heloïse' jusqu'aux approaches de la revolution,* (Brussels, 1922), p. 52.
3 In chapter 4, n. 6 we already pre-empted this: with the example of 'delicacy'.
4 A somewhat lengthier quotation should demonstrate that this logical problem was perceived quite clearly, but not *paradoxicalized.* Instead, it was *solved* noticeably *by latency.* 'La singularité n'est pas précisement un caractère; c'est une simple manière d'être s'unit à tout autre caractère, et qui consiste à être *soi,* sans apercevoir qu'on soit different des autres; car si l'on vient à le reconnaître, la sinularité s'évanoiut; c'est une enigme qui cesse de l'être aussitôt, que le mot en est connu.' (Charles Duclos, *Considérations sur les moeurs de ce siècle,* 1751, quoted from the 1970 Lausanne edition, p. 291f.). The author clearly makes an exception in the case of incomparability being based on services. Morality, in other words, still controlled the problem and forced it into the area of undeserved and therefore (?) affected particularity.
5 This doctrine of the ostensibly cosmic secret of love is still to be found in the seventeenth century. Supposedly, it would go against its nature to reveal the secret, for this would destroy it. But the same is not considered to be the case of communication between lovers. See, for example, 'La iustification de l'amour', *Receuil de Sercy,* (Paris, 1660), vol. 3, pp. 289—334 (p. 321f.). If it is true, as some have suggested, that this essay stems from La Rochefoucauld's hand, then the statement will have to be understood as ironic: as an indication of socially necessary discretion.
6 See 'Le scrupale ou l'amour mécontent de lui-même', from the *Contes Moraux* by Marmontel, quoted from *OEuvres complètes,* vol. 2, (Paris, 1819, reprinted Geneva, 1968), pp. 28—43.
7 On attributive differences in play here see above, p. 34f.
8 See above, chapter 10, n. 10.
9 This formulation is taken from Versini, *Laclos et la tradition,* p. 43.
10 This is assumed, although this topic had been extensively discussed immediately after *Pamela* appeared. The most important counter was Henry Fielding's *An Apology for the Life of Mrs. Shamela*

Andrews, (London, 1741), quoted from the reprint, (Folcroft Pa., 1969).

11 This is also anchored in the general social code of sociability — not without a knowledge of its obverse: 'Were we to dive too deeply into the sources and motives of the most laudable actions, we may, by tarnishing their lustre, deprive ourselves of a pleasure' advises the Countess Dowager of Carlisle in *Thoughts in the Form of Maxims Addressed to Young Ladies on Their First Establishment in the World,* (London, 1789), p. 81.

13 ROMANTIC LOVE

1 See, for example, the Abbé de Mably, *Principes de morale,* (Paris, 1784), p. 287ff, in the form of an analysis of the dangers of love marriages. The problem is, of course, an old one. Robert Burton debates seriously in his *Anatomy of Melancholy* (1621, quoted from the German translation of the third part, Zürich, 1952) whether he should leave the lovers to their will, if no other cure helps and thus allow them to marry. He refers to older evidence for this and adds melancholically: 'Freilich, . . . es kann nicht sein! aus vielen und verschiedenen Gründen' (p. 299).

2 Such distinctions clearly existed, but consisted more in the relation to *married life* than to *marriage.* The bourgeoisie set more stock on a close, homely relationship of the married couple and in so doing attempted to dismantle some of the traditional inflexibilities of the family structure, whereas the gentry was unable to find a capacity for family representation in the principle of closeness and therefore had to reject it from the outset.

3 See on this Jean-Louis Flandrin, *Les Amours paysannes (XVIe — XIXe siècle),* (Paris, 1975, collected case material).

4 See Levin L. Schücking, *Die Familie im Puritanismus: Studien über Familie und Literatur in England im 16., 17. und 18. Jahrhundert,* (Leipzig/Berlin, 1929); William Haller and Malleville Haller, 'The Puritan Art of Love', *The Huntingdon Library Quarterly,* 5 (1942), pp. 235—72; Edmund S. Morgan, *The Puritan Family: Religion and Domestic Relations in Seventeenth Century New England,* (New York, 1966); and now extensively Stone, *Family, Sex and Marriage.* On developments in France after about 1770 on the basis of English influences see Jean-Louis Flandrin, *Familles: parentés, maison, sexualité dans l'ancienne société,* (Paris, 1976), p. 165ff.

5 See Morgan, *The Puritan Family,* p. 47ff.; Howard Gadlin, 'Private

Lives and Public Order: A Critical View of the History of Intimate
Relations in the United States', in George Levinger and Harold
L. Rausch (eds), *Close Relationships: Perspectives on the Meaning
of Intimacy,* (Amherst Mass., 1977), pp. 33—72 (p. 40).

6 On the change in this notion at the turn of the eighteenth century
see Randolph Trumbach, *The Rise of the Egalitarian Family:
Aristocratic Kinship and Domestic Relations in Eighteenth-Century
England,* (New York, 1978), particularly p. 150ff.

7 See Rae Blanchard, 'Richard Steele and the Status of Women', in
Studies in Philology, 26 (1929), pp. 325—55; Stone, *Family, Sex and
Marriage,* p. 325ff.

8 Thus, for example, the famous reform text 'The Doctrine and
Discipline of Divorce', quoted from the impression in the 2nd
edition of *The Prose Works of John Milton,* ed. J. A. St. John,
vol. 3, (London, no year), p. 177, p. 194 and elsewhere. See also
Johnson, *A Society Ordained by God,* particularly p. 121ff.

9 This is shown by Trumbach, *The Rise of the Egalitarian Family,*
specifically with reference to the high nobility.

10 And the English colonies, one must add, with a view to what was
later to become the USA. See for the time-span of 1741-94 Herman
R. Lantz et al., 'Pre-industrial Patterns in the Colonial Family in
America: A Content Analysis of Colonial Magazines', *American
Sociological Review,* 33 (1968), pp. 413—26. The authors ascertain
with reference to industrialization that 'it may well be that
industrialization *facilitated* the development of a romantic love
complex already in existence.'

11 It is worth quoting the beginning of the *Vicar of Wakefield* (1766) in
this context: 'I was ever of opinion that the honest man who
married, and brought up a large family, did more service than he
who continued single, and only talked of population. From this
motive, I had scarce taken orders a year, before I began to think
seriously of matrimony, and chose my wife, as she did her wedding-
gown, not for a fine glossy surface, but such qualities as would wear
well . . . However, we loved each other tenderly, and our fondness
increased as we grew old.' Oliver Goldsmith, *The Vicar of
Wakefield,* quoted from the 1919 Bielefeld and Leipzig edition, p. 2.
Older proof of this is to be found in Morgan, *The Puritan Family,*
p. 29ff. See also Trumbach, *The Rise of the Egalitarian Family,*
passim, for the increase in marriages of love in the English high
nobility around the middle of the eighteenth century. For the
assumption that by the end of the eighteenth century marriage was
more or less freed from social control, see also Daniel S. Smith,
'Parental Power and Marriage Patterns: An Analysis of Historical

Trends in Hingham Massachusetts', *Journal of Marriage and the Family*, 35 (1973), pp. 419—28.

12 See for example Wilhelm von Humboldt's 'Theorie der Bildung' in his *Werke*, 2nd edition, (Darmstadt, 1960), vol. 1, pp. 234—40. A less convincing form of such an anthropology which hinges on an idealization of individuality states simply that humanity reaches its richest stage of development only by means of the individualization of all people according to specific unique characteristics, e.g. Friedrich D. E. Schleiermacher, 'Monologen 1800', III (Prüfungen), in *Werke*, (Leipzig, 1911), vol. 4, p. 420; but see also the monologue 'Weltansicht'. See on this, and specifically on the distinction between German and West European notions of individuality, Louis Dermont, 'Religion, Politics, and Society in the Individualistic Universe', *Proceedings of the Royal Anthropological Institute 1970*, pp. 31—41; Lilian R. Furst, *Romanticism in Perspective*, (London, 1969), p. 53ff.

13 See also Anne Louise Germaine de Staël, 'De l'influence des passions sur le bonheur des individus et des nations', quoted from *O Euvres complètes,* vol. 3, (Paris, 1820), p. 115ff.: 'L'univers entier est lui sous les formes différentes; le printemps, la nature, le ciel, ce sont les lieux qu'il a parcourus; les plaisirs du monde, c'est ce qu'il a dit; ce qui lui a plu, les amusemens qu'il a partagés; ces propres succès à soi-même, c'est le louange qu'il a entendue . . .' (p. 115). The quotation demonstrates that the world is evaluated *in relation to* someone else, but not (or at least not clearly) that this was taken to be a *projection of the world* that was subjective, particularly coloured and a distortion of the normal. Here, love does not yet mean that one together quits the normal world and enters a private world.

14 A clear expression of this progress is to be found in Schlegel's *Lucinde:* 'Sie [the French] finden das Universum einer in dem anderen, weil sie den Sinn für alles andere verlieren. Nicht so wir. Alles, was wir sonst liebten, lieben wir nun noch wärmer. Der Sinn für die Welt ist uns erst recht aufgegangen.' Friedrich Schlegel, *Lucinde,* (Berlin, 1799), quoted from the 1975 Stuttgart edition, p. 89. If love is included in the make-up of the world in this manner, then one can attribute permanence to it; love, at any rate, does not fail because it contradicts facts or interests from which it had rashly abstracted.

15 Thus, for Stendhal, communication is hardly necessary for love to 'crystallize', and, if communication occurs, it can destroy this magical configuration because it makes the 'no' possible. An example would be his heavily theoretical short novel *Ernestine ou*

la naissance de l'amour, quoted from the impression in *De l'amour,* pp. 352—78.

16 Allow me to draw your attention again to the *Sufferings of Young Werther,* Letter of 16 June.

17 See for the parallel area of the theory of education also Clemens Menze, *Leibniz und die neuhumanistische theorie der Bildung des Menschen,* (Opladen, 1980).

18 On analogous problems in the area of legal practice and educational practice see Luhmann 'Subjective Rechte: Zum Umbau des rechtsbewußtseins für die moderne Gesellschaft' in *Gesellschaftsstruktur und Semantik,* vol. 2, (Frankfurt, 1981), pp. 45—104 (p. 64ff.) and also Luhmann 'Theoriesubstitution in der Erziehungswissenschaft: Von der Philanthropie zum Neuhemanismus', ibid., pp. 105—94.

19 *Lotte in Weimar* is a later thematization of the problems that result from this. Another case is Schlegal's *Lucinde.* See also Alfred Schier, *Die Liebe in der Frühromantik mit besonderer Berücksichtigung des Romans,* (Marburg, 1913), p. 58ff.

20 The connection that obtained between literary production and marital problems at the time is admirably established by Kluckhohn, *Die Auffassung des Liebe,* p. 176ff. For an English parallel, the Griffiths, who published their correspondence and kept writing afterwards solely for the sake of publication, see Joyce M. S. Tomkins, *The Polite Marriage,* (Cambridge Mass, 1938, reprinted Freeport NY, 1969).

21 Thus, at any rate, Lascelle Abercrombie, *Romanticism,* 2nd impression, (London, 1927).

22 Compare this to Francis Hutchinson's argument which is very similar in form, namely that one had to recognize the *naturalness* of the 'kind and generous affections' (instead of deriving them from self-love) because only thus was 'improvement' attainable. See *An Essay on the Nature and Conduct of the Passions and Affections,* (London, 1728), in particular the preface. The argument can be thought of as a parallel to Bacon's conception of natural science: nature has to be recognized correctly if one is to be able to improve mankind's lot. The argument thus exploits self-reference in order to be able to reject it as self-love, and uses in contrast a structure, that (supposedly) is not to be found in nature.

23 See specifically Kant's strange notion that in sexual intercourse one reifies oneself and the other; whereas only in marriage is the reciprocal treatment of the partner as a person guaranteed (*Rechtslehre.* 1. Theil, 2. Hauptstück, Art. 25). See also the criticism in Johann C. F. Meister, *Lehrbuch des Natur-Rechts,* (Züllichau/Freistadt, 1808), p. 398ff.

24 See the 'deduction of love' as a purpose in itself in *Grundlage des Naturrechts,* (1796), quoted from *Werke,* vol. 2, (Darmstadt, 1962), p. 308ff.

25 What is more, from this vantage point the whole tradition of philosophical humanism can be devalued as animal, as 'brutal', which at the same time just goes to prove that the distinction animal/human no longer functions. See the material from the field of modern pedagogics in Rudolf Joerden (ed.), *Dokumente des Neuhumanismus,* vol. 1, (Weinheim, 1962).

26 'Qui alterum amat, is eundem considerat tanquam seipsum' is to be read in Christian Wolff, *Psychologica empirica Methodo scientifica pertractata,* (Frankfurt/Leipzig, 1738, reprinted Hildesheim, 1969), art. 659).

27 A characteristic document of this transition is to be found in Lessing's *Minna von Barnhelm* (1765), II, 7, (English translation Chicago, 1973): 'Müssen wir denn schön sein? — Aber, daß wir uns schön glauben, war vielleicht notwendig. — Nein, wenn ich ihm, ihm nur schön bin!' Virtue is still of the utmost importance here as the basis for love. It is sacrificed only at the very last moment.

28 'To forego' is perhaps too strong a term. Specifically Friedrich Schlegel devised a terminology (irony, jokes and levelheadedness) to describe the fact that self-reference continued to function simultaneous to the highest pleasure of unification. But because of its difference to the traditional claims of rationality this terminology also pinpoints the place, or at least the subordination of this element in a higher whole.

29 This was first stated, but without this signifying anything in Christoph Martin Wieland, *Gandalin oder Liebe um Liebe,* quoted from Wieland's *Werke,* 4. Theil, (Berlin, no year) pp. 149—231.

30 See Levana, art. 121, quoted from *Sämtliche Werke,* Abt. I, vol. 12, (Weimar, 1937), p. 341. See also: 'Alle *Liebe* liebt nur *Liebe,* sie ist ihr eigener Gegenstand,' in 'Es gibt weder eine eigennütziger Liebe noch eine Selbstliebe, sondern nur eigennützige Handlungen', in *Sämtliche Werke,* Abt. I, vol. 5, (Weimar, 1930), pp. 208—13 (p. 209).

31 We quote from the edition by Henri Martineau, (Paris, 1959), p. 95ff.

32 'car rien ne paralyse l'imagination comme l'appel à la mémoire,' *De l'amour,* p. 36.

33 'Il vaut mieux se taire que de dire hors de temps des choses trop tendres; ce qui était placé, il y a dix secondes, ne l'est plus tout, et fait tache en ce moment. Toutes les fois que je manquais à cette règle, et que je disais une chose qui m'était venue trois minutes auparavant, et que je trouvais jolie, Léonore ne manquais pas de

me battre' (ibid., p. 97).

34 It is precisely this transparency that now appears incompatible with momentary self-referentiality, for it presents the self more as an object of one's observation than as a previously (!) formulated text, the origin of which can no longer be returned to. 'Donc il ne faut pas prétendre à la candeur, cette qualité d'une âme qui ne fait aucun retour sur elle-même' (ibid., p. 99).

35 Ibid., p. 99.

36 Compare this with the problem of *soumission* in the seventeenth century. If it embodied annihilation and reincarnation, then the man could only assert his freedom by refusing his love (Corneile's 'La Place Royale', quoted from Pierre Corneille, *Œuvres complètes*, Paris, 1963, pp. 149—67) or more typically by beating a hasty retreat. If it was a 'galant' offer, then freedom lay in quietly not taking the offer seriously, in subverting communication on the basis of sincere or insincere love. It was Romanticism that first dared to postulate unity as freedom in the Other.

37 See, e.g., Adam Müller, *Von der Idee der Schönheit*, (Berlin, 1809), particularly p. 146ff., with a criticism of novels in which either the love affair or the novel ended in marriage.

38 1st edition 1816, quoted from *Œuvres*, (Paris, 1957), pp. 37—117.

39 To be exact and to do the novel justice one should say 'cannot be communicated sincerely', for a form of 'stolen' communication remained possible and in the final instance mediates the knowledge of reality.

40 A text like the following was no longer possible under Romanticism. In the context of the fashionable critique of modish devotion, de Villier states (*Réflexions sur les défants d'autruy*, p. 15): 'Quand la Comtesse D . . . a commencé à visiter les pauvres et à entendre les sermons elle savoit bien dans sons coeur qu'elle etoit une hypocrite, mais aujourd'huy elle se croit devote à force d'entendre les sermons et de visiter les pauvres, son coeur n'est pas mieux reglé; mais il est plus trompé.' Romanticism was to relinquish the capacity to distinguish between the genuine and the inauthentic on the basis of true factual definitions and was to trust the practice that had begun inauthentically, namely of developing *genuine* emotions a priori (i.e. not only in order to strengthen *inauthentic* emotions).

41 René Girard, *Mensonge romantique et vérité romanesque*, (Paris, 1961) responds to this ambiguity — which must be viewed as a unified complex — with the somewhat artificial distinction of *romantique* and *romanesque*.

42 See however also Schier, *Die Liebe in der Fruhromantik*, p. 122ff for the observation that precisely this abandonment of objective

reality leads to imagination, in the last instance remaining a monologue.

43 For example, Anonymous (Aphra Behn), *The Ten Pleasures of Marriage*, (London, 1682), and by the same author *The Confessions of the New Married Couple*, (London, 1683).

44 See, for example, E. T. A. Hoffmann, *Lebens-Ansichten des Kater Murr*, 'Einleitung zum Dritten Abschnitt', quoted from Hoffmann's *Werke*, vol. 9, part 9, (Berlin/Leipzig, no year), p. 193.

45 'Fragments divers', no. 21, in *De l'amour*, p. 246.

46 On the origin of this, particularly in relation to Prevost's *Manon Lescaut*, Erich Köhler, *Esprit und arkadische Freiheit: Aufsätze aus der Welt der Romania*, (Frankfurt, 1966), p. 97f., 172ff. This theme had for some time been passed down over the generations in a less elaborate form, above all in the topos of the unexpected *suddenness* of the genesis of a then *permanent* love. Thus one can read in the first of the famous 'Lettres portugaises': 'Je vous ai destiné aussi tôt que je vous ai vu' (Guillerages, *Lettres portugaises*, 1669, quoted from the edition by F. Deloffre and J. Rougeot, Paris, 1962, p. 39). The turn from a temporal (suddenness/duration) to a modal—theoretical (chance/necessity) version is noteworthy (e.g. in Friedrich Schlegel).

47 See also Aubert, 'A Note on Love', p. 213ff.

48 Being able to love on the basis of pictures or stories and then only having to make contact with the beloved was a constantly recurring motif in novels of the seventeenth century. This presumed implicitly the existence of a relatively small upper class.

14 LOVE AND MARRIAGE

1 There are numerous, both historical and comparative geographical studies of this tendency. Usually economic developments are (all too one-sidedly) presented as the reason for this change. From the special point of view of a Darwinian theory see Henry T. Finck, *Romantic Love & Personal Beauty*, particularly for the situation in America in the nineteenth century. See of the sociological literature especially William J. Thomas and Florian Znaniecki, *The Polish Peasant in Europe and America*, (New York, 1927), particularly vol. 2, p. 1159ff; Olga Lang, *Chinese Family and Society*, (New Haven, 1946), p. 120ff; Hiroshi Wagatsuma and George de Vos, 'Attitudes Toward Arranged Marriage in Rural Japan', *Human Organization*, 21 (1962), pp. 187—200; George A. Theodorson, 'Romanticism and Motivation to Marry in the United States, Singapore, Burma and

India', *Social Forces,* 44 (1965), pp. 17—27; Frank F. Furstenberg Jr., 'Industrialization and the American Family: A Look Backward', *American Sociological Review,* 31 (1966), pp. 326—37, particularly 329ff.; Robert O. Blood Jr., *Love-Match and Arranged Marriage: A Tokyo—Detroit Comparison,* (New York, 1976/7); Promilla Kapur, *Love, Marriage and Sex,* (Delhi, 1973); Greer L. Fox, 'Love Match and Arranged Marriage in a Modernizing Nation: Mate Selection in Ankara, Turkey', *Journal of Marriage and the Family,* 37 (1975), pp. 180—93; Barbara Lobodzinska, 'Love as a Factor in Marital Decisions in Contemporary Poland', *Journal of Comparative Family Studies,* 6 (1975), pp. 56—73; J. Allen Williams Jr., Lynn K. White and Bruno J. Ekaidem, 'Romantic Love as a Basis for Marriage', in Mark Cook and Glenn Wilson (eds), *Love and Attraction: An International Conference,* (Oxford, 1979), pp. 245—350.

2 The thematic innovations remain meagre and of little importance; only the changed constellation leads to the addition of a new form of attentiveness. In order to make this clearer we went into the classical code of *amour passion* in greater detail above.

3 A corresponding interpretation of Romanticism in Lothar Pikulik, *Romantik als Ungenügen an der Normalität: Am Beispiel Tiecks, Hoffmanns, Eichendorffs,* (Frankfurt, 1979).

4 Or so Mauvillon, *Mann und Weib,* p. 342 believes: 'that the highest perfection of the same [marriage] among human beings would be if marriage were always love and love always marriage.'

5 This can be shown using current data. See Lobodzinska, 'Love as a Factor', in particular p. 62f.

6 However, empirical research has repeatedly shown distinctions between men and women to exist, i.e. above all the tendency of men, at least at the beginning of a relationship, to fall in Romantic love much more than women. See, e.g., Charles Hobart, 'The Incidence of Romanticism During Courtship', *Social Forces,* 36 (1958), pp. 362—7, and by the same author 'Disillusionment in Marriage and Romanticism', *Marriage and Family Living,* 20 (1958), pp. 156—62; William M. Kephart, 'Some Correlates of Romantic Love', *Journal of Marriage and the Family,* 29 (1967), pp. 470—9; David H. Know and Michael J. Sporakowski, 'Attitudes of College Students toward Love', *Journal of Marriage and the Family,* 30 (1968), pp. 638—42; Alfred P. Fengler, 'Romantic Love in Courtship: Divergent Paths of Male and Female Students', *Journal of Comparative Family Studies,* 5 (1974), pp. 134—9; Bernard I. Murstein, 'Mate Selection in the 1970s', *Journal of Marriage and the Family,* 42 (1980), pp. 777—92 (p. 785). What remains unexplained, however, is both whether and the extent to which *this* difference

has a retroactive effect on the assessment of the motives of *the other person.*

7 See on this (perhaps already overtaken by current developments) the findings by William J. Goode, 'The Theoretical Importance of Love', *American Sociological Review*, 24 (1959), pp. 38—47 (p. 43ff.) or in Claude Henryon and Edmond Lambrechts, *Le Mariage en Belgique: Etude sociologique*, (Brussels, 1968), p. 129ff.

8 Perhaps one should say 'if it is supposed to convince the reading public!'

9 This formulation is used by Kevorkian, *Le Thème de l'amour*, p. 188 with regard to a novel by Gomberville.

10 'Puisque vous sçaves bien ma naissance, Madame, poursuivit le Pelerin, je ne vous parleray plus que des affaires de mon coeur' it is stated in a novela by Madame de Villedieu, *Annales galantes*, vol. 1, (Paris, 1670), p. 14f., quoted from the 1979 Geneva reprint.

11 See Alfred de Musset's one-act play: 'Il faut qu'une porte soit ouverte ou fermée', quoted from *Œuvres complètes*, (Paris, 1963), pp. 415—22. See also the Marquise's rejection of a declaration of love based on formulae: 'Heureusement pour nous, la justice du ciel n'a pas mis à votre disposition un vocabulaire tres varié. Vous n'avez tous, comme on dit, qu'une chanson . . . Cela nous sauve par l'envie de rire, ou du moins par le simple ennui' (p. 419). On the social control of the complex of courting love and steering towards marriage in nineteenth-century France see Finck, *Romantic Love & Personal Beauty.*

12 *De l'amour, selon les lois premiéres* (1808), quoted from 4th edition, 2 vols., (Paris, 1834). On the author and his works see Joachim Merlant, *Senancour (1770—1846)*, (Paris, 1907, reprinted Geneva 1970); André Monglond, *Vies préromantiques*, (Paris, 1925).

13 Op. cit., vol. 1, p. 56.

14 'Sans quelque idée secrète de la plus vive jouissance de l'amour, les affections les moins sensuelles dans leurs effets apparens ne naitraient pas, et, sans quelque espoir semblable, elles ne subsisteraient pas' (op. cit., vol. 1, p. 51).

15 See Destutt de Tracy, *De l'amour* (a planned, but not then published part of *Elements d'idéologie*), Paris, 1926), p. 17: not *'fureur'* but *'sentiment tendre et généreux'*. Similarly in Joseph Droz, *Essai sur l'art d'être heureux*, (1806, new edition, Amsterdam, 1827), p. 108ff. (p. 113).

16 See Senancour, *De l'amour*, particularly vol. 1, p. 104f., p. 147f., p. 153; vol. 2, p. 29ff.

17 See, ibid., e.g. vol. 1, p. 37ff., p. 277ff. (with recourse to the literary tradition).

18 Ibid., vol. 1, p. 148.
19 *De l'amour*, — a programme consciously aimed at reforming the institution of the family.
20 *Die Welt als Wille und Vorstellung*, Book 4, chapter 44 ('Metaphysik der Geschlechtsliebe'), quoted from *Werke*, (Darmstadt, 1961), vol. 2, p. 678ff.
21 Schopenhauer, ibid., p. 702.
22 Ibid., p. 682.
23 Particularly in Destutt de Tracy.
24 According to Darwin this can immediately be repeated in terms of a theory of evolution and can therefore be regarded to occur in strict accordance with scientific principles. See, e.g. Max Nordau, *Paradoxe*, (Leipzig, 1885), p. 273ff.' or Gaston Danville, *La Psychologie de l'amour*, (Paris, 1894): love — in the sense of a 'systematization exclusive et consciente du désir sexuel' — as the final form of the evolutionary differentiation of the reproductive process.
25 Formulations from Pierre Joseph Proudhon, 'Amour et mariage', *De la justice dans la Révolution et dans l'église*, 2nd edition, (Brussels/Leipzig, no year (1865)), part X, p. 11; part XI, p. 10. See also the criticism of an idealized love that leads one astray, that corrupts love: p. 48ff.
26 Typical of this is a mixture of Romanticism and anatomy, of aesthetic idealization and selective breeding: Finck, *Romantic Love & Personal Beauty*, or the mixture of poetry, physiology and 'twilight politics': Paul Mantegazza, *Gli amori degli nomini. Saggio di una etnologica dell'amore* (Milan, 1886). Sociologists also take part, for example Lester F. Ward, *Pure Sociology: A Treatise on the Origin and Spontaneous Development of Society*, (1903, 2nd edition, New York, 1925), p. 290ff., particularly p. 390ff.
27 Frederic Moreau's inability to act in Flaubert's *Education sentimentale* could be read in this way. A more daring interpretation would be that an education (development of the person) which does not actually take place in the novel, would now have to occur via a relation being struck between love and money, and that this would at the same time make education impossible, because money here (as ever) symbolizes inauthentic motives.
28 See the study 'Gesellschaftliche Struktur und semantische Tradition', in Luhmann, *Gesellschaftsstruktur und Semantik*, vol. 1, pp. 9—71 (p. 49f.).
29 Francis E. Merrill, *Courtship and Marriage: A Study in Social Relationships*, (New York, 1949), p. 25.
30 How little the code of passion can be used in real action is emphasized, among others, by Harry C. Bredemeier and Jackson

Toby, *Social Problems in America: Costs and Casualties in an Acquisitive Society*, (New York, 1961), p. 461ff. See also for French data *Patterns of Sex and Love: A Study of the French Woman and Her Morals*, (New York, 1961).

31 See her *De l'influence des passions sur le bonheur des individus et des nations*, p. 132; and, as confirming this, the results of the empirical studies given above (n. 6). Seen sociologically, the distinction in the man and woman's respective infection with Romantic love probably has something to do with the fact that the man's social status is not normally affected by marriage, so that the man can let himself be governed by romantic impulse, to a much greater extent than the woman, for whom the act of marrying will decide future status and who therefore has a reason and additional criteria for controlling her choice of a partner for the flight into Romanticism. See on this Zick Rubin, *Liking and Loving: An Invitation to Social Psychology*, (New York, 1973), p. 205f.

32 See Ernest R. Mower, *Family Disorganization: An Introduction to a Sociological Analysis*, (Chicago, 1927), p. 128ff.; Ernest W. Burgess, 'The Romantic Impulse and Family Disorganization', *Survey*, 57 (1926), pp. 290–4; Merrill, *Courtship and Marriage*, p. 23ff.; Paul H. Landis, 'Control of the Romantic Impulse Through Education', *School and Society*, 44 (1936), pp. 212–5. What is decisive here is the discovery that the functional problems of modern families, and particularly the difficulties of understanding between marital partners could not simply be ascribed to civilization or industrial society as a whole but were rooted precisely in the autonomy of the family as a functional unit, namely in the intensification of expectations triggered off by its coming about. What must be noted, however, is that 40 years later interest in such findings has been lost; they now count as mere 'opinion' and have never been systematically researched. See J. Richard Udry, *The Social Context of Marriage*, (Philadelphia, 1966), p. 192; Ernest W. Burgess, Harvey J. Locke and Mary Margaret Thomas, *The Family: From Traditional to Companionship*, (New York, 1971), p. 272f. Incidentally, the logic with which this 'opinion' is argumentatively presented is not completely convincing. Someone who marries after careful deliberation is not therefore safe from disappointment; he is indeed in a better position than the Romantic when it comes to determining that these are disappointments, and then comparing them with his expectations.

33 Willard Waller introduces the theme of divorce with these words, see *The Old Love and the New: Divorce and Readjustment* (1930, reprinted Carbondale, 1967), p. 3.

34 See the study by R. W. England Jr., 'Images of Love and Courtship

in Family-Magazine Fiction', *Marriage and Family Living*, 20 (1960), pp. 162—5, with a comparison of US literature between 1911 and 1915 and 1951 and 1955, which is especially fruitful with regard to 1) the coincidence (unregulated character) of the first meeting; 2) the short duration of the acquaintanceship (love alone decides immediately); 3) the insignificance of all other involvements in the life-world; and 4) the class-specific revaluation involved because of the location of such love in the realm of a higher class.

35 See Charles B. Spaulding, 'The Romantic Love Complex in American Culture', *Sociology and Social Research*, 55 (1971), pp. 82—100.

36 The existence of this trend has often been investigated and confirmed right up to the present day. See as typical B. K. Singh, 'Trends in Attitudes Toward Premarital Sexual Relations', *Journal of Marriage and the Family*, 42 (1980), pp. 387—93.

37 Thus Merrill, *Courtship and Marriage*, p. 52; G. Marion Kinget, 'The "Many-splendoured Thing" in Transition or "The Agony and the Ecstasy" Revisited', in Mark Cook and Glenn Wilson (eds), *Love and Attraction: An International Conference*, (Oxford, 1979), pp. 251—4. For an empirical study that could underpin this argument see Joachim Israel and Rosmari Eliasson, 'Consumption Society, Sex Roles and Sexual Behavior', *Acta Sociologica*, 14 (1971), pp. 68—82.

38 See Franz Dirlmeier, ΦΙΛΟΣ and ΦΙΛΙΑ *im vorhellenischen Griechentum*, doctoral thesis, (Munich, 1931).

39 Which was at least clearly formulated by the end of this tradition. See the remarks on Bourdaloue above, p. 69f.

40 Jules Michelet, *L'Amour*, (Paris, 1858), p. 17. Similarly (for marriage as an isle of happiness in a vulgar world) see Droz, *Essai sur l'art d'être heureux*, p. 108ff. On a corresponding ideology of the US family that utilizes such characteristics as 'retreat', 'conscious design' and 'perfectionism' see also Kirk Jeffrey, 'The Family as Utopian Retreat from the City: The Nineteenth-Century Contribution', in Sallie TeSelle (ed.), *The Family, Communes and Utopian Societies*, (New York, 1972), pp. 21—41, and in *Soundings*, 55 (1972), pp. 21—41. See for the nineteenth century further, Neil J. Smelser, 'Vicissitudes of Love and Work in Anglo-American Society' in Neil J. Smelser and Erik H. Erikson (eds), *Themes of Work and Love in Adulthood*, (Cambridge Mass., 1980), pp. 105—19.

41 See, e.g. Warren G. Bennis and Philip E. Slater, *The Temporary Society*, (New York, 1968), p. 88ff — which, however, presents only uncertain perspectives for the future.

42 See Elisabeth Bott, *Family and Social Network: Roles, Norms and*

External Relationships in Ordinary Urban Families, 2nd edition, (London, 1971).

15 WHAT NOW?

1 See 'Love and Adulthood in American Culture', in Neil J. Smelser and Erik H. Erikson, *Themes of Work and Love in Adulthood*, (Cambridge Mass., 1980), pp. 120—47.

2 Philip E. Slater, 'On Social Regression', *American Sociological Review*, 28 (1963), pp. 339—64. Note particularly the inversion of Simmel's approach: it is not the intrusion of third parties that is the problem, but their retreat from controlling and consensus-guaranteeing functions.

3 Evidence in Wilhelm P. J. Gauger *Geschlechter, Liebe und Ehe in der Auffassung von Londoner Zeitschriften um 1700*, doctoral thesis, (Berlin, 1965), p. 300f.

4 See, for example, Harriet B. Braiker and Harold H. Kelley, 'Conflict in the Development of Close Relationships' in Robert L. Burgess and Ted L. Huston (eds), *Social Exchange in Developing Relationships*, (New York, 1979), pp. 135—68 (noteworthy especially for the assertion that the tendency for conflict to arise increases when the partners intensify their relationship).

5 See the indicators in chapter 14, n. 32.

6 See the indicators in chapter 14, n. 7.

7 See for example: Irwin Altman and Dalmas A. Taylor, *Social Penetration: The Development of Interpersonal Relationships*, (New York, 1973).

8 Talcott Parsons, 'Religion in Postindustrial America: The Problem of Secularization', *Social Research*, 41 (1974), pp. 193—225. See also his 'Some Problems of General Theory in Sociology' in John C. McKinney and Edward A. Tirykian (eds), *Theoretical Sociology: Perspectives and Developments*, (New York, 1970), pp. 27—68 (p. 50ff.).

9 See Zick Rubin, 'Measurement of Romantic Love', *Journal of Personality and Social Psychology*, 16 (1970), pp. 265—73. For a seemingly more differentiated account (but without any adequate data on the items themselves) see Llewellyn Gross, 'A Belief Pattern Scale for Measuring Attitudes Toward Romanticism', *American Sociological Review*, 9 (1944), pp. 463—72.

10 Thus Morton M. Hunt, *Sexual Behavior in the 1970's*, (Chicago, 1974) distinguishes between two forms of sexual ethics: liberal—romantic and radical—recreational. A similar distinction appears in

Joachim Israel and Rosmari Eliasson, 'Consumption Society, Sex Roles and Sexual Behavior', *Acta Sociologica*, 14 (1971), pp. 68—82, in an empirical investigation.

11 See on these two aspects of the field of Romantic love, both of which inform literature, Aubert, 'A Note on Love'.

12 See the dual findings of Robert C. Sorensen, *Adolescent Sexuality in Contemporary America*, (New York, 1973), p. 108ff.: love as the compelling condition of sexuality *and vice versa*. In this context, homosexual relationships also become material for literature; and they are especially well suited to demonstrate this effect. See, for example, James Baldwin, *Giovanni's Room*, (London, 1956).

13 See for an account that is rather more parallel to developments in the novel, and which places too little emphasis on physical ties, Stanton Peele, *Love and Addiction*, (New York, 1975).

14 See the (highly telling) title of Ben Barker-Benfield, 'The Spermatic Economy: A Nineteenth-Century View of Sexuality', in Michael Gordon (ed.), *The American Family in Social-Historical Perspective*, (New York, 1973), pp. 336—72; or the recurrently capitalized 'Respectable' in Peter T. Cominos, 'Late Victorian Sexual Respectability and the Social System', *International Review of Social History*, 8 (1963), pp. 18—48, 216—50. For the lack of attempts at explanation see above p. 70, p. 115.

15 Particularly highly regarded: William H. Masters and Virginia E. Johnson, *Human Sexual Response*, (Boston, 1966); by the same authors *Human Sexual Inadequacy*, (Boston, 1970). See also the satire on Reichian prescriptions in Pascal Bruckner and Alain Finkielkraut, *Le Nouveau Désordre amoureux*, (Paris, 1977), p. 15f. If one also considers older erototechnical literature — e.g. L. van der Weck-Erlen, *Das goldene Buch der Liebe oder die Renaissance im Geschlechtsleben: Ein Eros-Kodex für beide Geschlechter*, (private impression, Vienna 1907, reprinted Reinbek, 1978), one might, however, doubt whether any new innovations are possible.

16 Thus, for example, the portrayal of the 'spectator role' owing to 'fears of performance' in Masters and Johnson, *Human Sexual Inadequacy*, p. 10f., p. 65f., p. 84 and elsewhere. Whereas the whole therapy continually creates a consciousness of performance or inadequate performance (or at least can hardly avoid doing so), the resulting observation of oneself and others is seen as a weighty barrier to performance. One is reminded somewhat melancholically of romantic irony and 'levelheadedness', which was clearly thought of as also being enjoyable, i.e. as a reflexivity of enjoyment; or of the old problems of the confessional: warning and stimulation at once.

17 Here the old theme of the inexplicability and suddenness of the

flaring up of love evidently helps no further; it was related to the *manner in which*, not to the *fact that* love had blossomed. A semantics is now needed that is oriented toward the difference of starting and not starting.

18 Thus Ted L. Huston and Rodney M. Cate 'Social Exchange in Intimate Relationships' in Mark Cook and Glenn Wilson (eds), *Love and Attraction: An International Conference*, (Oxford, 1979), pp. 263—9. See also Robert L. Burgess and Ted L. Huston (eds), *Social Exchange in Developing Relationships*, (New York, 1979).

19 See Sherri Cavan, *Liquor License: An Ethnography of Bar Behavior*, (Chicago, 1966); Zick Rubin, *Liking and Loving: An Invitation to Social Psychology*, (New York, 1973), p. 162ff.

20 See chapter 8.

21 'Blütenstaub 28', quoted from *Schriften*, vol. 2, (Jena, 1907), p. 117.

22 It is no accident that initially such a dry concept replaces the cult of self-ness, only to itself soon be remystified and to be treated with an ungrounded preference for itself. This is also true of 'intrinsic motivation', 'cognitive consistency' and other sorts of 'balance'; and, last but not least, emancipation.

23 See on this William J. Chambliss, 'The Selection of Friends', *Social Forces*, 43 (1965), pp. 370—80, following Morton Deutsch and Leonard Solomon's 'Reactions to Evaluations by Others as Influenced by Self-Examination', *Sociometry*, 22 (1959), pp. 93—112; Carl W. Backman and Paul F. Secord, 'Liking, Selective Interaction and Misperception in Congruent relations', *Sociometry*, 25 (1962), pp. 321—35; Theodor Newcomb, 'The Prediction of Interpersonal Attraction', *American Psychologist*, 11 (1956), pp. 393—404. See further Hanns Wienold, *Kontakt, Einfühlung und Attraktion: Zur Entwicklung von Paarbeziehungen*, (Stuttgart, 1972), p. 63ff.

24 Thus the title of Erving Goffman's *The Presentation of Self in Everyday Life*, 2nd edition, (Garden City NY, 1959).

25 This was already true of the code of *amour passion*, but here delimits sociable and/or marital obligations. See Bussy Rabutin, *Histoire amoureuse des Gaules*, (Paris, 1856; reprinted Nendeln, Liechenstein, 1972), vol. 1, p. 371f. English translation of the same name, Amersham, 1972. This criterion of spontaneity gains greater significance in modern versions; indeed, it becomes central for the perception and proof of love. See in particular Judith M. Katz, 'How do You Love Me? Let me Count The Ways (The Phenomenology of Being Loved)', *Sociological Inquiry*, 46 (1975), pp. 11—22.

26 See Lionel Trilling, *Sincerity and Authenticity*, (Cambridge Mass., 1972).

27 See, from a therapeutic and psychological point of view George W.

Bach and Peter Wyden, *The ultimate Enemy* (New York, 1970); further Sidney M. Jourard, *The Transparent Self: Self-Disclosure and Well-Being*, (New York, 1964); by the same author *Self-Disclosure: An Experimental Analysis of the Transparent Self*, (New York, 1971); Howard L. Miller and Paul S. Siegel, *Loving: A Psychological Approach*, (New York, 1972), p. 22f. Further, on the dissemination of corresponding notions see Zick Rubin et al. 'Self Disclosure in Dating Couples: Sex Roles and the Ethics of Openness', *Journal of Marriage and the Family*, 42 (1980), pp. 305—17. See also the analysis — from the point of view of a sociology of science — of 'self' theories by Ray Holland, *Self and Social Context*, (New York, 1977), which examines the assumption that authors (and especially Americans who have no European experience or skill in managing self-referentiality) when writing about the self have their own self in mind and therefore tend to generalize things positively, e.g. recommending a healthy personality development, sincerity, etc.

Self-evidently, this recent insistence on sincere self-disclosure has nothing to do with the literary obsession with sincerity, which both revolts against and is as a result destroyed by the Romantics' insight that sincerity is neither possible nor desirable. The most prominent example no doubt being André Gide and as a counter to him François Derais and Henri Ranbaud, *L'Envers du Journal de Gide: Tunis 1942—43*, (Paris, 1951). See also the analyses by Henry Peyre, *Literature and Sincerity*, (New Haven, 1963), p. 276ff. The therapists do not set their sights on the difference to the traditional experience but rather on the conjectured uses of the prescriptions.

28 See, for example, Madeleine de Scudéri, 'De la dissimulation et de la sincérité' in her *Conversations sur divers sujets*, vol. 1, (Lyon, 1680), pp. 300—22, where she poses the problem of how one can convince others to endure the sincerity shown toward them. Here (and for the seventeenth century as a whole) the theme is still placed in the context of analogies drawn between war tactics, courtly and successful behaviour as well as behaviour in love affairs. This also documents the beginnings of the development of an independent social morality that is reflected in the view of social considerations it takes. The conclusions that the eighteenth century drew from this were outlined in chapter 12.

29 This comparison is to be found in the Marquis de Caraccioli, *La Jouissance de soi-meme*, new edition, (Utrecht/Amsterdam, 1759), p. 52.

30 See, for example, Herbert A. Otto (ed.), *Love Today: A New Exploration*, (New York, 1973) for the maxim: 'the more you let yourself love, the greater the wholeness you bring to yourself and

others.' Note also the seven-rung love-ladder formulated for the organizational age, namely the demand 1) for an organization to call together 2) a commission to formulate 3) an action framework for 4) 'First Steps Toward 5) a Master Plan for 6) the Establishment of 7) a Loving Society' (p. 11).

31 *Lieben als Lernprozeß*, (Göttingen, 1975), p. 80ff.
32 Flaminio Nobili, *Trattato dell'Amore*, fol. 31 R, admittedly leaves the love—hate duality open to discussion, but then realizes that this is not possible. Nature, he claimed, did not want hate to be generated from ugliness just as love arose from beauty; 'anzi è tale odio più simigliante a privatione che a vero contrario.'

16 LOVE AS A SYSTEM OF INTERPENETRATION

1 See on this development Wallace Fowlie, *Love in Literature: Studies in Symbolic Expression*, reprint, (Freeport NY, 1972).
2 In other words, it is not just scorned. See also the indications in Luhmann, *Gesellschaftsstruktur und Semantik*, vol. 2, p. 210.
3 'Il faut renoncer à vous pour jamais, pour jamais! Grand Dieu! Et c'est ma propre bouche qui me prononce un arrêt qui peut-être sortirait point de la votre' the one text reads. And 80 years later after the loss of the heroic attitude that made this possible: 'Qu'exige-vous? Que je vous quitte? Ne voyez-vous pas que je n'en ai pas la force? Ah! c'est à vous, qui n'aimez pas, c'est à vous à la trouver, cette force . . .' See Crébillon, *Lettres de la Marquise de M.*, p. 181 and Constant, *Adolphe*, p. 113.
4 See chapter 12.
5 See Gregory Bateson et al., 'Toward a Theory of Schizophrenia', *Behavioral Science*, 1 (1956), pp. 251—64.
6 This assertion is made on the basis of empirical studies in Clifford H. Swensen and Frank Gilner, 'Factor Analysis of Self-Report Statements of Love Relationships', *Journal of Individual Psychology*, 20 (1964), pp. 186—88, (p. 187f.). See also Clifford H. Swensen, 'The Behavior of Love' in Herbert A. Otto (ed.), *Love Today: A New Exploration*, (New York, 1973), pp. 86—101 (p. 92f.).
7 Seldom, however, is this actually proposed. But see Elton Mayo, 'Should Marriage be Monotonous?', *Harper's Magazine*, 151 (1925), pp. 420—7.
8 The version characteristic for the seventeenth century was approximately: there are general, indeed technical rules on correct seduction; once love has been won, however, only what the beloved says and demands holds true; see for example 'La justification de l'amour', in *Receuil de Sercy*, vol. 3, pp. 289—334 (p. 314f.).

Index